Praise for *Peace Be With You*

"Religious extremists of all sorts—Jewish, Christian, Muslim—have distorted the best our faiths have to offer. Folks who blow up things and burn Qur'ans hijack the news—it is religion that has grown sick. But as Carlson reminds us, there is another thing stirring around the world. There is a movement of extremists for love and for grace that have been singing a different song. In the same war-torn deserts of the Middle East, there is an ancient movement of people who have left the old world to build a new one. The monastic tradition reminds us today, perhaps more than ever before, that there is a narrow way that leads to life if only we will have the eyes to see and the ears to hear."

—SHANE CLAIBORNE
AUTHOR, ACTIVIST, AND NEW MONASTIC
WWW.THESIMPLEWAY.ORG

"This is the kind of courageous wisdom that we need today! David Carlson's sources, his insight, his deep valuing of both past and future, his ability to say it well—all make this a must read if you care about the Gospel or if you care about the world—or both."

—FR. RICHARD ROHR, O.F.M.
CENTER FOR ACTION AND CONTEMPLATION
ALBUQUERQUE, NEW MEXICO

"A powerful, insightful guide addressing highly sensitive theological issues, this book may prove accessible and helpful to many who seek to counter terrorism with faith."

—STARRED REVIEW FROM
PUBLISHER'S WEEKLY

"This is the best book on its chosen subject that I have read in a very long time. It may, in fact, be the best book I have ever read on its subject. Just as important, however, is the fact that it is one of the richest, most insightful, and most instructive books I have ever read on the business of living the Christian life fully, biblically, faithfully, and non-dogmatizedly. It would be impossible to recommend *Peace Be With You* adequately, much less too highly."

—PHYLLIS TICKLE
AUTHOR, *THE GREAT EMERGENCE*

"Ten years after 9/11/01, maybe we're ready to receive the wisdom we weren't ready for when the attacks occurred. David Carlson sought that wisdom and offers it to us all in *Peace Be With You*. I just finished the book and feel I've experienced a pilgrimage and a retreat and a season of spiritual direction, all in one."

—BRIAN MCLAREN
AUTHOR, SPEAKER, AND ACTIVIST
BRIANMCLAREN.NET

"Compelling and thoughtful. David Carlson's *Peace Be With You* looks back at 9/11, and in looking back helps us find our way forward. A powerful story of who we are and who we could be."

—PHILIP GULLEY
AUTHOR, *IF THE CHURCH WERE CHRISTIAN*

"*Peace Be With You* brings forward the wisdom seldom sought in scientific research or in recent publications. The monastic tradition has a contribution to shed light for us to put one foot in front of another with confidence and poise. Peace is possible. This book provides an alternative to fear."

—SISTER MARY MARGARET FUNK
AUTHOR, *ISLAM IS... AND INTO THE DEPTHS*

PEACE BE WITH YOU

MONASTIC WISDOM FOR
A TERROR-FILLED WORLD

DAVID CARLSON

THOMAS NELSON
Since 1798

NASHVILLE   DALLAS   MEXICO CITY   RIO DE JANEIRO

Published in Nashville, Tennessee, by Thomas Nelson. Thomas Nelson is a registered trademark of Thomas Nelson, Inc.

Thomas Nelson, Inc., titles may be purchased in bulk for educational, business, fund-raising, or sales promotional use. For information, please e-mail SpecialMarkets@ThomasNelson.com.

Unless otherwise noted, Scripture quotations are taken from the Holy Bible, New International Version®. Copyright © 1973, 1978, 1984, 2011 by Biblica, Inc.™ Used by permission of Zondervan. All rights reserved worldwide. www.zondervan.com.

Scripture quotations marked KJV are taken from the King James Version of the Bible. Public domain.

Scripture quotations marked RSV are taken from the REVISED STANDARD VERSION of the Bible. © 1946, 1952, 1971, 1973 by the Division of Christian Education of the National Council of the Churches of Christ in the U.S.A. Used by permission.

Library of Congress Cataloging-in-Publication Data

Carlson, David, 1947-
  Peace be with you : monastic wisdom for a terror-filled world / David Carlson.
    p. cm.
  Includes bibliographical references.
  ISBN 978-0-8499-4718-6 (trade paper)
  1. Peace--Religious aspects--Christianity. 2. Monastic and religious life--United States. 3. Christianity and other religions. I. Title. II. Title: Monastic wisdom for a terror-filled world.
  BT736.4.C37 2011
  261.2'7--dc22

                          2011010272

Printed in the United States of America

11 12 13 14 15 RRD 6 5 4 3 2 1

Contents

Contents

Acknowledgments

To Kathy, my wife and first editor, I owe the most. She was a tower of strength and good sense throughout this project as she has been throughout our life together. My sons, Leif and Marten, were among the first to encourage me in this project, and their gift of humor was a greater help than they can know. Sara Camilli, my literary agent, offered wise counsel and support from concept through completion. I count Sara a friend. I also wish to thank Matt Baugher, Jennifer McNeil, and Jennifer Stair from Thomas Nelson for their invaluable assistance with this book.

Various others kept faith in this project when my own faltered. Stephen, Father Taso, David, Bill, and Drs. Jim, Greg, and Vikram—thank you. I am indebted to Khadija for believing that these interviews can open new conversations between Christians and Muslims. I am grateful also to the students in my "Religion and Violence" classes at Franklin College from 2005 to 2010 who asked probing questions and rejected shallow solutions to the complex problem of terrorism.

I wish to thank Franklin College, a gem of a liberal-arts college and my academic home since 1978. Through Franklin College's support from the Clifford and Paula Dietz Endowed Faculty Travel Fund and the Charles B. and Kathleen O. Van Nuys Dean's Chair in Religious Studies, I was able to travel from New Mexico to New York in 2007 to conduct these interviews.

Finally, I am indebted to all who agreed to be interviewed—the many monks and nuns, as well as a Mennonite minister and a potter. I came seeking a "word of life" for our age of terrorism and intolerance, and that is what these women and men generously shared with me. Because of their wisdom, I leave this project a different person. I am convinced that I was meant to listen to each of them.

Peace be with you all.

Author's Note

I began to understand in my formative years that following Christ would come with no clear map. There was to be no voice in the night such as Samuel heard, no blinding epiphany such as St. Paul experienced. Instead, there would be trial and error involved in discerning God's leading. Risk and uncertainty would always be present.

After meeting with me over a series of months, a spiritual guide pointed out that my tendencies were neither to remain in an old understanding of my life nor to move confidently into a new understanding. I was a "straddler."

This feeling of uncertainty has come up again and again throughout my faith journey. I felt the uncertainty strongly when I laid aside plans for law school to attend seminary. I felt that uncertainty again in my conversion to Orthodox Christianity in my middle adult years. Friends questioned my reasons for these hairpin turns in my life, but nothing I could say seemed as satisfying as the simple explanation that I was following Christ's leading.

Ironically, I only felt a sense of certainty with this book. Before, during, and after the interviews, I knew this project was one that I was meant to undertake.

Even in my Baptist years, I had begun to visit and then take retreats in monasteries. That proved to be an immediate love affair, as I discovered men and women of uncommon insight who had also, in a very radical way, followed the leading of Christ. While my vocation was clearly not to become a monk, my vocation did seem to be to converse with that world and let that world converse with me. Monastic and contemplative writers—from the desert fathers and mothers to saints Anthony, Pachomius, and Benedict, to authors Thomas Kelly and Thomas Merton—became guides whom I trusted to tell the uncommon truth.

Monasteries are often misrepresented. They are not hermetically sealed bubbles where men and women flee to escape the world. Monks and nuns take being "in the world" as seriously as the command to not be "of the world" (John 17:14). And as we all have, they, too, have lived through more than a decade of religious hatred and intolerance. But I also knew that their training would give monks and nuns a different angle of perception on our suffering.

As Thomas Merton described his own time in history, so I understand our age as one where the better question is not "What will happen next?"—tempting as that question is—but rather "How shall we live?" So even as early Christians headed into the deserts in search of a "word of life" from the desert fathers and mothers, I began a journey to monasteries across the country in search of a "word of life" for our troubled age.

I did not take this journey as an academic, a professor gathering data for an objective research project. Rather, I came to these interviews as a pilgrim or seeker, without a thesis to prove but needing answers that would satisfy both mind and heart. I credit the monks, nuns, and others whom I interviewed for reading my need correctly. They spoke from their hearts to my heart and, in the process, this journey changed my life.

I ended this journey a different person of faith than I was at the beginning. At the beginning of my travels, I was keenly aware of the potential of religious faith to produce massive hatred and intolerance. By the end, I had to confront and transcend my own hatred and intolerance.

I began this journey with anger and confusion. By the end of it, I had to confront my impoverished understanding of forgiveness—that most taboo of words after 9/11—in order to make room for the radical power of that holy act.

I began this journey with a sense of a divided world, the "them" whom we wish to annihilate on one side, and the "us" whom we wish to protect on the other. By the end of the journey, my own divided heart was beginning to heal. The process was painful, but I eventually and gradually found myself waking to a new reality, where the divided worlds of enemy and friend have been replaced by only one category— the neighbor who has sacred value.

I began this journey with a hope that what I would hear in these interviews might help fellow Christians who were also searching for a spiritual response to hatred, fear, and terrorism. By the end of the journey, Muslim friends familiar with the project convinced me that the interviews would offer comfort and hope to people of other faiths as well.

What is my hope for *Peace Be With You*? My hope is that readers will sense that the questions I put to monks, nuns, and others about faith, fear, hate, hope, and forgiveness are ones that you have wanted to ask someone over our decade-long, and still continuing, struggle with intolerance, terrorism, and uncertainty. And I hope that the insights these monks, nuns, and others shared will transform you as they have changed me.

Terrorism and intolerance are not concerns restricted to only one theological perspective. My conservative friends, politically and religiously, are as troubled as my liberal friends at how we as people of faith should pray and act in these uncertain times. So whatever faith tradition you belong to, and wherever you would place yourself on the theological spectrum, I hope that you will find in *Peace Be With You* renewed hope for a spiritual and God-honoring response to what plagues our world.

And finally, as the Orthodox liturgy expresses my prayer, "Peace be with you, O reader."

In Search of a "Word of Life"

This book was born out of three stories that were told to me seemingly by coincidence between 2001 and 2006—three knocks at a door that, when I opened it, led to the writing of this book. By the time I heard the third story, I was ready to begin the journey.

THE FIRST KNOCK—BROTHER ISAAC

In November 2001, ten weeks after 9/11, I flew with two college students to New Mexico to visit the Monastery of Christ in the Desert. A grant that had funded a project on faith development among young adults brought us to this isolated Benedictine monastery to interview one of the monks. The trip was my first time on an airplane since 9/11, and I remember feeling a rush of joy as we lifted off the ground. The flight seemed a personal victory over al-Qaeda.

At the end of our interview with Brother Isaac, a young, outgoing monk whom I had met on a previous visit to Christ in the Desert, he made a passing reference to how the events of September 11 had affected the monastery. Retreatants who happened to be at Christ in the Desert at the time, he explained, reported that they could not imagine being at a better place during that tragedy.

Brother Isaac's own recollection of those days was somewhat different. He described his wrestling with the gospel text for September 12, a text in which Jesus commands His followers to love their enemies.

"That gospel was hard for me," Brother Isaac confessed, "but Jesus is always right."

Brother Isaac's comment was the first knock on a door, the first connection between terrorism and monastic life, but I hardly heard that knock. Like most Americans that fall, I was still in shock over 9/11, and, like some Americans, I was trying to downplay its long-term significance. By November, US troops along with international support had gone into Afghanistan, and the outcome of that action seemed initially encouraging.

THE SECOND KNOCK—FATHER MATTHEW KELTY

In early March 2002, I traveled to Gethsemani Abbey in Kentucky on a personal Lenten retreat. There, as I had many times before, I left the last service of compline to catch Father Matthew Kelty's evening talk. Until recently, Father Matthew offered nightly reflections for retreatants. Mixing the poetry of John Donne and Francis Thompson with Scripture and monastic insights, Father Matthew offered a kind of spiritual dessert before guests retired for the night.

On that evening in early 2002, Father Matthew departed from his usual remarks about living the Christian life with wonder and humility to talk about his response to 9/11—specifically, his decision to cut an American flag out of the newspaper and tape it to his door. A few days later, after he'd noticed a few raised eyebrows from fellow monks to his patriotic gesture, he scrawled the word *Peace* across the flag. His actions attracted the attention of a reporter and photographer from

Louisville, and within a few weeks, the photo of Father Matthew with the peace flag along with a story about Gethsemani Abbey's response to 9/11 appeared in the *New York Times*.

Father Matthew's flag story was the second knock on the door, the second connection between 9/11 and monastic life, but it meant as little to me at the time as had Brother Isaac's remark at Christ in the Desert.

THE THIRD KNOCK—KATY RALPH

In the summer of 2006, I met Katy Ralph while on vacation in northern Wisconsin. Katy is an artist, a gallery director, a granddaughter of a theologian, and by her own admission, a "red diaper baby" (the daughter of American communists). This graceful, soft-spoken woman fascinated me with her firm conviction that art itself could be a spiritual path.

In a conversation later that summer, Katy shared her experiences of being at a New Age retreat center in the California desert when 9/11 occurred. This time, I heard the third knock on the door. While Katy was by no means a nun in the Christian tradition, her experience of isolation from the world on this day got me thinking. Brother Isaac's and Father Matthew's similar reminiscences came back to me, and it struck me that I could hardly be the only person interested in how monks, nuns, and retreatants had reacted to 9/11. Monastic culture is widely different from our consumer one, and I was intrigued by how that tragedy looked through such different lenses.

But curiosity was not the only, or even the main reason that I was drawn toward monastic communities. We were now five years past 9/11, and in an era of increasing terror and uncertainty, I had a mounting and unsettled feeling that we had headed down the wrong path from the beginning. But this feeling was vague. All I could articulate at the time was that if revenge and retaliation were the best responses our nation could muster after 9/11, then Jesus did not have to come, live among us, and preach a radical understanding of "neighbor" that includes the enemy.

RESPONSES TO A NEW KIND OF WORLD

Although I had initially accepted the incursion into Afghanistan as justified to dislodge the Taliban—a group about whom I knew little—I joined other Americans in being skeptical about the invasion of Iraq in the summer of 2003.

Conservative friends told me that I was missing the bigger picture. To them, the war in Iraq provided an opportunity to plant the seed of democracy in the midst of one of the most troubled areas of the world. With regime change, we could create an ally in the region, a consistent source of oil, and a neutral nation for Israel not to lose sleep over. I was told that the desire for democracy beat within the breast of every living person. I was assured that our troops would be welcomed by the Iraqi people. But we were not welcomed, and my skepticism about the war on terror only increased as the conflict wore on.

Of course, there had been a religious response to 9/11 from the Christian community, but that response reduced rather than strengthened hope. Instead of encouraging their churches to pursue a much-needed study of Islam, one of the world's largest and fastest-growing religions, some prominent conservative Christian voices were exploiting 9/11, using that tragedy as an opportunity to spread fear and disinformation about Islam. Pat Robertson called Islam "the enemy." For Billy Graham's son Franklin, Islam was "evil." For the late Jerry Falwell, Muhammad was a "terrorist" and the Qur'an comparable to *Mein Kampf.* For Jerry Vine, Muhammad was "demon-possessed" and a "pedophile."[1]

Those slanderous comments exploded like bombs in the hearts of Muslims around the world. The accusations also worried me deeply. Islam and Christianity have had a long history of contact, sometimes peaceful, sometimes belligerent. Part of the tension between the two faiths is that both are "fulfillment religions." Christianity has historically understood itself as the fulfillment of Judaism, even as Islam views itself as the ultimate fulfillment of both Judaism and Christianity.

This common feature of "fulfillment" theology has also contributed to an imbalance in understanding between the traditions of Christianity and Islam. Many Muslims have an impressive knowledge of Christianity, some able to out-quote the New Testament in dialogues with Christians. Most Christians, however, have ignored Islam, leaving them open to such calumnies as "Muslims worship a different God than Jews and Christians" and the conviction that "all Muslims are violent." Also common among many Christians is the distorted view that al-Qaeda is synonymous with Islam.

IN SEARCH OF HOPE

Being an academic, I initially turned to the scholarly experts to try to find some clear thinking on this age of terror and uncertainty. At first, I was enthusiastic about what I was reading. The war on terror is a war of ideas, the experts argued, and by believing that, I grew confident that an answer to terrorism lay at the bottom of some think tank.

The following fall, I offered, with a sense of the experts' confidence, a course on religion and violence. Over the last months of 2005, the class focused on six trouble spots in the world. By the following semester, I had to add three nations to that list. Clearly, religious violence was a virus both rapidly growing and highly resistant to current treatments.

THE DANGER OF ISLAMOPHOBIA

Too many of my college students grew up convinced that Islam is the enemy of the United States and all democracies. They were in junior high school when the planes hit the towers and the Pentagon. If they had not seen the nightly war footage from the streets of Baghdad, they certainly had seen numerous films featuring fanatical Muslims, such as *Executive Decision* and *The Siege*.

While my career has given me numerous opportunities to address and dispel such misconceptions, I found their prevalence among my students suggestive of a dangerous national trend of what was termed *Islamophobia*. Evidence of this moral disease was available at the local, national, and international levels. I received a phone call from a parent in a nearby town who had removed his children from the public schools because the curriculum included an unbiased intro-duction to Islam. Laws were and are being passed in Europe, but also in Canada that restrict the wearing of the *hijab*, or veil, by Muslim women. And there were disturbing stories from Guantánamo, alleg-ing deliberate abuses of the Qur'an in a practice than can only be termed *religious hazing*.

The readings about religion and violence were sobering, and as the semester progressed, I felt some pressure to conclude the course with some grounds for hope. But by the end of that first semester, I realized that we did not yet have a hopeful answer. The experts offered brilliant analyses of the problem. In contrast, their solutions seemed vague and, the more I studied them, unlikely to work.

I began to feel that I'd taught myself into a corner.

Who, I wondered, had the Christian stature and credibility to address this climate of fear and hatred? Previous visits to monasteries convinced me that in these communities I would at least find men and women who had responded differently to 9/11 and who held very dif-ferent viewpoints from those of political pundits and TV evangelists.

I also hoped that in monasteries and retreat centers I would uncover wisdom, the type sorely missing in our terror-filled world.

A NEW PATH TOWARD HOPE

I consequently began this project with only two questions in mind. First, how did monks, nuns, and retreatants respond when first learning of 9/11? And second, how have they continued to respond to our world of violence and terror, given their spiritual resources and training?

As the project progressed, I realized that the second question was far more significant for those of us who seek a hopeful way forward. But as I expanded on both questions, I also realized that the questions were related. The initial response of monks, nuns, and retreatants often revealed the potency of spiritual resources that we do not use in the general culture.

As the idea of the project began to take shape in my mind, I realized that I was following an ancient Christian pattern. Out in the stark desert regions of Egypt in early Christian history had lived desert fathers and mothers, men and women known for their spiritual wisdom. These forerunners of modern monks and nuns attracted hundreds of Christian pilgrims who were searching for a transforming "word of life."

I awoke the day after my conversation with Katy, the one in which I heard the third "knock," with a sense of excitement. I realized that for some time I had been ready to take this journey. With my students, I had studied the diverse causes of religious violence. Now, in search of a remedy, I would interview the best spiritual doctors I knew.

LOVE IS A DISCIPLINE OF THE MIND

Of course, my friend Katy was not a nun, but she had been in similar spiritually based isolation at the time of 9/11. When I contacted Katy and asked to interview her, I did not tell her that our conversation would be a test balloon of the project.

Katy came a bit late to the interview, complaining of a headache, which struck me as a bad sign. I breathed a sigh of relief when it became clear that Katy's memories of 9/11 and the following days were vivid. She had awakened early on September 11, 2001, with a feeling that something was wrong. In the middle of the morning yoga class, someone began pounding on the door. A moment later, Katy heard someone gasp and then begin sobbing. One of the leaders informed the group of the tragedy and added, "The only thing we can do is surround everyone on both sides, on all sides, with love."

Love—love as a discipline of the mind, not a feeling—was the major theme in Katy's interview. Again and again in those initial days, she said, when retreatants felt overcome by fear, the leaders brought the focus back to love.

Katy explained that she was on staff for that session as travel coordinator for the retreatants and staff. The assignment should have been a simple one, but with 9/11 canceling flights and closing airports, Katy quickly felt overwhelmed. That was when the sickening headache began, one that wouldn't subside until Sunday, September 16, when she was at the airport herself for her flight home. Headaches are rare for her, Katy said, but the one she was feeling on the day of our interview was eerily like the one she'd had in the days following 9/11.

Upon her return to Wisconsin, Katy felt fortunate to have experienced those odd and terrible days in the isolation of the California desert but also out of step with her friends. "I could see [the need to] love everyone in a whole different way."

Love everyone—what did that mean? I wondered. Katy had struck me as hardly being naive or a romantic dreamer. I asked her to offer an example of what this love meant. Putting her hands down slowly on the table, Katy paused for a moment before replying. "I symbolically have George [W.] Bush on my altar, and send him love [every day]. This is where we have to go," Katy continued, "to honor everyone even if we totally disagree with them."

Okay, I probed, that may work for you as an individual as an alternative to revenge, but what direction should we be taking as a nation? Katy again paused before answering. "More and more of us [need] to lose our sense of self-importance." She quickly added, "It's about power. [It's] to have personal power without needing to have power over anyone else." That was clearly a distinction, I realized as she spoke, that we as a nation have not understood.

If exercising personal power rather than global dominance is the key to peace, did that mean that peace was more than a far-off dream? Katy nodded. "If we don't dream up peace, if we don't [dream] more and more and more, to the tipping point . . . we're not going to have it. We're certainly not going to have it [by] waging war."

The interview ended on that note. My first response was to feel encouraged but also more than a little troubled. One initial concern of mine had concerned how much people would remember about 9/11, as we were now five years beyond the crisis. Yet Katy's memories had returned with vivid clarity, and I was encouraged by her comment that more memories had come back to her as the interview progressed.

But her language, specifically her repeated emphasis on *hope, peace,* and especially *love,* troubled me. Those words flit like butterflies across greeting cards and yellowing posters from Woodstock. Along with *happiness,* these three terms are some of the most despoiled in our current culture. How could they possibly offer a remedy?

A BATTLE WITH WORDS

Words are not defined by dictionaries but by communities. In Katy's experience in the desert of California, I could see that *hope, peace,* and *love* were attitudes that had been as specifically applied to the crisis as medicine is to a disease. To her, these words were not fragile butterflies but bricks. They were solid, capable of building walls. And behind that wall of words and the practicing of those attitudes, Katy had experienced 9/11 far differently than I had.

During her stay in the retreat center, Katy had seen no news coverage of that terrible day, while those looped images were all that I and most Americans did see. Despite her limited access to the media, she had focused on something about the tragedy that I had not: she sensed that spirituality offered the only path through 9/11 and our fearful situation. And on that spiritual path, hope, peace, and love matter. They are as real as bricks.

I thought back to the first knock on the door, Brother Isaac's description of his battle with Jesus' command to forgive the enemy. In Christian circles, we recite and read Jesus' words of forgiveness easily—too easily. Brother Isaac balked at those same words from the gospel because, in his community, members know they have to live by the words they say. In monastic communities, words matter.

In contrast, my culture has made a science out of trivializing language, using *love* to sell toothpaste, *peace* to sell CDs, and *hope* to cover up failed military operations. Little wonder that I struggled as I tried to visualize what it would be like to make the painful sacrifice of placing my enemies on my spiritual altar—the sacred center of my life—and sending out love to them every day.

The interview with Katy offered the first of many struggles that I would have with language over the course of the project. The cloister walls that separate monastic culture from the outside world also protect that community's language from being despoiled, from falling into the verbal sin of sentimentality. Katy was my first exercise in having to listen with fresh ears, in taking very seriously, and often in new ways, words that tend to be trivialized in my culture. I also realized that I would need to know much more about the monastic communities themselves if I were to understand their language, and it was something I needed to discover firsthand.

Religious studies scholar Robert Ellwood has offered an insightful description of religion as both an X-ray and a drummer calling dancers to the floor.[2] I was convinced that monastic communities would offer "X-rays" into what was wrong below the surface of our world, especially what we in the United States had missed in our response to 9/11 and in our continuing war on terror. But I would very likely distort those insights unless I stepped onto the dance floor—that is, unless I stepped inside those cloister walls myself.

As I drove home from the interview with Katy, I tried to imagine the journey ahead. I pictured numerous visits to monasteries and many interviews in my search for a "word of life." Some of that wisdom would undoubtedly be painful to hear. But I was ready to listen.

"DON'T LOSE HEART"

When I returned to the college in the fall of 2006, I began the process of sending letters to monasteries requesting visits and interviews. As I awaited their responses, I watched the political game unfolding as one politician after another established a presidential exploratory committee and made sure to ask God to bless America as they boarded planes to take zip trips to Iraq. Here there was no discussion of the difference between personal power and power over others. Every candidate assumed that a renewal of American strength and influence was what the world needed. American dominance, which contributes so much to the tension in the world, would remain an unquestioned plank in both parties' platforms.

Also sobering that fall of 2006 were the world events that nearly overwhelmed my course. The civil war in Iraq, the Muslim reaction to Pope Benedict XVI's challenge in September, the renewal of war in Somalia, and the Taliban returning in force in Afghanistan proved beyond a doubt that religious violence had lost none of its virulence.

The last month of that semester can only be described as grim. Palestinians were now fighting both Israelis and one another. In Lebanon, a high-ranking official and leader of the Christian community was assassinated. About the same time, a Russian ex-spy critical of Putin's policies against Muslims in Chechnya was mysteriously poisoned.

A sense of bleakness settled over my class as we saw how ubiquitous were the conditions that foster religious violence around the world and how puny the efforts to curb it. I admit that I was not surprised when some students in the course had stopped engaging the issues by midsemester. I supposed that they were simply calculating how much of the material they needed to remember to pass the course. *Globalization, Kashmir, Hamas, Hezbollah, Islamic jihad, Kahanists,* and *Muslim Brotherhood* were simply terms to hold in the brain for a few weeks, like *the Battle of Bull Run, the Taft-Hartley Act,* and *the Pleistocene era.*

One student wrote in her journal: *"Thinking about all these questions makes me feel hopeless. . . . We all know that we have sent out armies to stop terrorism. Even though we have done this it is not helping us at all."*

I scratched *"Don't lose heart"* in the margin. But this student and others like her were simply staring into the same abyss that I was.

IN SEARCH OF A NEW PATH

In the nick of time, I received the first positive responses from monasteries. The Benedictine Monastery of Christ in the Desert in Abiquiu,

New Mexico; the Orthodox Skete of St. Michaels in nearby Cañones, New Mexico; as well as the Trappist Abbey of Gethsemani in Kentucky had invited me to visit in January to conduct interviews.

I jumped eagerly to the preparations and found the interview questions surprisingly easy to formulate. My eagerness was bolstered by a comment made that same month by Nathan Dungan on NPR's *Speaking of Faith*. He observed that 9/11 had offered our country an opportunity for reflection, a chance to step back and consider who we are and what we are about.

I found myself in agreement with Dungan's conclusion that this opportunity had been missed.

If reflection had occurred anywhere in this country, it had occurred in monastic communities dedicated to contemplation and prayer.

In January 2007, some seventeen hundred years after early Christian pilgrims journeyed into the desert and five and a half years after 9/11, I gathered my notepads, tape recorders, and plane ticket in search of that for which the desert fathers and mothers had searched— a word of life.

I was a Christian looking for Christian wisdom. What I found was indeed Christian, but it was also a new way for all people of faith— Christians and Muslims especially—to work together in building a compassionate human family.

PART ONE

Voices from the Desert

CHAPTER 1

"Where Are the Prophets?"

The Monastery of Christ in the Desert
Abiquiu, New Mexico
January 11, 2007

I began my travels to monasteries fully aware that monks and nuns might not wish to offer advice to the outside world. I was prepared to reply that I was not asking them to lecture American culture but rather to respond to the thousands of others like me who are seeking some light, some way forward, in an increasingly dark world. This hope for light was precisely what drew me to monastic communities.

Nearly all religions have a contemplative branch, an option that encourages reflection and solitude. Very early in Christian history, men and women chose to live apart from society where they could devote their lives to the disciplines of prayer, reading, and manual work. Even before Christianity was legalized in AD 312, these men and women found the Christian life in urban areas to be too lax and too comfortable. The first religious desert dwellers were hermits living alone in caves, but soon communities formed around a leader, an abbot or abbess, who led the group in a common rule for life.

Monasteries that go bad, as many monastic houses have done in Christian history, go bad for the same general reason. The monastic salt loses its savor when the community loses its seriousness, sacrifice, and solitude. When monasteries find it easy to conform to the surrounding culture, monasteries lose their reason for existence.

Nearly every monastic community I visited expressed the same worry, that its life was in danger of becoming too comfortable, its sacrifices too few, its contrast to the culture too faint. Father Columba Stewart of Saint John's Abbey in Collegeville, Minnesota, expressed a concern of all monks and nuns: "In common with most monasteries of our kind, we are finding that our forms of entertainment are becoming more and more like those of the culture around us. We see the same videos and TV shows, read the same books, visit the same restaurants, stores, and websites. With the coming of the Internet, 'separation from the world' has become even more challenging."[1]

While planting a monastery in a remote forest or desert does not by itself protect a community from these dangers, physical isolation brings with it certain logistical challenges—food, shelter, medical care—that make life more difficult. The Monastery of Christ in the Desert, lying thirteen miles off the highway down a forest road in northern New Mexico, is just such a place. Founded in 1964 by Father Aelred Wall, the Monastery of Christ in the Desert was deliberately set in an inconvenient location.

From the moment this project became real in my mind, I knew that my first visit would be to Christ in the Desert. This Benedictine house in New Mexico was where I had heard the first "knock on the door" while doing research there in 2001. I also believed that the extreme solitude of the place would help me find my footing with the project. In that hope, I was echoing the belief of Father Aelred, who, in 1964, understood the desert to offer "a place where one sees the true proportion of things, a place of purification and repentance, a place where God's providence becomes unmistakably clear."[2] Finally, my previous work with Brother Isaac in 2001 led me to believe that Abbot Philip might be open to my request to interview in the community.

In early November 2006, I wrote to Abbot Philip, explaining the project and asking permission to visit. Not long after Thanksgiving, I received word that my request to come in mid-January had been granted. About the same time, I received an invitation to conduct interviews at St. Michael's Skete, an Orthodox monastery located about forty miles away in another canyon near Cañones, New Mexico.

The prospect of beginning the project began to affect not only my waking hours (composing interview questions, making travel arrangements, and applying for grants), but also my dream life as well. In late December, I dreamed that a colleague, a counselor at the college, was telling me that I needed heart surgery. Something very deep in my upbringing, he said, needed to be repaired.

Clearly, my psyche was aware that something major in my life was coming, something demanding a deep change. At least, that was what I hoped the dream meant.

THE JOURNEY TO CHRIST IN THE DESERT

One unexpected change in my plans occurred when our older son, Leif, expressed a desire to accompany me to Christ in the Desert. He had become acquainted with Christ in the Desert through a program on the Learning Channel entitled *Monastery*, a series that Leif then drew to my attention. A cross between a documentary on monastic life and *Survivor*, the program followed five young men as they struggled for forty days in monastic life at Christ in the Desert.

When Leif asked if he could tag along on my visit, I told him he was welcome to do so, if he could get time off from work at the Peace Learning Center in Indianapolis. At the time, I had no way of knowing that Leif's own experience at Christ in the Desert would contribute so much to my own.

On January 9, the day before our flight, US planes bombed Somalia. While the war on terror gave birth to yet another battle-front, Leif and I arrived safely in Albuquerque and learned of record snowfalls in the northern canyons. To be on the safe side, we rented a four-wheel-drive vehicle and headed north.

Several hours later, we found the turnoff and followed the forest road for thirteen miles down to the Chama River and then to the monastery. The road was as bad as I remembered it from my trip there six years earlier, and the drive was breathtakingly frightful. Later that evening, at compline, the last service of the evening, the monks prayed for guests and monks who had to travel in and out on the road. The prayer is necessary. While we were there, one guest straggled in on the morning after she was supposed to arrive, her truck having gotten stuck in the two feet of snow that had fallen overnight.

During our stay, the skies alternated between blinding sunlight and heavy snow showers. At times, we could not even see the church from the guesthouse, while at other times we were overwhelmed by the cliffs and canyons that surround the monastery. Some of these rock formations are jagged. Others are so smooth and striated that the canyon seems to be made of Neapolitan ice cream.

As is true of many monastic houses, the history of Christ in the Desert has been one of financial struggle. This reality is obscured, however, by the stunning adobe buildings, particularly the wondrous church by the noted architect George Nakashima.

The visitors' center and refectory are also new and impressive, the massive frescoes alone contributing to a sense of luxuriousness. Leif and I entered the building and found the bookstore open. Hoping to make contact with someone, we ran into Prior Christian. Tall, bearded, and sockless in sandals despite the cold, Prior Christian sent my heart into near arrhythmia when he confessed to knowing nothing about my visit.

But as I briefly explained the project, Prior Christian brightened and immediately shared his own memory of being in Mass on September 11 when the planes hit the towers. Why, I wondered, had I not brought my tape recorder?

Prior Christian described how the monastery, with no radio or TV on that morning, had first heard about the tragedy via the Internet. Then he mentioned a column he'd just finished writing for the monastery's newsletter, the subject of the column being why *World Trade Center* and *Flight 93* were his two favorite movies of the past year. "What will be hit next?" he asked. "The Golden Gate Bridge?"

My heart was racing. I'd not been at the monastery more than thirty minutes and hadn't even asked one question, but this monk was talking about the very subject that I'd come to discuss. I took it as a good omen that I'd run into the monastery's leader (the prior is in charge when the abbot is away, which was the case during our visit) and that he was giving me gold without my even having to pan for it. I pictured the two of us sitting down for a longer chat, when, with my tape recorder running, he could share to his heart's content—and mine—his memories and thoughts.

When I told him of my hope, the prior shook his head. My heart took another dive as he told me that I was asking the impossible. With the abbot away on a much-needed sabbatical and with one of the monastery's key board members arriving the next day for an important financial meeting, my request was completely out of the question.

I could hear the desperation and impatience in my voice as I asked him to consider finding fifteen minutes—which, in truth, would have been useless—in the four days of our stay. No, he repeated kindly but firmly. He wished my project the best but said that I should not count on him at all. But as he left the bookstore, he called back that he'd try to find a copy of his newsletter column on 9/11 before I left.

A PRAYER AT THE EMPTY ALTAR

I left for vespers feeling ashamed and chastened. In my first hour on the job, I had betrayed my own vow to be a patient listener and had tried to force my will on the project. I recommitted myself to taking whatever the stay at Christ in the Desert would give me, though it would not be the last time during the project that I would try to force matters to go my way.

At vespers, I scanned the small clusters of monks on both sides of the stone altar as they chanted my least favorite psalm. Psalm 137 is a lament of the exiles in Babylon and ends with a prayer for God to bring the day soon when Babylonian babies would be dashed against a rock.

I did my best to forget the words as I focused on the church itself. Built in a Greek cross plan, the stunning church has four wings that jut out from the central open space. Guests sit in the west wing, their eyes drawn to the massive windows soaring upward to the sheer cliff face outside. In the early morning, the cliff face seems to hold the sun back as it rises to light the valley, while in the evening the same cliff catches the day's last rays. The stunning sight was what I most remembered from my two previous visits.

But that night, my focus remained in the church and on the empty altar in the center, set precisely where the two arms of the cross intersect. The altar's stone base rises out of the ground like some ancient pillar. Rough-hewn, the stone base looks as if it had been transported halfway around the world from a catacomb of Rome. The altar top is a slab of stone as well, but smooth.

I aimed a prayer at the empty altar. "Lord, help me not to be so hungry for this work that I forget to wait upon You."

On the way to dinner after that service, Leif and I met Brother André, the guestmaster, who was my contact for the project. Short and bespectacled, Brother André looks a lot like Bob Newhart. And with Newhart's deadpan face and with the problem of another winter storm on the way, Brother André looked like a man shouldering many concerns, with my interviews being pretty low on the list. "We'll talk about the interview tomorrow," he said.

The interview? Was he saying there was only *one*? Yes, he replied, explaining that many of the monks at Christ in the Desert are from Southeast Asia, Africa, or Central America (as I'd noticed at vespers). They had told Brother André that they did not feel comfortable being interviewed. And the older monks had begged off, saying that their memories of 9/11 were too fuzzy. What about Brother Isaac? I asked, referring to the monk I'd interviewed back in 2001. Gone, he said. He'd left monastic life.

At the evening meal in the new refectory—monks sitting on one side, guests on the other, the prior sitting alone at the head table—I assessed the situation. We had flown out of Indiana at six o'clock in the morning and driven the crazy road to the monastery for one interview?

I remembered my prayer a few moments before in the church. "Lord, help me not to be so hungry for this work that I forget to wait upon You." I amended the prayer. "Okay, Lord, if it's one interview, it's one interview. But how about making it a good one?"

A CALL TO CHANGE—BROTHER ANDRÉ

Brother André and I sat down for the interview after the morning work period on January 11, 2007, my first full day at Christ in the Desert. He had avoided meeting my gaze earlier that morning, and I grew worried that he might cancel the interview. But I was also curious about his behavior. Brother André had e-mailed me several months before, inviting me to visit and to interview. Why the reticence now?

At the agreed-upon time, we met in Brother André's office, where a computer and phone provide the monastery's sole link to the outside world. I set up my recording equipment and explained briefly the origins of the project, all the while aware that this was the first official interview of the project. How many interviews would follow before the project was completed? I wondered. Ten, twenty, maybe more? *Or maybe just this one.*

Brother André began with a comment that I would hear several times over the life of the project: he was not the person to ask about how the community of Christ in the Desert had responded to 9/11 because he had been away at the time.

Monks and nuns do take vows of stability, meaning that they promise to remain at their particular monastery until death or until reassignment by the abbot. But monastics also take a vow of obedience. As the voice of Christ in the community, the abbot or abbess can send a member away for further education or to conduct needed work. In September 2001, Brother André had been sent to St. Anselm University in New York to take course work.

As Brother André shared his memories of 9/11, I realized that we had experienced that tragedy not very differently, as I had assumed, but quite similarly. We had both learned of the tragedy while in an educational setting. He heard the news from his professor, even as I, as a professor, knew that I would need to talk to my students about what had happened.

After attending a special noontime Mass at the university, Brother André retreated to the student pub, where he watched the same footage the rest of us around the country and world were watching. But Brother André focused on a smaller and perhaps more manageable memory of the day. The mother of one of Brother André's fellow monks in New York (he was staying at a monastery adjoining the university) had died the previous weekend, and her funeral was held the night of September 11. "It wasn't bad enough with 9/11," he said, "but I had to go to a funeral of someone I didn't even know." He described how disoriented he felt at the reception, trying to be pleasant to people whom he did not know, all the while struggling to grasp what had happened in New York City, at the Pentagon, and in Pennsylvania.

That evening, Brother André remembered writing in his journal, *"Why did this happen? Why?"*

But after writing *"Why did this happen?"* in his journal, Brother André wrote another question, one that few Americans considered on 9/11: *"Why not?"* While he was quick to say that he did not condone the actions of the hijackers, he realized, when he considered the radical Islamic view of the West, that, from their point of view, "they're getting back at us for the way we're living."

I could not tell at this point if Brother André was simply trying to view the tragedy from another perspective, or if he'd agreed with some aspects of the radical perspective. My confusion cleared when Brother André explained that 9/11 made him recall the ancient covenant between God and Israel. "When you look at the Old Testament . . . when the people strayed from Yahweh, things would happen to them. [God] let the enemy come in, or they'd be sent to Babylon in exile."

The West, in Brother André's view, is in the same shape as Israel during the days of the early prophets. He shook his head, saying he couldn't accept the thought that God had directly caused 9/11, but he did believe that "God lets things happen . . . I think we're paying for our sins. I think of that a lot." He shook his head again at the irony of our nation forcing change on Iraq when we need to change ourselves.

The belief that God could use a nation's enemies to punish His own people was a perspective rarely mentioned in our day, I remarked. Rhetoric from pulpits, as well from Washington, preferred to view the war on terror as good versus evil. Compared to al-Qaeda, the Taliban, and other radical Islamic groups, the West views itself as at least relatively innocent. It is assumed that God, in weighing the two sides, would side with the West.

It was not that simple for Brother André. "What God [was] doing with Israel," he replied, "was always trying to bring them back, and sometimes the only way to get the people back is to get them on their knees." He compared present-day America to those in recovery programs who have yet to hit rock-bottom before they will begin to change.

Although I had not mentioned Iraq, Brother André said how greatly the present war troubled him. "I was really sad yesterday when I found out that the president wants to send twenty-one thousand [more] troops to Iraq. That really put me down the rest of the day."

It dawned on me that I had misread Brother André. He was not reticent about the interview but troubled.

"Twenty-one thousand," he repeated. "And for what?"

And why, he continued, had Americans not grasped from the beginning the deep animosity between the various factions in Iraq? Instead of solving anything, Brother André believed that our involvement was only making matters worse.

This interview project would dispel one misunderstanding after another about monks and nuns. One of the most common is that monks and nuns are "separate from the world," and, as such, are out of touch with modernity. Brother André was more informed about current events than most people in our culture.

A CRY FOR GOD TO END INJUSTICE

I asked Brother André how his Benedictine practice had strengthened him and might offer something helpful to others. Besides the prayer life and the daily immersion in Scripture, Brother André drew particular attention to the Psalms, which Benedictine monks chant seven times a day. "You can equate what's going on in a lot of these old psalms, these psalms of struggle and war and 'Help me, God.'"

It became clear that 9/11 and the war in Iraq have profoundly affected what Brother André ponders as he chants those psalms. He explained, "You can look through the eyes of what's going on . . . and put that into your prayer."

To illustrate his point, Brother André brought up the cursing psalms, including the one that troubled me most, Psalm 137. Brother André suggested that I needed to listen to those psalms in a different way. I should not hear them as bloodthirsty requests for vengeance or, as I have thought, dangerous theology for a world already drowning in violence. Instead, these psalms are the cry of the oppressed for God to end injustice.

How different those psalms would sound, he suggested, if we picture an Iraqi whose child has just been killed by Allied troops or whose house has just been bombed. "These are the people who are actually in that situation of these cursing psalms," he explained.

He mentioned a photo he had recently seen on the Internet that had moved him deeply. The photo was of two Iraqi men eating lunch together at an outdoor café, laughing as they enjoyed each other's company. "These are real people," he said, as if this were a revelation. Even if their ideology is different from ours, Brother André added, he couldn't get past their basic humanity. "They have mothers and sisters, you know."

I was not listening to a curmudgeon, I realized, but to a tormented man. Here was a man who understood that the tragedy of Iraq is not summed up in the number of US casualties. Here was a man who agonized about the untold number of Iraqis who have died or who suffer on a daily basis. Here was a man who was "in Iraq" when he chanted the psalms—seven times a day.

HOW AM I CHANGING MY LIFE?

I shared Nathan Dungan's observation, made on National Public Radio in November 2007, that 9/11 had been an opportunity for needed introspection on the part of the American people, but that opportunity had been largely missed. And yet, I added, it seemed to me that Brother André had not missed that opportunity. I asked if he could explain why more people did not wrestle with what was happening.

"It hasn't hit home for most people," he replied. "[The tragedy] hit home for those who got killed, and it hit home for those whose families [were] involved, and friends," but not for most of us.

I thought also of many of my students who live their college years in a bubble, largely unaware of what is happening in their world; 9/11 and the suffering in the Middle East have not changed reality for most of them. Life goes on as usual, even though life is no longer that.

My reverie was interrupted by Brother André's next comment, a chilling one, perhaps one that I'd been afraid to let myself think. "[Americans] are going to need more of this [type of tragedy] to change their way of living." After a moment, Brother André asked me to imagine what happens when a monastery loses its devotion to the rules, to its observance, and to its practice of listening to God. "If you lose that observance, it's very hard to get it back. I don't care how good the monks are." This was how he saw American society at the present time.

I shared my observation that most Americans do not understand 9/11 and the continuing war on terror as a call to rethink our way of life. Outside of security measures, I could not recall one aspect of our way of life and our way of being in the world that has been curtailed because of 9/11. The mind-set of many has seemed to be that they count on the military to fix the problem and return life to what it was before 9/11.

His hands flew up at my comments, his voice booming as he said, "I tell God, 'Where are the prophets?' I say to God, 'Save America. Bring the prophets.'" Brother André raced on. "No one is saying anything! You go to the churches; they don't preach anything about this stuff . . . They don't talk about issues anymore. They're afraid people are going to leave the church. [The congregants] don't want to hear it."

Brother André immediately turned the focus back on himself and his vocation. "It makes me think as a monk . . . how am I living my life? Am I true to my vocation?"

He continued, "I was thinking yesterday about [our military] sending all these young men to Iraq again. I say, 'How am I changing my life?' Here we pray to God all the time. 'Oh, help this person; help my friend who is sick.' But I tell the monks sometimes, 'Yeah, we ask God for all these neat things to help people out, but if we don't live our lives the way we're supposed to, do we think God is going to listen to us?'" I could sense his pain as he added that he believed that God is often limited by human beings, including the monks at Christ in the Desert.

Brother André was well aware of how many people dismiss his vocation as useless and even selfish, assuming that all his efforts are for his own spiritual welfare and benefit. "[But] we're not here for ourselves . . . We're here for the world . . . But how can we expect the world to behave if I can't do it myself?"

Author and former Trappist monk Thomas Merton made a similar observation on his first visit to the Abbey of Gethsemani at the outset of World War II. "This is the real capital of the country in which we are living," Merton wrote. "This is the center of all the vitality that is in America. This is the cause and reason why the nation is holding together. These men, hidden in the anonymity of their choir and their white cowls, are doing for their land what no army, no congress, no president could ever do as such: they are winning for it the grace and the protection and the friendship of God."[3]

Such a notion will undoubtedly sound ridiculous if not superstitious to many who equate power with influence and lobbying strength. Monasteries have neither. Yet those with a monastic vocation believe, nonetheless, that there is an interconnected web of responsibility. What we do and do not do matters beyond our own lives. "I believe in corporate sin," Brother André said, "if that's the right word . . . I tell everybody, 'What we do here [that is] wrong affects the world.'"

DEALING WITH HATRED

I asked Brother André what response we should make to those who hate us and our way of life. First, he said, it is necessary that we seriously ask why others hate us and simply not assume that such hate is without reason. "But if they are hating us for a real good reason, then it is our responsibility for us to say, 'Okay, I need to change.' If they hate us because we're immoral . . . then something is wrong in our society."

I focused on the issue raised by Merton, the issue of freedom. Merton revived the Augustinian understanding that real freedom lies in doing the good, the will of God, not in doing whatever we want. Had the West lost sense of limits to guarantee true freedom? I asked.

"Oh, yes," Brother André replied emphatically and offered an example from monastic life. "[People] think you lose your freedom when you come into a monastery. Now you're under obedience, just can't do what you want anymore, can't go out when you want, can't spend money like you want, all these other things we lose, you know . . . But [this life] gives us a greater freedom, the freedom to live our life in God."

I thought of the last stanza of T. S. Eliot's *The Wasteland*, where Eliot compares human life to a sailboat under masterful control. The boat achieves its end, reaches its destination, when the rudder and lines to the sails are controlled. Chaos and confusion, not freedom, are achieved in letting go the lines and leaving the boat to the mercy of the wind. Monastic life is all about taking hold of the ropes—these ropes of discipline that lead to freedom.

Brother André pointed to the daily trial in a monastery of living in close community with others. With monks from Southeast Asia, Latin America, and Africa, Brother André pointed out, Christ in the Desert faces the same challenge of cultural diversity as does our society as a whole. "When things go a little rough here, we say, 'If we can't do it, how do you expect the rest of the world to do it?' We have to show the rest of the world an example that, yes, it can be done."

BEING REAL, FREE, AND BLESSEDLY TORMENTED

As our conversation was wrapping up, the phone rang. Brother André excused himself to interrupt his own voice on the answering machine (*You've reached the Monastery of Christ in the Desert. You may leave a message . . .*). He had evidently surprised the caller, for he next said with a laugh, "Yeah, yeah, I'm a real person."

A real person. One of the key questions of our time, especially in the West, is "What does it mean to be real?" A monk who is also an American, Brother André is troubled and searching for answers. He lives his life every day, in every psalm that he chants, in sharp contrast to a culture that rolls along as if 9/11 had posed no questions for us to consider.

In one of her books, Madeleine L'Engle cites a cardinal who wisely states that a "witness [consists] . . . in being a living mystery. It means to live in such a way that one's life would not make sense if God did not exist."[4]

For many, Brother André's life in his remote canyon of New Mexico, his austere schedule of prayer, and his torment over events in our world make no sense. But if God exists, his life makes more sense than we might want to admit.

The real problem for us in *normal* society, even those of us in the church, is that much of our way of life makes sense only if God does *not* exist. For the majority of us, it is Mick Jagger, not Brother André, who in a popular credit card commercial in 2007 invited Americans to exercise our freedom by doing whatever we want, whenever we want.

Brother André believes that he is a truly free man. I would argue that he is free because he is a *blessedly tormented* man. He is tormented because he finds himself unable to turn away from world events. And he is tormented because he views those events through the lens of the biblical witness, a lens that is anything but rosy.

Brother André reminded me of the eighth-century prophet Amos.

The religious establishment of Amos's day viewed Israel as relatively innocent compared to the gross sins of her enemies. Resting on their covenant with God, Israelites assumed they had special, favored status. If they were ever attacked, they assumed that God would fight on their side.

The prophet Amos, however, probed beneath Israel's surface confidence and found the core rotten. The nation was living far from her covenantal responsibilities, especially mercy toward the poor and powerless. Perhaps Amos's message was dismissed in his day as "blame Israel first," even as Brother André's comments could be dismissed as "blame America first."

But Brother André is harder on his community and himself than on the American society. Living by his community's covenant, the Rule of St. Benedict, Brother André ponders how faithful he and his fellow monastic brothers and sisters have been. Even his daily immersion in the Psalms creates less spiritual comfort than a painful link with the Iraqi people. As God keeps track of the fall of even the sparrow, a monk must also track the pain of this world.

But if Brother André is tormented, he is also *blessed* because he has embraced this vocation. He has chosen to live with his eyes open, and I found his writhing over world events to be oddly comforting. My sense of unease about 9/11 and its aftermath had led me to search for a "word of life." That, I came to realize over the span of 2007, was part of my own vocation. And I consider it fortunate that my search for a "word of life" led me first to Brother André.

CHAPTER 2

Caught Between Paradise and Wilderness

The Monastery of Christ in the Desert
Abiquiu, New Mexico

In the end, thanks to Brother André's intervention, he was not the only person at Christ in the Desert whom I interviewed. He had asked Mother Julianne, a senior nun I'd briefly met that morning from the adjoining Monastery of Our Lady of the Desert, to consider being interviewed. Later in the afternoon of the next day, Brother André told me that Mother Julianne was willing. But she would not be available until after Sunday Mass—three days later.

The next day, when I ran into Mother Julianne as she was coming up to the bookstore and refectory to offer ESL training with several novices from Southeast Asia, it was on the tip of my tongue to ask her to move the interview forward. But I had learned my lesson from my first afternoon when I had tried to force an interview with Prior Christian. To push would be to risk losing everything.

So I waited, and the days offered me an unexpected chance to make my own retreat, listen to Leif's reflections on the experience, and watch the winter storms, like freighters, glide down the canyons to drop inch after inch of snow. Those days of quiet waiting also brought an unexpected and mysterious development within me.

LEIF'S OBSERVATIONS

My son Leif has his issues with the church. With a master's degree from Earlham School of Religion in Peace and Justice Studies, he has questioned the church's relevance in a world of such desperate need. An internship in Palestine after graduate school working with kids clarified his hope of returning there as soon as was possible to work for Palestinian rights.

Given his frustration with what he considers the complacency of the American church, I wondered if Leif would be as critical of the monastic pattern of prayer, chanting, work, and silence. Of what use was that to a needy world?

Monastic life has always occasioned that type of skepticism and ridicule, not only from non-Christians, but also from those within the church who favor "active" ministry. Thomas Merton himself had an ongoing conversation with the Catholic theologian Rosemary Reuther, who in the turbulent 1960s tried to goad him to come out of "hiding" and join those marching in the streets. I don't think Reuther ever grasped Merton's response that he was more engaged in the world from within the monastery than if he had left it and tried to meet her standards of relevancy.

But Leif surprised me again and again. When do our children, no matter what age, not surprise us? When he comes down to spend a weekend at home, he usually passes on our invitation to join us at church. But at the monastery, Leif began that first morning by attending the earliest service, at 5:45 a.m. I expected that level of commitment to last a day, but he proved me wrong. It was often Leif who pushed me to get out of bed and trudge through the snow, ice, or mud to the church.

I was pleasantly surprised a second time when in the services I heard him very quietly chanting psalms with the monks. Often, I would stop and just listen.

Out of the corner of my eye, I could see Leif, during those services, scanning the rank of monks sitting on the two sides of the altar. Being a prankster himself, Leif noticed that several of the younger monks, men about his own age, were trying to get other younger monks to laugh.

Sure enough, at the next noon meal, three of the younger monks, all sitting together, tried to make each other laugh. I heard Leif chuckling quietly next to me as one of the monks started to pass the salt to his neighbor, only at the last moment to pull it back like Lucy with the football in the *Peanuts* cartoon. The face of one monk turned red, that strange color when one is trying with all one's might to suppress not just a snicker but a hopeless guffaw.

I glanced to see what the prior was making of all this, but he seemed to be looking toward the heavens—for help? I then looked to some of the older monks, but they, too, didn't seem to be paying attention. I waited for the explosion as now another of the younger monks was fighting a losing battle to stay in control. Suddenly, that monk pulled up the generous cloth at his neck of his habit to cover his face from nose downward. Only his eyes showed that he was weeping with silent laughter.

A BALANCED LIFE

As our days passed at the monastery, I noticed from Leif's comments and questions that it was not the oddity of the community that impressed him, but its normalcy—the laughter of young men trying to get something by their elder. But even more than the prankishness of the younger monks, it was the community's approach to work that most impressed Leif.

At the time of our visit, Leif was working for a not-for-profit agency that taught conflict resolution to inner-city schoolkids. He'd been quick to note the sniping and power games that are so common in our working society.

Part of making a retreat at Christ in the Desert is the expectation that retreatants will work as well during the later morning and early afternoon. Leif was assigned the first day to assist Sister Kateri in the monastery's bookstore. Nobody was likely to drive the treacherous road in the dead of winter to shop in the bookstore, so Leif's primary work was to help Sister Kateri package Internet orders for books, candles, and music.

The bookstore is situated in the front of the new refectory and becomes, even without walk-in business, the center of social life during the two work periods. Monks and nuns came through to talk on their way to classes, such as Mother Julianne's ESL class.

At the end of his second day of work with Sister Kateri, Leif whispered that he'd never seen this approach to work. He'd worked at enough jobs to notice what happens whenever a supervisor stopped by a work site. Conversation stops or is, at least, altered. And even without a supervisor coming through, workers talking "too long" will eventually say guiltily to the other, "Well, I guess we'd better get back to work."

In the monastery, Leif noticed how work "worked." The appearance of the guestmaster or prior brought the opposite result. Work stopped, and conversation began. The next day, I watched as a lay worker associated with the monastery brought his dog into the main building. All work ceased as the dog moved from person to person, collecting scratches.

In the Rule of St. Benedict, the requirement of daily manual work is made very clear.[1] Assigned work is part of accepting the vow of obedience, with simple and necessary work being valued, as prayer, as promoting contemplation of God. But work is never an end in itself, nor the purpose of a monastery. A balanced life lived with God in every moment is the goal.

With my work shift scheduled for the afternoon, I would spend the mornings reading on a couch in the main gathering area. I could hear Sister Kateri talking to Leif in the back room of the bookstore. She would break from telling him what had brought her to the monastery to ask his advice on expediting a shipping order. Once I heard her ask Leif what he hoped to do with his life. She seemed particularly taken with his hope of working with the Palestinian people.

Leif noted that something very human is at the heart of monastic life. St. Benedict counseled that Christ could come in the form of one's fellow monk, nun, or guest. Christ is with the community in prayer, in chanting, but also in work. Monastic life is a training to look and listen for Him.

But in our streamlined, maximally efficient, and profit-driven work environment, the personhood of the worker is inconsequential. Few workers listen to anything but their own thoughts. From a monastic point of view, such work is "Christless," for where the person of the worker is denied, Christ cannot be present.

EMOTIONAL SEESAW

In the days between my interviews with Brother André and Mother Julianne, two emotions began to battle within me. The first was a sense of wonder at the beauty of Chama Canyon and the wildlife abounding within it.

Periods of intense sunlight, so bright that my eyes squinted no matter in which direction I looked, alternated with snow squalls during our time at the monastery. The snowfall was heavy and quiet, borne by none of the wind that comes with the snowstorms of the Midwest. Weather would shift by the hour. We would trudge through mud on the quarter-mile path from the guesthouse to the church for one service, only to be up to our calves in snow the next.

The footing could be treacherous, forcing us to keep our eyes on the ground as we walked. We noticed the animal and bird tracks, and if we stood still, the wildlife showed itself as well. The rabbits and birds—the magpies were particularly numerous—were almost tame, moving away from us very leisurely if at all. It was as if we were a natural part of their world.

At night, we could hear the wilder sounds of owls, coyotes, and wolves, reminding us that the fight for survival continued in the canyon. But during the day, with Rio Chama flowing only several hundred feet away and not a sound of machinery to disturb animal and human life, I found it easy to believe that a bit of Eden still existed in our violent world.

During the morning and evening hours, I had the feeling that the best of being human was right here. I felt not a moment of hurry during those days, a great contrast to life in academia. Along with Leif, I attended almost every service. I also read a lot, yet still had time for everything else that I desired.

But the afternoons were a different matter. Come noon, almost like clockwork, and lasting until four or five in the afternoon, I felt overcome with unexpected sorrow. The feeling seemed to roll back and forth through me, only to leave at dusk as quickly as it came. Next day, right on schedule, it would return.

Perhaps it is my background in counseling, but nothing frustrates me as much as feelings that I do not understand. I analyzed the situation from every angle, but without any resolution. A thick knot lodged in my throat, as if I were grieving a loss. Was it something connected with the project? Was it something prompted by being with Leif, some regret at not being a better father?

I knew that the mysterious feeling was something in my spiritual core, but the more I tried to dig it up, the deeper I seemed to fall into the hole. Yet with each evening, the feelings seemed to depart like birds.

My days at Christ in the Desert became this strange mix of paradise and wilderness. In the midafternoon service in the church, my own inner struggles seemed to open me to noting the pain on the faces of some of the monks. One monk seemed particularly burdened by something far heavier than my private mystery. His face bore a patient heaviness and exhaustion, as if he were living his vocation one line of the psalmist at a time. I read the lines we were chanting and wondered how each one was touching him, if at all.

I began to think of my leaving Christ in the Desert on the upcoming Sunday in the same split way. Part of me knew that I would miss the quiet of the canyon, the luxury of time to talk with Leif in our room or to hear his baritone voice blend with the monks' during services. But part of me was growing ready to leave, as I hoped that I could leave the odd midday sorrow behind me in the canyon.

As the project unfolded, the mysterious feeling of loss and sorrow would disappear only to resurface later, not only in my own heart and mind but also in the words and tears of those whom I interviewed.

CHAPTER 3

9/11 Should Have Been a Bridge to the World

The Monastery of Christ in the Desert
Abiquiu, New Mexico
January 14, 2007

Mother Julianne makes an impression just by entering a room. I first saw her when, stamping snow from her feet, she came into the refectory from the nuns' nearby quarters of Our Lady of the Desert monastery. Waiting for her and their ESL class were three newly arrived novices from Southeast Asia. A sturdy woman in her seventies (she told me later, with obvious pride, that she is a fifth-generation Texan), Mother Julianne was dressed as nuns of my childhood—in a black habit with white trim and matching wimple. Only a wisp of white hair was visible on Mother Julianne's forehead.

In the next hour, while I was doing my work detail in the bookstore and reading a history of Christ in the Desert, I experienced a moment of synchronicity. As I heard Mother Julianne's booming voice offering English phrases for the novices to repeat (very meekly), I came across a story about her in the book. The account told of Sister

Julianne ("Mother" is an honorary title) marching into the American consulate in Guatemala City to deal with the visa of a Guatemalan sister which had been held up for three years. "Wearing her sternest high-school-principal face, she informed the consul that Sister Hilda's presence in the United States was solely in the interest of serving God. The face must have sufficiently impressed the consul, for abruptly everything was straightened out."[1]

The story matched the voice behind the heavy door. I recognized a teacher's tone as Mother Julianne assigned the words and phrases to be practiced before the students' next session. It was a voice to be obeyed.

But her strictness was tempered by a boisterous sense of humor. As the group left the session, Mother Julianne found a way to make a joke across the language barrier, perhaps about the challenge she faced of walking with a cane through the snow and ice.

After Mass on Sunday, Mother Julianne met me for the interview in the same room where she teaches her ESL classes. As we began, I could hear the happy sounds of community—introductions and explosions of laughter over the buzz of conversation as the monks and guests met for refreshments after Mass. Joy is an aspect of monastic life that breaks the somber stereotype, but is one that I have met in nearly every monastery I have visited.

As the community of Christ in the Desert schedules this relaxed time of refreshments and conversation for only a few hours after Sunday Mass, I felt a bit guilty pulling Mother Julianne away. Mother Julianne, however, assured me that she did not mind, and she was clearly keen to share her thoughts.

"IT'S NOT JUST AN AMERICAN PROBLEM"—MOTHER JULIANNE

Mother Julianne's memories of September 11 were extraordinarily vivid and reflected the confusion that permeated the country along with shock and sorrow. "[Abbot] Philip and I were supposed to leave on [September] 12, take a flight out," she explained. Not grasping the enormity of the tragedy, the two drove down to Albuquerque the afternoon of September 11. But at the motel, Abbot Philip and Mother Julianne found themselves with other travelers who were stranded by the national "no-fly" policy. "It was so unreal that I found myself just watching [the events of 9/11] constantly on the news until I went to bed. And only later did it fully dawn on me what had happened."

With all flights canceled, Mother Julianne and Abbot Philip had no choice but to drive back to the monastery on September 12. As did the majority of Americans on the "day after," the two listened to the news the entire way home.

Mother Julianne's account of 9/11, however, took a quite different turn when she described her return to the monastery. She noticed the effect that the tragedy had on Sister Hilda, a Guatemalan survivor of persecution and the nun whom Mother Julianne had helped bring to the United States. "I've been to her village," Mother Julianne said, "and they showed us where they'd . . . killed the people and thrown them into like a canyon there, the bodies. And you never knew who'd be taken from the village and killed . . . What 9/11 brought back [to me] were strong memories of violence."

Mother Julianne spoke next about another sister of the order, a nun from Rwanda who had witnessed people being slaughtered in that country's terrible civil war. The Rwandan nun had told her sisters in the United States how they had disobeyed the authorities and hidden nuns from other orders who were being hunted by the military.

"Those places were no longer just cold, distant places for me. They became more real—what the people were suffering. And that was all before 9/11," Mother Julianne said.

I was unexpectedly moved by Mother Julianne's connecting 9/11 with the suffering in Guatemala and Rwanda (and later in the interview, Bosnia). She was articulating something that had saddened me about our nation's reaction to 9/11. Our grief could have become a bridge of understanding and empathy to others in the world who have known (and continue to experience) horrendous suffering. But that had not happened. I had yet to hear anyone ask, "Was 9/11 something like what the Japanese experienced in Hiroshima and Nagasaki?"

Instead, 9/11 only seemed to isolate us further from the world. To most Americans, the tragedy of 9/11 was experienced as a bubble of suffering so unique that only we could possibly feel the severity of the pain. Our grief seemed to become our private possession.

Yet here was a nun, living in a remote canyon of New Mexico, who had responded quite differently. Why was it, I asked, that she could not talk about 9/11 without connecting it to the pain of Latin America, Africa, and the larger world?

Mother Julianne shook off any personal credit. Instead, she credited her previous order (Sisters of St. Mary of Namur) which, being an international order, has provinces or chapters all over the world. The order's diversity and sharing of experiences made the community continually aware of the suffering of people, especially the poor in Third World countries. "I think that's why 9/11 took on a whole international [meaning]—it's not just an American problem. It's a problem of our present [global] society."

When I first arrived at Christ in the Desert, I was frustrated that I might only have one interview. The trip seemed a large investment in time and grant money for that meager result. But in hearing Mother Julianne speak, I knew that if I had heard only this one insight, the trip would have been worth it. I could have kissed Mother Julianne at that moment.

Few would doubt that September 11 changed our relationship with the world forever. For many of us, the world in those terrifying moments became too small and too threatening. In fear, we labeled as "the axis of evil" those cultures that we understood least. We tried to secure our borders against all outsiders. The world had suddenly become too close for our comfort. And in the United States, *comfort* is accepted not as a feeling but a right.

But there were other Americans who, like Mother Julianne, knew long before 9/11 that the world has always been unsafe, especially for the poor and powerless. This minority of Americans have touched the world and its suffering not as tourists or as part of a military presence but as fellow human beings. 9/11 was as great a tragedy for these Americans, and perhaps even more so, but the intense suffering of those days brought them closer to the plight of others. For them, our nation's decision to further isolate ourselves while simultaneously lashing out aggressively is an equally great tragedy. Instead of bridges, we built walls.

Mother Julianne listened patiently to my comments before responding with the story of another Rwandan sister, one whose entire family had been killed during the civil war. At a later time, the nun was able to trace her family's killer to a prison where he was unfed and uncared for. In obedience to Christ's command, Mother Julianne said, the nun became that man's caregiver. She also started a group in Rwanda similar to those in South Africa that are dedicated to healing the wounds of war through forgiveness.

"And I think I would probably . . . be arrested by the FBI or National Security if they heard me say this," Mother Julianne added, "but I think we have no sympathy for those men that . . . did this. I don't think that they were malicious . . . [They were] like this man who killed the [nun's] family."

How out of sync was this nun from the macho mantras that have circulated throughout post-9/11 American culture? We have no "Forgiveness Matters" T-shirts to compete with the popular T-shirt that brags, "Pain Is Weakness Leaving My Body."

Once again, I was aware that monasteries live in a different language pool than the outside culture's. While the same words, such as *love, compassion,* and *forgiveness,* are used, their meanings are different for monks and nuns, and those different meanings lead to different responses. In the outside culture, *forgiveness* is restricted to person-to-person relations, not nation-to-nation. After 9/11, the war in Iraq, and the war in Afghanistan, forgiveness seems synonymous with surrender and weakness, and, worse yet, is viewed as dangerous, even treasonous. We have become the new Sparta, and, as I repeatedly had to consider throughout this project, Jesus' radical message of forgiveness of the enemy does not fare well in Sparta.

But Mother Julianne has not concocted her "weak" philosophy of forgiveness in the quiet and peaceful confines of Chama Canyon. She has gone to a place that many of us, including me, had yet to visit. Ten months after 9/11, she traveled to New York City and visited Ground Zero. Here again, she seemed unable to view that tragic site in isolation but rather connected it with another place, the Holocaust Museum in Washington, DC. In both places, she recalled, she had been struck by being in "sacred space," a place that demanded silence. "It was not any place you could go through quickly . . . I even get goose pimples now . . . I didn't want to talk after I left there . . . even the site had the memory of people who had suffered and died."

Why had she chosen to go to Ground Zero? I asked.

"Because I began to feel that we were handling, the government was handling, everything in the wrong way." This "wrong way," she explained, was what happens when human beings and governments make decisions about groups before they understand them.

As we are learning by necessity, there is a long history of hostility between the Sunni, Shia, and Kurds that remains a key factor in Iraq. Mother Julianne explained, "We went in, I feel, without understanding the history of Iraq . . . Boy, you've really gotten me started—it's the anger in ourselves that we don't deal with, so we project our anger upon other people . . . I don't think our government has understood that whole psychological process."

Mother Julianne was struck with how quickly after 9/11 our nation moved to blame the tragedy on someone else, "and not look at the fact that [we] could be wrong, [our] approach could be wrong." She agreed "100 percent" with Nathan Dungan's comment that 9/11 was an opportunity for introspection by our country, but an opportunity largely missed. Instead of 9/11 being a time of self-reflection, Mother Julianne felt that it became an opportunity to "go out and find your enemy and get rid of them."

And, she went on to say, the very way that Americans reacted to 9/11 and the ensuing war on terror reflected our conditioning by the media, especially the consumer culture. "We'll get instant gratification by going over, finding these people, and killing them."

At the heart of Mother Julianne's comments was her conviction that the United States continues to operate as a colonial power in a post-colonial period. America feels this compulsion to change other cultures, she said, even as we lack a basic understanding of the rich diversity of the world. We know ourselves, our answer, our solution, and that seems enough.

"I think one mistake Americans make," she said, "is that we decide for every culture that it would be absolutely a little Eden if we could make them have a democratic government."

She compared our nation's presumption to a foreign-born nun who always washed dishes in cold water. Mother Julianne remembered shielding this nun from the anger of a superior who was certain that the entire community would become ill unless the dishes were washed in hot water. Mother Julianne reminded the superior that their fellow nun probably never had hot water available in her home country. And not one member of the community became ill, Mother Julianne shared with a smile. Life grows unnecessarily difficult, she added, when we cannot imagine another way but our own.

Her story was a perfect opening for me to share Thomas Merton's conviction that hell is where we hate those from whom we cannot get away. "Is that where we are now as a world?" I asked her. "Are we in hell?"

"That's an interesting description," she admitted after a moment. "Not very theological." But on second thought, she agreed that our nation's response to 9/11 had moved us closer to hell. "It is a hell, because if we try to counteract violence with violence, we're simply creating hell. That's all we're doing."

As I was turning off the recorders, Mother Julianne did something that seemed an unexpected postscript to our interview. She spun around a full 360 degrees in the swivel chair. Perhaps, I thought at the time, she was turning away from the folly that she had described. But to me, Mother Julianne was the world, an entire globe of people, spinning on its axis.

LEAVING THE CANYON

After the interview with Mother Julianne, Leif and I hurriedly packed the car and headed out of the canyon to Albuquerque in an attempt to beat the next snowstorm. Leif would fly back to Indiana the next day; I would drive up another canyon to another monastery.

Our visit had been an encouraging beginning to the project. I came to New Mexico with a knot of fears. If I had feared that the monks and nuns would remind me curtly that their vocation does *not* include lecturing society, I also feared the opposite, that I would only hear bits of homilies, dried pieties, and broad generalities.

I also came to New Mexico with my pat answers to those concerns, should they arise. I would reply that I was not asking them to lecture American culture but rather to respond to the thousands of others like me who are seeking some light, some way forward, in an increasingly dark world.

But those fears were unfounded. Brother André and Mother Julianne received me openly, recognizing that I was, in my own way, another guest at the monastery who was seeking spiritual direction.

In Brother André, I had met a Christian in torment. Paradoxically, that had been a relief, for there has been nothing so troubling to many American Christians (and, no doubt, non-Christians) as the jolliness of current church life. We pray for our troops but rarely for the enemy, despite Jesus' mandate, and then we happily return to our preoccupations of work, shopping, sports, and entertainment.

OUR SHARE OF SUFFERING IN A SUFFERING WORLD

My visit to Christ in the Desert challenged me in my thinking, leaving me a different person than I was when I arrived. Through Brother André, I saw that much of our way of life makes sense only if the God of the Bible does not exist. Brother André's torment stems from his conviction that this God does, in fact, exist.

Mother Julianne also left me with much to ponder. She seemed psychologically unable to think of 9/11 without relating it to other pain and sorrow in the world. Never did she discuss 9/11 in isolation. She made me wonder if our nation's response to 9/11 had been determined decades, maybe centuries before, by the way we have sought to live above the suffering of the outside world. How ironic that the isolation of which active Americans often accuse monks and nuns is, in fact, *our* way of relating to the wider world. Monks and nuns are not the *least* connected with the suffering of the world but some of the *most* connected.

In a letter to Pablo Antonio Cuadra, Thomas Merton accused the West of dealing with the world as conquistador, traveling businessman, and tourist.[2] We in the West operate on the assumption that we have something the world needs, which is, of course, true. Much of the world suffers needlessly because they do not have the basic infrastructure of a functioning society. But what we never consider, Merton charged, is that other cultures, particularly those we label as Third

World or primitive, have spiritual wisdom that we in the West desperately need.

9/11 thrust us into the world from which we have so often insulated ourselves. But given our historic pattern, we could do little else with 9/11 but retreat deeper into our grief and anger.

If 9/11 means anything, as Mother Julianne believes, it means that Americans now share the same grief that so many in the world, sadly, know all too well. In her view, in our rush to war and our need to punish someone, we missed the opportunity to build a bridge to the suffering world.

But perhaps the most surprising aspect of the two interviews at Christ in the Desert, which I noticed only in listening to the interviews again, is the absence of any reference to Islam or Muslims. The question of the tension between Islam and the West, which had colored so many analyses of 9/11, was simply not the key issue for Brother André and Mother Julianne. As they looked out at the world through the lens of their monastic training, they saw not a sectarian world but a *suffering* world.

As I began to come to terms with their perspective, I was left with a question. Does the Christ whom I worship see the world with its religious divides, or does Christ see beyond that to the suffering of our world? I packed for my next trip, hoping to find an answer to that question.

CHAPTER 4

Here We Have No Lasting City

St. Michael's Skete
Cañones, New Mexico
January 15–17, 2007

On January 15, 2007, I dropped Leif at the airport for his flight back and headed north to St. Michael's Skete, an Orthodox monastery in the canyons near the village of Cañones. At the Albuquerque airport, I had fought an urge to return home myself. It was a little past noon, and my afternoon demon was still with me. My confusion with this midday malaise might have been dispelled had I read by that point Kathleen Norris's *Acedia and Me*, which explores this common phenomenon in monasteries.[1]

Over dinner the night before, Leif and I had traded impressions of our time at Christ in the Desert. Not knowing how to explain my odd afternoon sorrow, and feeling a bit ashamed at having to force down the tears, I decided not to mention it.

In our conversation over dinner, Leif was more honest. Some of the monks and even the prior had invited him to stay longer, and he admitted feeling a real kinship with the younger monks. He asked if

I thought he could offer the monks his training in ESL for a week or two every year.

But then Leif turned to his major problem with our time at the monastery: the cursing psalms that had been chanted in several of the services he faithfully attended. I shared what I had read about those troublesome psalms in a guest handbook I had found in our room. Apparently, I said, other guests were bothered about those ancient psalms as well.

As he can do when he feels his dad is starting to lecture, Leif looked slightly over my shoulder as I summarized the article. But when I shared how Brother André heard in those cursing psalms the cries of the Iraqi people, their longing for God's justice, I noticed tears forming in his eyes. He looked down at his food, and for a few moments, we both were silent. I yearned to hear my son explain what his tears meant, but given the lack of honesty about my own sorrow, I had not earned that right.

MANNA FOR MY JOURNEY

As I drove out alone from the airport, I placed the directions to St. Michael's along with a New Mexico map next to me and forced myself to focus on what might lie ahead. My expectations were as fuzzy as the directions that Father John had e-mailed me. I had been an Orthodox Christian for fourteen years at the time, but the visit to St. Michael's would be my first to an Orthodox monastery. I wondered how the place would compare with the Benedictine houses with which I was more familiar.

Christian monasticism traces its roots back at least to fourth-century Egypt. Those first monks, such as the hermit St. Anthony of the Desert and St. Pachomius, the father of cenobitic or community monasticism, were neither Orthodox nor Catholic but part of undivided catholic ("universal") and orthodox ("right doctrine") Christendom.

All Catholic and Orthodox monasteries consequently consider the monks of the Egyptian desert to be their spiritual forefathers. The very term *skete* that some Orthodox monasteries prefer derives from one of the earliest monastic locales in Egypt. And those earliest patterns of prayer, work, and praise from the deserts of Egypt and Syria form the basis of the later Rule of St. Benedict in the West and similar monastic rules in the East. All this I knew from reading histories of Christian monasticism. But I wondered how different Orthodox and Catholic monasteries would be in practice.

As I drove northwest out of Santa Fe toward Cañones, the radio gave yet another forecast of record snow and cold for the area. The weather seemed to be the big news of the day. Dejectedly, I hit the radio's scan button and expected the usual choices of music—country, rock, or classical—and news. Instead, I heard a tribute to Martin Luther King Jr. on one station and, with a start, remembered that today was the national celebration of his birthday. Within moments, Dr. King's own voice filled my car, and for the next half hour, I listened to a speech remembered as "The Drum Major Instinct."

On February 4, 1968, exactly two months before he would be assassinated, Dr. King gave the speech at Ebenezer Baptist Church in Atlanta, Georgia. I was familiar with the more famous of Dr. King's speeches, and realized as I listened that I had heard parts of this speech before, but not in its entirety. "The Drum Major Instinct" was exactly what I needed to hear. The slow, rhythmic cadence of King's voice resonated through my rental car.

I do not know if it is possible to practice *lectio divina* when listening to the radio, but that is how I concentrated on Dr. King's words. *Lectio divina* is a distinctly monastic way of reading sacred Scripture, a method that differs from both the rigid literalism of fundamentalism and the critical textual analysis favored by academics. *Lectio divina* invites the reader to read slowly, to reread, and, most of all, to listen with the heart. What the reader is listening for is a very personal bit of wisdom.

With my mysterious afternoon sorrow still dogging me, I felt open to what might be addressed to me. And as Dr. King addressed the crisis of his time, the Vietnam War, he seemed to be speaking to our current dilemma.

"God didn't call America to engage in a senseless, unjust war as the war in Vietnam. And we are criminals in that war. We've committed more war crimes almost than any nation in the world."[2]

In that turbulent year of 1968, Dr. King described our nation as suffering under the power of the "drum major instinct," that basic egotistical desire to be out front, to be superior and to dominate others. America was, he said, "the supreme culprit" of this sickness. It was at that point of his address that Dr. King's words began somehow to ease my sorrow.

I thought of Brother André's anguished cry, "Where are the prophets?" *Here is one,* I thought. King's words are as alive and compelling now as they were nearly forty years before. And Brother André would have certainly recognized how his own thoughts about the prophets of Israel were echoed in Dr. King's warning.

"But God has a way of even putting nations in their place. The God that I worship," Dr. King said, "has a way of saying, 'Don't play with me.' He has a way of saying, as the God of the Old Testament used to say to the Hebrews, 'Don't play with me, Israel . . . And if you don't stop your reckless course, I'll rise up and break the backbone of your power.'"[3]

Just as Dr. King was uttering the final words of his speech, ". . . so that we can make of this old world a new world," the radio station faded out in snowy static. As I turned off the highway onto the canyon road, I realized that I had just received manna for my own journey. My sorrow was with me but quieted. Dr. King's strength remained in the car as if he were my passenger, calming me even when the directions I was following to St. Michael's became confusing. Two women who happened to be standing in front of the tiny Catholic church in Cañones corrected my mistake, and ten minutes later, I pulled up before the unplowed entrance of St. Michael's Skete.

A BIT OF RUSSIA IN NEW MEXICO

St. Michael's Skete is as remote in its own way as is Christ in the Desert. Both lie far up in the canyons of New Mexico's high desert and give a similar feeling of being cut off from society. As I stared up at the high canyon walls that closed in around St. Michael's, I remembered reading Mother Julianne's comment that guests at Christ in the Desert sometimes become so claustrophobic in the canyon that they have to be driven out to the nearest town.[4] And St. Michael's Skete was a much smaller community within even tighter walls than Christ in the Desert. I wondered how many guests and how many monks had thrown in the towel at this place.

As I opened the gate and drove into a parking area with no other visible tire tracks, I feared that I'd missed some vital communication from Father John. Exiting my vehicle, I skirted the deeper drifts and trudged through knee-high snow toward the one-story building. An icon of the archangel Michael on the wall looked down on me as I passed through a small opening and came into what seemed to be the courtyard of a small motel. Along one wing was a series of doors, while the other wing held a larger common room with a kitchen.

I knocked on the doors, one after another, but heard nothing. Dr. King's inspiration was waning as I stamped my feet in the silence and considered my predicament. Was it really possible that I had come all this way for nothing? But at that moment, I heard another vehicle come through the gate. Hurriedly retracing my steps, I met a subcompact with four men and a dog crammed inside.

First out from the backseat was a tall man in his twenties, with untrimmed beard, dressed completely in the black Orthodox monastic robe, or *riassa*. He greeted me, but the barking dog made it impossible to catch his words. Assuming he was a novice, I shook his hand politely. An older man in his seventies, dressed in a heavy coat and stocking cap, pulled himself out next and introduced himself as Stewart. The third to appear was a small man in his forties who was also dressed in practical civilian winter gear of a heavy coat over flannel and denim. In a quiet voice, he introduced himself as Brother Vincent, a novice.

I waited to meet the monastery's leader, Father John. Finally, exiting from the driver's seat was a venerable-looking man in his late sixties, also with untrimmed beard and in full monastic garb. Saying how pleased I was to finally meet him, I moved to kiss Father John's ring in respect. He laughed loudly and pointed to the young man in his twenties. "That's Father John," he explained.

Father John smiled at my mistake and waved off my apology. The older monk with the big laugh turned out to be Brother M (name withheld by request).

We all moved back to the building, where Brother M showed me to my room. As he left me to unpack, he promised to return in an hour to drive everyone to the church for vespers.

The simple adobe room held a bed, desk, wardrobe, and a niche in the wall for another icon of St. Michael the Archangel. Seeing my breath with each exhale in the frigid room, I immediately searched for the thermostat.

But there was no thermostat in the bedroom or in the adjoining bathroom. I opened the wardrobe and found a tall column of blankets. *So this is how they live*, I thought, as I pulled the blankets out and layered them on the bed. Quickly shedding my coat, I crawled under the pile and felt their weight pressing heavily down on me. I thought of the weather forecast of record overnight cold and reached for my stocking cap. *If these monks don't freeze out here, I won't freeze*, I told myself.

But as I tried to write in my journal and felt my fingers stiffen, I began to doubt that I could sleep through such cold. I crawled out of bed, put on my coat, and headed through the snow for the community room, with its fireplace and kitchen. There was no central heat there either, but at least I found several electric heaters. I looked at the couch and made a backup plan for the night.

True to his word, Brother M returned at the appointed time. I entered the passenger seat of the Subaru and smelled animal. Turning around, I saw Stewart, Brother Vincent, and the large Labrador retriever. Father John had already gone to the church, one of the men explained.

Brother M talked nonstop on our ride through the trees to the church. I could have walked to the church, he explained, but, given the deep snow and the fact that I would have to cross a slippery bridge across a mountain stream, it was better that I accept the ride. The car paused at the top of the hill as if Brother M had forgotten something back at the rooms. "Here we go," he said a moment later, punching the accelerator. The car shot down the hill toward the stream. I noticed the car tracks on the other side of the water, but, I wondered, where was the bridge?

The car splashed into the stream and, its front tires catching on the other side, crawled up the incline. "Have to get up some momentum there," Brother M explained. I glanced down at the dashboard and at a string of digital words that cycled across the radio's display. *Glory to Jesus Christ, Glory to Jesus Christ, Glory to Jesus Christ . . .*

"You live a pretty austere life out here," I offered. With their laughter, I realized that the men thought I was referring to speeding by car through a stream.

"I mean, not having heat in the rooms," I continued. "That has to be tough on a night like this."

Brother M looked over at me with surprise. "You don't have heat? The pipes must have frozen when we were down in Albuquerque." Not to worry, he assured me. They would sort the problem out after vespers.

The car rounded the final curve and stopped in a clearing. *I am in a Russian postcard*, I thought, as I looked toward the small rectangular church with an onion dome on top. Painted glossy blue with golden stars, the dome bore an Orthodox cross, also golden.

Entering the dark church, I could see nothing except the faint glow from a wood-burning stove. I edged toward it, trying to find the right distance to thaw out without being scorched. A moment later, I heard a match strike. A small gleam from a kerosene lamp appeared over a reader's stand.

My eyes adjusted slowly, so it was a few moments before I grasped that I was surrounded by hundreds of icons adorning the simple wooden walls and the iconostasis (icon screen) at the front. Behind the icon screen and lit by the candles on the altar, I could see the tall form of Father John as he, with his back to us, began the service.

Throughout vespers, one side of me warm, the other side cold, I felt deliciously disoriented as I listened to the chanted readings and prayers. Outside the church, I had gazed up at the clouds of stars in the winter sky and felt again that I could be in Russia. Or we could all be on Mount Athos, I thought, the spiritual center of Orthodox monasticism, although I doubted that that island peninsula in Greece ever knew this kind of cold.

Within minutes, I noted the differences between this Orthodox service and those at Christ in the Desert and other Benedictine houses. In the services of the Catholic daily office, the mind of the worshipper focuses like an arrow that passes cleanly though the chanted psalms, readings, and prayers. Nothing is repeated, every word uttered or chanted slowly for the heart to ponder. In contrast, Orthodox services are lengthy and repetitious, the prayers and readings like birds spiraling closer and closer to the divine flame. The patient worshipper experiences exhaustion before passing into an unexpected state of lightness and clarity.

That evening, the readings and prayers circled around the chains of St. Peter, a theme that triggered memories of my visit to the very different church of San Pietro in Vincoli in Rome. There I always return when in Rome to stand before the chains believed to be those that held St. Peter in prison in Jerusalem (Acts 12) to venerate what are considered holy relics by both Orthodox and Catholics. In the early centuries of Christianity, one strand of chain ended up in Rome, the center of Western Christianity, and the other in Constantinople, the center of Eastern Christianity. The two strands of chain are considered miraculous because, according to the story, the two linked together when reunited in Rome in a later century.

Ever since I first heard the story of the chains, I have considered them a sign of a miracle yet to happen, that being the reunion of Orthodoxy and Catholicism. And having just come from the Benedictine monastery of Christ in the Desert to this Orthodox skete, I took the commemoration of those chains that first night as a good omen.

I will also never forget another moment of that cold vespers service, the moment when Father John left the altar to cense each of the hundred icons in the room. Beginning with the major ones on the icon screen, he continued his tour of the room, one wall at a time, giving each icon his brief but full attention. It is Orthodox belief that in every service of worship, no matter how many or few people are present, the room is considered full because of the invisible army of saints that always joins us. Father John made that belief very real as he bowed to each of the saints present with us that night.

"*Eerily beautiful. True peacefulness*" were the words I wrote about the service later that night in my journal.

After vespers and back in the community room, Brother M worked on preparing supper while Father John and Brother Vincent attended to the furnace outside. Stewart stood by and entertained me with stories of having run a bookstore near Catholic University in Washington, DC, one frequented by Robert Drinan, Avery Dulles, and Jeanne Kirkpatrick.

Making supper proved to be a challenge, as the frozen pipes meant no water in the kitchen as well as no heat in the rooms. The shrimp were cooked in bottled water on top of the electric stove while the microwave did a good job of fusing the tater tots into a caramelized mass. Eventually, Father John entered the room, accompanied by his dog, and announced that the real culprit turned out to be the empty oil tank. There would be no water or heat until they could be resupplied the next day. That brought a quick prayer from Brother M that the pipes would not burst in the frigid nighttime hours.

Grace was offered solemnly by Father John before the five of us sat down to eat together and swap stories. We talked for hours, leading me to wonder if guests brought some welcome relief from the isolation and routine of the place.

As we talked, I made mental notes about the personalities of the four men. Father John was easygoing and quiet. With his long hair, beard, and good looks, he could be mistaken for a member of a rock band. He shared that he had been a film studies student in Chicago before moving to New Mexico. And like so many of his generation, he had been completely unchurched and ignorant of Christianity. But in his young adult restlessness, Father John had discovered Orthodox Christianity through the Holy Trinity parish of Albuquerque. His conversion to Christian faith and Orthodoxy had led very rapidly to his becoming a novice monk, embracing that vocation, and after further education, being ordained a priest monk, or hieromonk.

Stewart, the oldest of the four and a lay member, sat with a ready smile and seemed to be an optimistic spirit in the community. When the challenge of sleeping in the cold rooms was brought up, he noted wisely that each room could take one of the small space heaters, and in that way we'd all get through the night just fine.

The novice, Brother Vincent, was the quietest of the group. Clearly competent about things mechanical, he spoke rarely and, when he did, with humility. His unconcern about the night ahead contributed to a mood that seemed to me to be one of practiced patience. Noticeably absent from our conversation throughout the entire evening was the issue of who was to blame for the oil running out.

Brother M was the most affable of the group and a gifted story-teller. Speaking with a slight Western-tinged accent, he put me at ease. While cooking supper, he gave me a running account of his background in another denomination and his attraction to what he referred to as the seriousness of Orthodoxy. A recovered alcoholic and former addictions counselor, Brother M had lived for some time on the property as a solitary hermit and still lived alone in a small hermitage deeper in the canyon. Yet he seemed positively delighted to have an extra mouth to feed and new stories to hear.

Over dinner it was decided that I would interview both Brother M and Father John the following day. Later that night in my cold room, I thought about the differences in age and life experience between the two monks. They were clearly different in personality, the one quiet and thoughtful, the other unabashedly outgoing.

Yet despite these differences, the two monks had much in common. Both were converts to Orthodoxy, and both lived by a very demanding common rule at St. Michael's. As the two who primarily shared leadership at St. Michael's, conducted together the lengthy services of the day, and were the community's hope for growth, Father John and Brother M lived in daily contact with each other and obviously were well acquainted with each other's views.

I suspected that the two men would offer me a good opportunity to compare how monks of the same community but of different generations assessed the crisis facing our world. Had their life in common contributed to their forming common attitudes?

PRAYING FOR THE COUNTRY—BROTHER M AND FATHER JOHN

Having slept as well as could be expected, I returned the next morning to the common room. In the few minutes before morning prayers, I scanned the periodicals on a coffee table and was pleased to find an

Orthodox newspaper celebrating the November visit of Pope Benedict XVI to Ecumenical Patriarch Bartholomew in Constantinople (Istanbul). My mind linked the photo of the two leaders' hands raised together in unity to the miracle of the chains of St. Peter we had commemorated the night before. I wondered, *Will those hands ever be clasped in a permanent bond?*

Moving to a bookshelf, I noted the various books written by or about saints of the Orthodox Church. *The spiritual all-stars*, I thought, as I turned my attention to a collection of CDs at the end of the bookshelf. My eyes skipped past the expected titles of Byzantine and Russian chant to catch on Barbra Streisand's *A Happening in Central Park*.

I could hardly imagine a greater contrast to Central Park than this remote canyon outpost, or a 1960s "happening" to these quiet, hypnotic services. But I was also relieved to picture these men on one of the lonelier nights at St. Michael's imaginatively joining Barbra Streisand and thousands of her fans in that other world.

In the two interviews I conducted after morning prayers, I was not surprised to hear that both Father John and Brother M remembered 9/11 and the community's response in nearly identical ways. After matins on September 11, 2001, Father John had been busy making candles, a main source of the monastery's income. He was hurrying in the task, as the community had plans to travel to Colorado to visit a nun. He had just completed the third dipping of the candles when Brother M burst into the room with news of the tragedy, sent via e-mail by a college student in Santa Fe.

Brother M confessed that what first came to mind as he looked at the e-mail was a verse from the Bible: "For here we have no lasting city" (Hebrews 13:14 RSV). His second thought was that the community needed to return to the church. Arriving at the church, they found the building locked in anticipation of their trip to Colorado and so opted to prostrate themselves on the ground outside for prayer.

Without their prayer books, which were also inside the church, the men recited a few familiar psalms as well as the chief Orthodox Trisagion prayer ("Holy God, Holy Mighty, Holy Immortal, have mercy on us"). "Mostly, [we] just prayed a long extemporaneous prayer for the country," Brother M recalled. "I can remember it like it happened yesterday."

While the community had acted in unison in those first minutes, the generational gap between Brother M and Father John provided widely different perspectives on the tragedy. For Brother M, the shocking news brought back his seminary days in November 1963 when John F. Kennedy was assassinated.

"I start crying when I talk about this," he said, as he recalled the seminary bell calling professors and seminarians to the chapel to recite the prayers for the dead. "Everybody was crying like a baby . . . That was part of my instinct [with 9/11]—to go pray immediately."

Born decades after the Kennedy assassination, Father John viewed 9/11 through a different and direr lens. What he remembered most vividly was a conversation with a friend his own age who was staying at the monastery at the time. "We both were sure that something bad was going to happen as a result, like we were going to nuke someone or we were going to flip out . . . meaning we were going to flip out as a nation."

What concretely did he and his friend fear? I asked. "A police state," as well as more attacks, Father John replied. "We were gripping for a possible World War III sort of thing."

No one on that terrible day knew what would happen next as rumors gave birth to irrational fears. An aura of vulnerability traveled with the monks of St. Michael's as they drove north to Colorado for the visit with the nun. Father John remembered wondering what men in the long, black robes (*riassas*) and the stovepipe hats of Orthodox monks would look like to a country in shock. Would they be mistaken for Muslims?

Father John's worry was not far-fetched. In ordinary times,

Orthodox monks would remind most Americans of characters from Hogwarts. But 9/11 wasn't an ordinary day. In nearby Arizona, a Sikh was killed, a victim of a religious hate crime. His turban led his ignorant assailants to assume that he was Muslim.

Brother M also remembered the trip north to Colorado as ominous. At a gas station, he was struck both by the extreme quiet of the place as well as the strange looks that their group was receiving. "In fact, we took our crosses out [of our *riassas*] and put them on the outside," he recalled.

Both Father John and Brother M noted the odd absence of planes and their telltale contrails in the western sky that day. But as the group from St. Michael's approached the nun's hermitage near Pikes Peak and NORAD Mountain, both monks distinctly heard the drone of a jet plane. The sound continued for some time, though no plane was ever visible. "Apparently the president was there for part of the time . . . in one of these stealth bombers," Brother M surmised.

While at the nun's hermitage, the group decided to take a slow hike together. "We went . . . to a place called 'the Top of the World,' about two miles away," Brother M recalled. He found himself asking the same questions over and over again. "What in the world is this? What's happening?"

EVERYBODY IN THE WORLD IS WITH YOU WHEN YOU PRAY

For those who dismiss monasticism as a colossal waste of a human life, no moment in recent American history would seem to prove the ridiculousness of such a life as much as September 11. The world's last superpower had been hit and hit hard, and the entire globe seemed to be on fire. There was no shortage of prayers on that day, but the crisis in which we had all been so suddenly thrust would make the monastic life of solitude seem to many a selfish retreat from the pain of the world.

At the outset of this project, I did not expect to discover that monasteries experienced a mass exodus of monks or nuns after 9/11, but I did imagine that the tragedy would have prompted a questioning of vocation. Father John and Brother M, as did their Catholic counterparts at Christ in the Desert, Brother André and Mother Julianne, testified that 9/11 had the opposite effect on them. Rather than causing them to question their vocation, the tragedy instead made them reaffirm their commitment to it.

In the immediate aftermath of the tragedy, Brother M told Father John that the two of them must redouble their efforts as monks, to fast more and with greater willingness, as well as to commit to a deeper participation in their daily services.

"You know your vocation is to be on one of the cutting edges of the church's mission," he explained. "It's the prayer mission. You have a mission to people, and you have a mission to God. And after 9/11, everybody said . . . 'What can I do about this?' Well, I have to take my vocation more seriously."

While most people Father John's age are in their first careers or serving in the military, the young monk was not tempted by 9/11 to join them. "I do have to tell you that at the time of 9/11, I was a novice, and I could have left," Father John explained. He had already experienced a "direct call, a personal call" to monastic rather than married life, but 9/11 only confirmed that decision. "I [can] say that the events of 9/11 sort of hit home about everything I was taught . . . about the monastic life . . . [and] the world."

Perhaps sensing that his comment left much unexplained, Father John shared an adage from St. Maximus the Confessor that had helped him come to grips with 9/11. "Man is a microcosm and . . . the world or universe is a macroanthropos [enlarged humanity]." Then Father John paraphrased, "When you look at the one, you see the other."

A person's sin, he suggested, is like a pebble thrown into a lake, the ripples going out to affect everyone. "In the same respect," he added, "one person repents . . . Renewing that relationship with others also has the same effect. It goes out like ripples and affects everyone else."

When a monk is weeping in his cell over his sins, Father John explained, that monk is not self-absorbed. "When we're weeping for our own sins, we may realize that suddenly we're weeping for the world at the same time." He added that a prayer for the world is also a prayer of repentance, even as a prayer for one's own repentance is a prayer for the world. "Everybody in the world is with you when you're in your cell alone, praying."

With that language, Father John had raised one of the most persistent misconceptions about monastic life. When monks and nuns talk about being "separate from the world," they do not take that separation to be a rejection of their solidarity with humanity or even with the mess that we as humans make of the world. A monastery in a canyon of New Mexico is as much *in* this world as a "happening" in New York City's Central Park. The separation from the world that monastics are seeking is a disconnecting from the *way of the world*, from life devoted to feeding our appetites without thought or discipline.

But I did not comprehend the extent of Father John's sense of solidarity with the world until he offered a personal reflection on 9/11. "When I contemplate 9/11 . . . I think of my stuff from my past, and then I look at, you know, the Twin Towers coming down, and that's why the [church] fathers can say, 'I did that.'"

I did that? I found his comment unsettling. It was not a feeling I had had on 9/11. Al-Qaeda, not I, had brought about 9/11 as a bold rejection of Western governmental policies. And it was not I who decided to invade Iraq. My hands were clean, my conscience clear, I had told myself. Now, I found myself wondering which one of us, Father John or me, was separate from the world?

THAT AWFUL VOID WITHIN US

It was obvious in his interview that Father John's recent theological training had taught him more than the intricacies of Orthodox worship. In Orthodoxy, Father John had found a way of understanding the problems of human life, from the inner life of the soul to the tragic turns of human history.

He had come to understand 9/11, he explained, by returning to the story of the Fall in the first chapters of Genesis. He pointed out that while we usually interpret the passage as Adam and Eve being expelled by God from Paradise, what really happened, and happens to all of us, is that humanity in its original sin expelled God from our lives. And that decision has created a void in every human being.

But because human beings are made for wholeness, Father John continued, we cannot live with this sense of inner emptiness. Life becomes an endless search to fill that void with a host of earthly matters, from possessions to appetites to addictions. All conflicts with others, including wars and attacks such as 9/11, arise from the desperate need to fill that void. Yet nothing we will find on this earth will solve our problem, for this inner emptiness can be satisfied only by God.

To that point, the young priest's thinking had struck me as conversant with standard Christian thought from St. Augustine to Paul Tillich. But Father John was more inventive in his application of the concept of the inner void to 9/11 and our present crisis.

He began by recalling the early church fathers who saw in Islam a "Christian heresy." As Father John expressed his basic agreement with this appraisal, I thought how politically incorrect such a statement sounds today. Pope Benedict's challenge to Islam in November was minor in comparison to this early Christian dismissal of Islam.

For Father John as an Orthodox Christian, the answer to the void within us is not a "what" at all but a "Who." We will find rest when we know the triune God revealed in Christianity, he said, a view of God that Islam has rejected from its very beginning.

But Father John wanted to make it clear that he did not view 9/11 as the bad religion of Islam attacking Christian America. The secular culture that the radical Islamists attacked is simply another false attempt to fill that void with materialism, individualism, and sensuality.

His face brightened as if he recognized something new in what he had just said. "And that, I think, is what Muslims are responding to." Quickly, he added, "But, of course, not in a Christian way."

9/11 was, he argued, one religious group—radical Islam—striking out against another religion—secularism. Each sees the other as providing no real solution to the human problem, and both groups, Father John believed, are right in drawing that conclusion. "In the one [radical Islam], you want to murder those who are not of your view, and then in the other [secularism], you want to consume others, literally. I see our culture," he added, "as quasi-cannibalist[ic] . . . Everybody devours everybody else in order to fill the [void]."

As we neared the end of our interview, and perhaps sensing that his outlook on the present conflict did not offer much hope, Father John paused for a moment. He considered it significant, he said, that our interview was taking place on the feast day of St. Anthony of the Desert, the first Christian monk. As his final thought, the young priest said he wanted me to consider a saying from St. Anthony: "A time is coming when men will go insane. And when they see one who is not insane, they will look at him and say, 'He is insane. He is not like us.'" To which Father John added, "I think we're there."

But please do not assume, he quickly added, that he considered himself yet sane. "God willing, 9/11 made me see that I'm not doing [everything I say], that I am contributing to the problem, and that makes me want to weep because I'm in the same position as every other person."

LIFE IS NOT A BIG GAME

"I began to learn in AA," Brother M. stated, "that some changes are absolutely necessary, and, if you don't [change], you'll die." As we talked, I realized that in this comment, Brother M had supplied me with far more than a biographical footnote. "Change or die" is the choice that Brother M sees before the world, especially the United States at this time.

Brother M's reading of the church fathers had taken him in a different direction from Father John's. In those readings, Brother M had found a respect for truth wherever it is to be found, even outside the Christian faith. He noted as an example that the early church held the pre-Christian Greek philosophers in great esteem. In their own way, these philosophers, too, had prepared the way for the coming of Christ. And such openness to truth, he added, accounted for the historically quite cordial relations between Eastern Christianity and Islam, where it was not unusual for Muslims and Christians to ask for prayers from one another.

"In Orthodox theology, grace is God at work." Smiling, Brother M added, "How can you say where grace is not?" This has led him to believe that "God can obviously work outside the covenant. I'm sure He works with Muslims, people of good will."

Brother M's criticism falls more heavily on contemporary Western culture, which he described as becoming a "gigantic Walmart." The West assumes, he argued, that its very "lackadaisical" way of life alone holds truth.

For Brother M, as an Orthodox monk and recovered alcoholic, life is serious. But the prevailing attitude in America is that "life is a big game." A tone of sadness, rather than bitterness or anger, accompanied his grim assessment of our society.

As had been the case with Mother Julianne of Our Lady of the Desert, Brother M was struck by the commitment the 9/11 hijackers.

"To kill yourself like that is impressive. I mean, it's wrong, wrong, wrong, but it's still impressive."

Wrong as it may be, the seriousness of the hijackers contrasted sharply for Brother M with the "life as a game" mentality of American culture. "The president didn't help [by] saying, 'They're jealous of our prosperity; they hate our democracy.' I mean, give me a break . . . What I think 9/11 says is, 'You [American] people are arrogant, hypocritical slobs.'"

It was not difficult, as we ended the interview, to grasp that in this extreme comment was Brother M's own assessment of our culture. Later, as I listened to his biting words on tape, I wondered if Brother M was suggesting yet something else, something akin to the conclusion drawn by Brother André of Christ in the Desert. Did *God* see us as "arrogant, hypocritical slobs"?

Brother M would not be the first American monk to aim such an arrow at the heart of American culture. In the 1960s, Thomas Merton took a similar tack. Merton argued that when a culture presumes to hold the truth that others need, but feels no need to listen to the truth of others, arrogance results. As I considered Merton's and Brother M's point, I wondered how many Americans could name even one truth that the world owes to Islam. How many Westerners remember that the Renaissance that shaped our modern world would have been impossible without Islamic libraries and centers of learning where ancient Greek and Roman texts were carefully and lovingly preserved?

AT THE BASE OF EVERYTHING: FORGIVENESS

In visiting St. Michael's Skete, I felt that I had traveled back to the beginnings of monasticism. Life at St. Michael's was basic and, from one perspective, harsh. From the time of St. Pachomius onward, small groups of men or women had retreated to the deserts of Egypt and

Syria to form communities much like St. Michael's. As had Father John, Brother M, Stewart, and Brother Vincent, these earlier monks had been drawn to a serious life of sacrifice. The uncompromising and blunt comments given by the two monks in their interviews echoed the uncompromising rule by which they lived.

This was brought home to me on my last morning, when plans to celebrate the Divine Liturgy had to be changed because the church lacked sufficient heat. Father John and Brother M decided that we should, in lieu of Divine Liturgy, hold a prayer service by the fireplace in the common room. With my bags packed to leave after the service, I imagined getting an earlier start on the snowy roads. But it was two hours later, having stood for cycle after cycle of prayer, before I said my good-byes and departed.

To emphasize the rigor of St. Michael's or even the intricacies of Orthodox rule and practice, however, would be to miss what is the foundation of their life together. All monasteries in contemporary culture, no matter the size or stage of development, are plagued by similar problems of declining vocations, rising health insurance costs, and the increasing flood of guests. The added burden of St. Michael's Skete is that these tasks are shouldered by so few. It seemed a miracle in itself that a community so small could absorb the strain of sickness, discouragement, loneliness, and the natural friction of personalities. While at Christ in the Desert, I had read that that community, at a similar early stage in its life, had nearly folded when the abbot and another monk stopped speaking to one another.[5]

The "rule" followed by monastic communities recognizes this danger and yet does not permit our society's common tactic, that of distancing ourselves from colleagues or neighbors who simply will not be neighborly. Reconciliation, the requesting and offering of forgiveness, is not an abstract goal but an action in the monastic day as real as eating.

In most monasteries, these moments between monks and nuns would more commonly take place outside the view of guests. At St.

Michael's, I was in the middle of the community's life and consequently was able to witness such real-life, real-time forgiveness.

On my first evening, over the supper without heat and water, the five of us had swapped anecdotes about people we knew in common as well as bits of our own stories. I was ending a brief summary of my own spiritual journey and how I had come to this project when Brother M invited Father John to tell how he had come to Christian faith.

Father John seemed pressured by the request, but the momentary awkwardness was quickly covered by the rest of us. That next morning, Father John and Brother M decided, in light of the extreme cold, to hold morning prayers in the warmer community room. In preparation for the service, Brother M and Father John were discussing various issues of texts and prayers when Brother M suddenly stopped and asked Father John to join him outside. There was a feeling of tension in the room as Father John quietly nodded.

Outside was twenty degrees below zero, but both men left the warmth of the room in silence. My mind raced as I imagined the possibilities. Had my coming somehow caused a problem? Were quarrels between these two very different men, of different generations and different personalities, common? Was the peace of the previous evening a facade for my benefit, one that was now melting away? Would I hear shouting next or someone stomping off to his room?

In a few moments, the two monks returned to the room, and the service started. I listened for some indication of their moods, but all that I could discern was a deeper, relaxed tone in Brother M's voice.

It was only later that Brother M told me privately what had happened. He shared that he had such love and respect for Father John, a man in his twenties who was yet his spiritual father, that he never tired of hearing the young priest tell guests how he had come to religious faith. That was why the night before, over supper, he had tried to give Father John that chance.

But he had forced the moment, he realized, and that had put the more reticent Father John in an awkward position. Brother M confessed that he had a tendency to do that with people.

Such a faux pas is trivial in my world. But Brother M had carried his regret through the night and felt the memory still standing between Father John and him as they were about to pray together.

Outside in the cold, Brother M had asked for and been granted Father John's forgiveness. They had embraced as brothers, kissing the other's cheeks. As he told the story, it occurred to me that monasteries had endured over the centuries not because of brilliant leaders or inspiring locales, but precisely because of such humble moments.

Friction is present in every human community. In my world, we build protective walls and call that tolerance. And if someone is so rude as to breach our walls, we bring up clever, cutting comebacks to put that person in his place.

But in a monastery, the offending brother or sister's "place" is your place as well. Monastic life is completely life in common. Unaddressed grievances that we would dismiss as petty are deadly in monasteries.

One conclusion, of course, is that monasteries encourage an abnormal emotional sensitivity. The other possibility is that such grievances are just as deadly in our families, high schools, colleges, cities, and our shrinking world. But to admit that would demand painful changes, such as standing out in the cold.

TAKING HUMAN LIFE SERIOUSLY

Think tanks abound in the First World nations, with the United States undoubtedly funding the most. We gather together the best-educated minds and pay them large salaries to advance the nation's or a particular group's interests.

I left St. Michael's sensing that monasteries are "contemplation tanks," places where another, equally serious, type of thought is practiced every day. But for some very understandable reasons, most Americans are oblivious to the wisdom that monasteries have to share.

Monasteries embrace values of celibacy, poverty, and obedience, values antithetical to those of the surrounding culture. And while death is ever present in TV dramas, the constant awareness of one's own death that is stressed in monasteries is foreign to most of us. It is little wonder that many view monasteries as divorced from the real world.

But herein is the stunning paradox of monasticism. While monasteries do not see this world as enduring, they also take life in this world *more*, not *less*, seriously than the rest of us do. Every moment of life in this world is to be lived consciously, and our interactions with others are to be treated as potential encounters with God Himself.

A closer look at monastic communities indicates how they concentrate on three of the most important aspects of human life.

First, monastic communities take it as their calling to make visible God's dream for the world. They know that genuine peace and wholeness are as fragile as the rarest flower, as complex in construction as the most intricate machine. The minimal tolerance that we settle for in even the most democratic societies would be the death of monasteries. Their survival depends on unrelenting commitment to a much higher vision.

This has led monasteries to a second focus, to understand the subtle workings of the human heart. The only path to eternity with God leads through knowing ourselves in this life. Monasteries are *incarnational* communities, for to join Christ in heaven, monks and nuns understand that they must follow Christ in becoming *fully human* in this world.

And third, monasteries focus on what lies between God's dream for the world and the human heart—concrete life in community. Centuries of practice have given monasteries a keen awareness of the emotional and spiritual obstacles to living together, as well as the remedies for overcoming those barriers.

I drove away from St. Michael's with a question that I would ask repeatedly throughout the project: do monasteries, by their very patterns of community life, hold wisdom that could help the human race survive the twenty-first century?

The answer to that question will be no as long as we as a nation insist on being the world's "drum major," the nation out front, demanding that others follow our lead. The answer will also be no as long as we believe that arming the planet, from the smallest nation to the largest, is the path to global security and peace. And the answer will be no as long as we settle for the low hurdle of tolerance in our own troubled and violent country. As long as we have this frame of mind, monastic wisdom will seem utter foolishness.

But the answer to that question—do monasteries offer a model for survival?—will become a yes when we drop our need to dominate and instead commit ourselves to Dr. King's vision of the Beloved Community, where adversaries are reconciled through peaceful conflict resolution.[6] In that vision, Dr. King foresaw not only God's answer to America's legacy of racism but also God's dream for our post-9/11 world.

Of course, Dr. King's vision of the Beloved Community was hardly new. The Beloved Community is the goal of the gospel, the kingdom of God which we as humans are created to hunger for. And the Beloved Community is precisely what monasticism has striven to make visible throughout its long history.

I had come to the canyons of New Mexico with a need to find some hope for the future. What the interviews gave me was far more than inspiring words. In praying, working, eating, laughing, and shivering with these monks and nuns, I witnessed a very human wisdom being lived out. I left the canyons knowing that if we ever commit ourselves to Dr. King's prophetic call to "make of this old world a new world," the wisdom of monasticism will be an essential guide.

9/11's Most Taboo Word—
Forgiveness

Center for Action and Contemplation
Albuquerque, New Mexico
January 18, 2007

I was restless. I had scheduled two more days in New Mexico in the hope that another monastery in the area would agree to participate in the project. But once back in Santa Fe from St. Michael's Skete, I checked my e-mail and realized that I was out of luck.

What to do in the intervening days before my flight home? Northern New Mexico is a beautiful part of the country, a place my wife and I had visited many times, but I was not in the mood to be a tourist.

My restless mood stemmed from more than just unexpected free time. After the two desert monasteries, much of life back in "normal" society seemed abnormal. The past week, when I had been completely out of contact with the outside world, seemed like a month. Now, back in the motel room, I found the endless cable channel choices numbing.

Particularly insane seemed the high-energy shopping networks, but the highlight films and jock analysis on the numerous sports channels also seemed odd. I wondered how much of my life I had spent watching people on TV trying to defeat one another at something.

What blessed relief to come upon a channel showing Richard Attenborough's *Gandhi*. Here was another example of a disciplined, spiritually directed life. I had no doubt that Gandhi would have felt right at home at Christ in the Desert and St. Michael's Skete, and the monks and nuns would have undoubtedly welcomed him, but Gandhi's path was different. Besides being Hindu, Gandhi pursued his quest for truth (*satyagraha*) not in an isolated setting but in the very center of India's social and political life.

The movie brought to mind a conversation that I'd had a few days before my flight out with my colleague David Chandler. Upon hearing my planned itinerary, David asked if I had thought of visiting Richard Rohr's Center for Action and Contemplation in Albuquerque. Richard Rohr's name seemed only vaguely familiar, and in the rush to get ready for the trip, I had not followed up on the suggestion.

Watching Gandhi's life led me back to the name of Richard Rohr's organization—The Center for Action and Contemplation. The order of those two human endeavors—action, then contemplation—struck me as deliberate. The feminist theologian Rosemary Reuther once berated Thomas Merton for his seclusion from the world as a Trappist monk. The action was in the streets, she wrote him, and that was where Merton belonged. Although Merton wrote a clear justification of his monastic vocation, his journals reveal that he was always sensitive to the tension between contemplation and action. Fittingly, a posthumously published collection of Merton essays was entitled *Contemplation in a World of Action*.[1]

What would be the contrast, I wondered, between a center devoted to action and contemplation, in that order, and two monasteries that might better be described as centers of contemplation alone?

I found a computer in the motel lobby. Finding the Center's website and contact information, I e-mailed a request to visit. Almost immediately, I received a reply from Michael Bennett, a staff member. Yes, I was welcome to stop by, even though Michael Bennett was unsure, with Richard Rohr being away, if anyone at the Center would be suitable to interview.

I followed Michael's directions from Santa Fe to Albuquerque and drove down a busy street into what seemed a tough neighborhood. I passed the Center before realizing that I had missed it. Turning around and being successful on my second try, I appreciated how Rohr, a Franciscan friar, had emulated St. Francis by choosing an urban setting, rather than monastic isolation, to locate his ministry.

After locking the car, I entered the complex of low buildings. I could have been at a United Way office, where small groups of people were working together in rooms and others were working individually at computers. Monasteries promote quiet. Even the chanting of the monks and nuns in the services of the daily Divine Office has a solemnity to it. The Center for Action and Contemplation, in contrast, seemed to be bustling with what its title promised—action.

I was soon met by Michael Bennett, who ushered me to his office. Michael, a contemporary of mine with a soft-spoken voice, is, I soon learned, the director of men's programming. Later readings from Richard Rohr's books would testify to the important place that men's workshops have at the Center. And the spiritual and psychological health—and unhealth—of men in our culture would be at the heart of my conversation with Michael Bennett.

Michael repeated his belief that he would be a poor substitute for the well-known and dynamic Richard Rohr. I explained that missing Father Rohr was not a calamity from my point of view. I was not interested in interviewing persons of such renown that their name recognition would swamp the contributions of lesser-known but also insightful persons. And I shared that Michael's reticence seemed a good sign to me, as I had not met (and would not meet) anyone in the project who said, "I'm just the person for you to interview." What I had found to be true, I told Michael, was that most people did not believe that they held compelling perspectives on our post-9/11 world until they were interviewed.

FILING BANKRUPTCY OF THE SOUL—MICHAEL BENNETT

Painful personal experience, Michael Bennett said to begin the interview, had led him to be sitting in that office. "I came home for lunch, and she [his wife] was gone. And I see this bank statement for a credit card that I didn't even know I had." For Michael, the entire world he had known collapsed in those moments back in 1998. Soon after, he was forced to declare bankruptcy.

The shock of that "crushing blow" pushed Michael into attending one of Richard Rohr's initiation weekends for men, an experience that he credited with helping him survive his double disaster without lingering resentment. In a way, the loss of his wife and financial solvency had stripped Michael of everything but God. "And the God that I had was still in this box. And this initiation really smashed the box on who I thought God was and actually who I thought I was as a man."

Two major themes in Richard Rohr's work, as Michael described it, are the distorted sense of God and sense of manhood out of which many men in the West live. And those misperceptions are closely intertwined. "The God that the church had taught me . . . [Him] I just couldn't love." It was only after Michael's five-day initiation weekend that he realized that the true God loved him as he was, flawed and even broken, and that this God had no interest in Michael being what the community, his ego, or even the church told him he must be.

Michael's response to 9/11 was a direct result of his life-changing initiation experience. Working as a FedEx driver at the time, Michael recalled that he had viewed that tragedy "from a completely different point of view probably than I ever would have if I hadn't had this, what you might call a conversion experience or a new idea of who God was."

As he delivered packages during those first days after 9/11, Michael shared the initial reaction of so many others that "we have to get them." But he soon found himself asking over and over again, "Why would someone do this?" He sensed very strongly that "there [was] another story here."

On the Internet, Michael found Richard Rohr's various responses to 9/11 and knew that Rohr was expressing what he was feeling. Rohr had called the nation to consider a "third way" of responding to the tragedy, avoiding both flight and fight. That third way is to reject the dualistic temptation to blame others or ourselves, but instead, to let the tragedy teach us as a nation about our way of being in the world. This third way was to enter "liminal space," a zone of mental activity where the fog clears, where light and insight can surface. Liminal space is where we become open to change.

"I feel it [9/11] was an opportunity for us to realize who we really were and to face . . . as a country . . . what we have done in the world," Michael explained.

THE TABOO OF EMPATHY

How, I asked, had Michael's initiation experience affected his thinking about what we *might have* learned from 9/11? "My whole experience with God [helped me] put myself in their [the hijackers'] place."

It was clear as we talked that Michael had thought considerably about the hijackers, refusing to dismiss them as insane or culturally so different from us as to be incomprehensible. This empathy for the hijackers, I was surprised to discover, was not uncommon among many whom I would interview throughout the project.

Here, a potential misunderstanding must be dealt with. In no interview in the entire project did I find sympathy with what the hijackers had done. No one condoned the horror of their act or said that the United States deserved 9/11. But as with Brother M at St. Michael's Skete, Michael Bennett offered a rare willingness to ponder what the hijackers must have gone through to come to that horrible decision.

Michael's experience of initiation had trained him to break through the taboo against empathy for the enemy. Putting himself in the shoes of the Other, in this case the hijackers, Michael did not sense in their deed an act of mind-numbing brainwashing—a common post-9/11 accusation—but an act of *conviction*, of faith. That act of faith was one distorted by hatred, but it was an act of faith nonetheless. "There was a certain admiration," he confessed, "because I've looked at myself and the things that Jesus tells me to do, and I know that I'm just not doing them. I can't even do the little things, and these guys are flying into buildings to prove their point."

Michael's empathetic tendency also affected his view of the violence in Iraq against American and coalition troops. What would be our response as a people, he asked, if Iraqis invaded our country "for our good"? Wouldn't we be doing whatever we could to force them out?

Michael apologized for what he considered his simplistic viewpoint, but I found his reversal of images striking. Why has it been so difficult to shed our illusion that we would be, and should be, welcomed into Iraq by the people? Why has it been so difficult to do what Michael has been willing to do, to imagine ourselves as Iraqis as they saw the tanks of another country roll down their streets?

Our lack of empathy, Michael believes, is a failure of our moral imaginations, and that failure is rooted in our national confusion of God and country. As is true of the Taliban, al-Qaeda, and specifically the hijackers on 9/11, we imagine ourselves as Americans to be the instruments of God. But Michael suggested that the problem goes even deeper. Not only do we uncritically maintain that we are doing the will of God, but we also see our country itself as a sacred entity—in fact, a god—incapable of making a mistake. With such an understanding, why would we even care what our actions mean to those affected by them?

THE DANGEROUS IDEA OF FORGIVENESS

I asked Michael to describe how we would be different as a nation if we abandoned what he considered to be our arrogant thinking.

Michael responded by citing the transformation in South Africa, where Nelson Mandela had risen to the presidency after decades in prison. After so much suffering, that profound and nonviolent change had taken place "because the blacks were willing to forgive. That's powerful stuff for me—to see how things like that happen."

Before even realizing where the question would take us, I said, "Are you saying that offering forgiveness for 9/11 would be a good thing?" I may have whispered my question; I certainly sensed that we were discussing something dangerous.

Michael responded almost immediately. "It [forgiveness] is the only thing, the only thing that is going to change things in this world. Somebody has to take the initial step, and I guess it has to be us. We've been so privileged that, why not? Why not us?" Michael thought for a moment before adding, "But I don't know if we'll be able to go deep enough to see that."

Michael continued, "I have hope, but the only hope I have is in the kind of work that I'm doing here. Each individual person has to be somehow transformed, has to really be introduced to who God really is. And not the God that religion has told us He is."

Michael paused and shook his head. "There are days I sit in here with men and . . . men need it more than anybody because men are the problem . . . They need to understand that who the world, especially our culture, says we are as men is not who we are." As Michael spoke, I thought of the guards at Abu Ghraib prison. How had I missed the similarity between their arrogant postures and the stances of athletes as they cavorted in the end zone after a touchdown, or celebrated after a rim-shaking slam dunk?

I looked up from my notes and thought of Michael's journey from bankruptcy, spiritual as much as financial, to his present, more open point of view. "So God is not," I asked, "who we've been told, and we as men are not who we've been led to believe, and the world that we have is the outcome of those two things?"

"Yeah, yeah, it is," he replied, but he went on to explain that we don't have to live with these distortions. He spoke of the awe that he has felt in his role in the initiation experiences offered by the Center. "As a team member, I kind of sit behind them and just watch the transformation. And I realize . . . it is nothing that we have said or done—it's just the Spirit and God that by Saturday [brings] a total transformation." Michael stopped and looked down. I realized that he was fighting back tears and losing the battle. "These guys just kind of melt into who they really are."

I repeated the expression back to Michael—"Men would melt into who they really are." Was that the basis of his hope for the world?

"Who they [men] were created to be," Michael clarified. "Who they are in God's eyes. To be able to see God in them."

Tears again welled up in Michael's eyes. "That's some powerful stuff, to recognize the God in me and to see, my God—He is there. I *have* been made in His image."

I felt as if I had been given a clue to a complicated puzzle. If we as human beings want a world without hatred, fear, and terror, we will have to understand God's relation to ourselves—and to our enemies—in a radically different way.

THE OTHER 9/11—REV. ANITA AMSTUTZ

Despite my natural Scandinavian reserve, this project has taught me to be opportunistic. At drop-in sites such as the Center for Action and Contemplation, I would often have no more than a minute or two to explain the project and request someone's participation. Any fatigue or a personal preference for quiet reflection had to be put aside.

That was the case with Anita Amstutz, who was clearly skeptical when I first made my request. Although on the staff of the Center for Action and Contemplation, Anita assured me that she was neither a nun nor even a Catholic. In fact, she was an ordained Mennonite minister.

But I was persistent. At the end of my time with Michael Bennett, I asked who else at the Center might be a good subject to interview. He had been quick to suggest Anita. I was intrigued. The Mennonite community is one of the historic and consistent "peace churches," which suggested to me that Anita might offer uncommon and strong opinions about our current crisis.

"Where else am I likely to hear a Mennonite perspective?" I explained to her. That caused Anita to pause, but after looking at her watch, she once again begged off. She had only a brief lunch break before afternoon appointments at her church.

I played my last card. "How about if we talk over lunch? My treat."

Anita weighed the offer, consulted her watch again, and finally agreed. The nearby restaurant she chose turned out to be filled with people and to have the noise level of a junior high school cafeteria. And when we were seated near the swinging doors to the kitchen, I wondered if my two recorders would pick up anything above the din of clanging plates and competing conversations all around us.

In her midthirties at the time, Rev. Amstutz was trim, alert, focused, and equipped—thank God—with a penetrating speaking voice. She began by explaining her association with the Center. Fr. Richard Rohr's work had wide ecumenical appeal, she said, as several of the Center's staff are non-Catholics. And the Franciscan orientation of the Center for Action and Contemplation, with its focus on peace and justice issues, was a natural draw for her as a Mennonite.

TERRORISM AS THE UNWELCOME WAKE-UP CALL

As with previous interviews, I began by asking Anita to recall where she had been in the fall of 2001. She explained that she'd been a recent seminary graduate from the Pacific School of Religion at the time. But not feeling drawn to parish ministry, she had been working for a natural food corporation outside Oakland, California.

"And I hated it [the job]," she said. "So I knew that I had to begin exploring vocation again. Back to the drawing board." A consultation with a vocational counselor led her back to the key question. "Why aren't you thinking about doing church work?" the counselor asked. The next day, as if to confirm the new direction, a friend told Anita of a Mennonite church in Albuquerque, New Mexico, that was losing its pastor.

Later in the fall of 2001, Anita accepted the half-time position at the small church, and, having heard of Richard Rohr's work, she visited the Center. Participating in the community's daily prayers at 7:40 a.m. soon followed, and that, in turn, led to her applying for the outreach coordinator position at the Center.

Anita's memories of September 11 back in Oakland began with an early phone call from her mother instructing her to turn on her TV to see what was happening in New York City. "All I heard all day long [at work] was, I mean, people were horrified and there was a lot of revenge. It was a pretty mainstream kind of a 'corporate America' place to work."

Despite the presumed liberal bent of the natural food industry, Anita found only one or two others in the corporation who held a viewpoint similar to hers. "I remember thinking to myself, *How am I going to be at work because I come from a pacifist tradition, and I do not believe that we need to go to war, or reciprocate violence with violence? So what am I going to do, because I'm going to look like a freak?"* Anita's response was to sympathize with the grief that her coworkers naturally felt, but to remain silent when the conversation turned to how the United States should "blow people up."

As was true of other Americans, Anita found that it took a few months before she could begin to reflect theologically and politically on 9/11. One of her first thoughts centered on the symbolic significance of the targeted locations. It seemed "archetypically clear that they were hitting the Pentagon and the Twin Towers, our financial might, our military might, and the White House . . . [would have been our] political might . . . I remember talking about that with friends and just saying, 'The writing is on the wall.' I mean, it's so clear that the terrorists . . . were waking us up. And were we willing to be woken up?"

"Waking up" was a frequently heard expression in this country in the aftermath of 9/11, but Anita hardly meant it in the usual sense of 9/11, like Pearl Harbor, calling America to wake up militarily. "Because of my understanding of the gospel and my understanding of reality," she said, "because of my faith and because of the training I've had, I suddenly started to put it all together in terms of the global, economic reality, in terms of the devastation that's happening ecologically and how that's impacting poor people all over the world." And a large portion of those in poverty in the world are Muslim, she noted. "But it's not just Islamic . . . it's people without power. And I began to really understand how the Islamists are, for better or for worse, trying to give us a message."

OUR ENEMIES HAVE SOMETHING TO TEACH US

My initial hope that Anita might offer an uncommon perspective was fulfilled by her next comment. "That's why Jesus asked us to

85

invite our enemies to the table, because our enemies have something to teach us." My pen paused above the notepad. Al-Qaeda had something to teach us?

Anita referred to Richard Rohr's emphasis on the shadow, which seems similar to Jung's use of the same term. That is, what we don't want to know about ourselves is projected on the Other, who becomes our enemy. What the attackers on 9/11 were doing, Anita suggested, was "showing us a side [of ourselves] we refuse to see or accept or understand."

As I listened to Anita, I thought of how tempting it has been to interpret 9/11 as a depth of inhumanity beyond our civilized country's capacity. We viewed the attackers' choice of weapon (domestic airlines) and the loss of so many innocent lives as proof that al-Qaeda is barbaric, a charge for which we could never be indicted. And the justifications for the attacks presented to us by the Bush administration—that the Taliban and al-Qaeda resent our freedoms and our prosperity—were conveniently reasons that *flattered* rather than *indicted* us.

What Anita was proposing was difficult to swallow, not because her charge was patently false, but because the charge was so repugnant, however true. Perhaps that is always true of the shadow, whether that shadow is personal or national. The shadow contains truth that we do not want to admit and truth that our feelings of outrage conveniently block. For Richard Rohr, facing the shadow is part of that "third way," one that rejects the dualistic tendency to view the world as white versus black, good versus evil.

Facing the shadow, then, means that we seek to understand the lessons to be learned through events rather than simply to assign blame. In this alternative analysis, the horrible disregard for human life exhibited by the hijackers on 9/11 is not foreign, but instead akin to what we have also done in the world. Our methods would differ—given the weapons that we have at our disposal, we would have no need to turn civilian aircraft into missiles—but the results of our actions have been similarly devastating to others in the world.

I thought of Secretary of State Madeline Albright's response when asked about the nearly half a million Iraqi children who had died during our sanctions against Iraq in the 1990s. She weighed that loss with weakening Saddam Hussein and concluded, "We think the price is worth it." But could not al-Qaeda justify and dismiss the tremendous loss of innocent life on 9/11 with a similar claim of acceptable collateral damage? And doesn't that justification simply and conveniently hide the shadow side of the warrior mentality?

I thought, too, of Thomas Merton's description of hell, where "no one has anything in common with anybody else except the fact that they all hate one another and cannot get away from one another and from themselves."[2] Merton certainly caught the claustrophobic feeling of our post-9/11 world, where the Other crowds our space and robs us of any sense of invulnerability.

At that moment, I was glad for the din in the restaurant, the noise level so elevated that we could barely hear one another. How would other patrons react if they heard Anita's perspective? Would her words be considered treasonous? Were they blasphemous? In even considering this perspective, were we dishonoring the victims of 9/11, or were we, paradoxically, honoring the sacred value of all humans, and especially the victims' dignity and sacred value, by seeking the truth?

Anita realized that what she was saying about our national shadow would constitute a terrifying awakening for us as a country. Yet she was hopeful. "There is a portion of humanity that is starting to wake up to that, and that is the only reason that I have hope." She spoke of a fellow Mennonite student who, during her seminary years (pre-9/11), had seemed to anticipate something catastrophic on the horizon. "She always said, 'The surf's up, and some of us are going to swim and some aren't. There is going to be something that's happening, and there's a whole part of our culture [that] will not be able to go along with us.'"

Those best able to "swim" in the turbulent surf of our times are, for Anita, those spiritual communities that realize that the West's preoccupation with acquiring "stuff and more stuff" has led to both spiritual emptiness and global destructiveness. "I'm not just [talking about] Christian communities, but spiritual communities that are sensitive to what's going on and are teaching each other and beginning to find new ways of living and calling other people to do that."

Anita affirmed that her own hope as a Christian lies in Jesus' message of the coming kingdom of God. But, she added, her faith is in "the kingdom here; the kingdom is now."

If we are to experience the kingdom of God "here and now," Anita said, we will have to take another, and even harder, step. That is, "we will have to listen to those we view as enemies and those whom we judge to be misguided." Such a step would demand greater humility and compassion on the part of First World nations, she suggested. We, the privileged, can no longer view ourselves "at the top of the food chain" but take "our place within the community of life."

JESUS' UNNATURAL DEMAND

I asked Anita to imagine a scenario of being asked to give a sermon to the entire nation on primetime television, all channels. What would she, as a Mennonite, preach?

Anita held my gaze as if something had become suddenly clear to her. "I think all we'd have to do is show a clip of what happened in the Amish community . . . For the Mennonite and Amish communities, who are cousins, that event was like our 9/11. That something so horrible could happen to innocent children."

Anita wiped away tears before finishing her thought. "But then the way they [the Amish] chose to respond."

Along with most Americans, I was familiar with the tragedy Anita was referring to. On October 2, 2006, Charles Carl Roberts entered the Amish West Nickel Mines School in Pennsylvania and executed five girls between the ages of seven and thirteen and wounded five others before killing himself. What had stunned the nation almost as much as the tragedy itself had been the decision of the Amish community to contact Roberts's widow only hours after the tragedy and ask what they could do to help. Over half of those attending Roberts's funeral were reportedly Amish.

While that unexpected Amish reaction had led to a national debate on the appropriateness of forgiveness as a response, Anita wanted to emphasize something that few have considered—that the Amish response of forgiveness and compassion had occurred while their community was still numb with shock. Forgiveness and compassion are not *feelings* but are *actions* required by God. "All they know is that [forgiveness] is what the Bible teaches; this is what my community teaches me; this is why I must do it."

In later interviews, I would hear echoes of this belief, that the Amish response to their personal tragedy—what Anita called the Amish and Mennonite 9/11—had been a timely sign to the nation and to the world of the power of forgiveness. "I don't know how that is even practical on an international stage," Anita admitted, "but all I know is that the world was riveted, at least this nation was riveted, by that example." And that example was not limited to the concrete gifts of food and money to the traumatized widow. "They [the Amish] wanted to make sure that cycle [of violence] is not continued, for her children and her family."

"I don't know if the world gets it," Anita said sadly, "that violence is a cycle . . . and that someone has to stop it somewhere."

STRIPPING DOWN

That evening, I sat in the silence of my motel room and thought back over my conversations with Michael Bennett and Anita Amstutz. I was grateful for their frankness, their willingness to be spiritually naked with a stranger. And although they surely knew how unpalatable their views would be to a majority of American readers, they had both stripped away what they considered our national illusions.

Both Michael and Anita assessed our nation's reaction to 9/11 as one of action with negligible, if any, contemplation. Out of a desire for revenge, America had struck back, as if that desire had not also been al-Qaeda's rationale for the attacks. To al-Qaeda, 9/11 had also been a response to US abuses in Iraq and Saudi Arabia during the Gulf War as well as the treatment of Palestinians. And just as al-Qaeda expected, we fell into the cycle of violence and revenge as surely as they had.

In our seeking payback, we missed what Michael and Anita saw as an opportunity for self-reflection. Hate, in the form of exploding airplanes, had crashed into our national psyche on the morning of 9/11. And that hate awakened our own appetite for revenge, a vengeance that felt viscerally pure and morally justified. As we watched body parts being removed with the rubble of the Twin Towers and the Pentagon, we concluded that if any nation had a right to hit back with full force, that nation was us. Al-Qaeda and the Taliban had cut the cord of human connection between us, and acting as animals, they had become the Other who must now pay.

For Michael and Anita, our nation limited its options the moment we saw ourselves as warriors with a sacred mission. With few doubts, we believed that a just God—yes, a warrior God—would hate al-Qaeda and the Taliban as much as we do.

What was so clear from my hours with Michael and Anita was how different is the goal they are pursuing. While we, as a nation, considered the destruction of all terrorists to be the optimum outcome to 9/11, we had been seduced into believing that vengeance would lead to peace for our world.

Both Michael and Anita have their eyes on a different horizon, one that has left room for Jesus' radical message of love of neighbor *and* enemy. As much as any American, Michael and Anita longed for a future without terrorism, but they understood that such a future would come only by our addressing the level of desperation in the world that leads to desperate acts.

Therein was the insight that I took away from my time with Michael and Anita. I felt that I could be an American after 9/11 and ignore Jesus' message of radical forgiveness, but I could not do that and still be a Christian.

There was no way to get around the fact that Jesus makes a very *unnatural* demand on His followers. He asks us to remain forever turned *toward* the Other, to seeing my worst enemy as my neighbor.

I did not conclude that Michael and Anita were asking our country to let down our defenses. In fact, I took their comments to mean that we, as the most powerful nation on earth, have an obligation to extend that protection to the innocent no matter where they live.

But coming through their responses was this clear message—Jesus would not permit His followers to turn away from anyone, even if the enemy were to attack us seventy times seven times.

PART TWO

Voices from America's Heartland

CHAPTER 6

Thomas Merton:
The Man at the Intersection

On September 11, 2001, every American wanted to talk with someone. We know that many passengers on those planes used cell phones to call loved ones, as did those in the burning towers.

Those of us who watched the horrors of 9/11 from a distance also felt a need to call those we loved, to share our grief and confusion, or to simply hear their voices. Just after the second plane hit, my older son, Leif, called from Fargo, North Dakota. More than anything he said, I remember the fear in his voice, and I did my best to assure him that whoever had committed this horrible act would be tracked down. We talked a long time, even after we had nothing more to say.

And because fear and sorrow are not rational, many of us desperately wanted to talk to someone close to us, even though that loved one was no longer living. I wanted to call my father-in-law, Nils, who had been dead fifteen years. I simply wanted to hear his voice.

But in the weeks and months following 9/11, it was Thomas Merton, the Trappist monk and writer who had died in 1968, more than any other person whom I most wanted to talk to. I have read

Merton's writings avidly for spiritual wisdom and direction. As the months after 9/11 became years, the desire persisted, and I realized that Thomas Merton might still have something to say to our age of terror.

When I brought my fears and concerns about our post-9/11 world into a conversation with Merton's writings, it was as if he had been waiting for me.

THE ODD SENSE OF BEING KNOWN

I did not meet Thomas Merton until after he had died. As far as I remember, his sudden death in Bangkok in late 1968 went unnoticed at evangelically conservative Wheaton College, where I was in my senior year.

Seven years later, after seminary and doctoral studies abroad, I was hired by Loyola University (Chicago) to teach a course on St. Paul at the local Baptist Campus Ministry, in DeKalb, Illinois. Before beginning to teach, I was asked to come to the local Newman Center on the campus of Northern Illinois University to meet the program director. As I waited for my appointment, I browsed a book table and found a cheap edition of Merton's *Seven Storey Mountain*.

I opened the book to read those famous first lines, and I was hooked.

> On the last day of January 1915, under the sign of the Water Bearer, in a year of a great war, and down in the shadow of some French mountains on the borders of Spain, I came into the world. Free by nature, in the image of God, I was nevertheless the prisoner of my own violence and my own selfishness, in the image of the world into which I was born. That world was the picture of Hell, full of men like myself, loving God and yet hating Him; born to love Him, living instead in fear and hopeless self-contradictory hungers.[1]

Seven Storey Mountain is an odd book, an autobiography written by a monk barely thirty years old, yet written as if the author were looking back over a long and troubled life. After the appointment, I took the book home and read it straight through. What I most welcomed in Merton's writing was his ability to write about spiritual matters without the usual tone of piety or any of the "Jesus is just all right" hippie language of that era. Though written in the 1940s, *Seven Storey Mountain* spoke to the crisis of meaning of my era and my own life. I found it simply incredible that Merton was of my parents' generation. I felt like Benjamin Braddock (Dustin Hoffman) in that other famous scene in *The Graduate* when he dives into the swimming pool to escape the swarming adults and their advice. Only in my case, I found a witty and sardonic monk swimming at the bottom of the pool.

That was the beginning of my friendship with Thomas Merton. As so many other Merton readers can testify, this cloistered monk seemed somehow to know me better than my closest friends. Chronicling the changes in his own life through books, articles, and journals, Merton encouraged me to understand my own life as a journey.

There was a time in the late 1980s and the 1990s, after the Soviet Union dissolved in a whimper and the United States emerged as some sole surviving superpower, when Merton's Cold War essays seemed passé. Then 9/11 occurred, followed by the subsequent wars in Afghanistan and Iraq. The same essays now read as commentaries on our time.

THE WOUND WHERE OUR HEALING MUST BEGIN

In biblical studies, scholars talk about determining the "canon within the canon." With the Bible being so vast and complex, the reader must first decide on the proper touchstone, or starting point. Once the touchstone is established, be that a particular book of the Bible or even a chapter of a book, the reader is able to "read out" from that starting point and make sense of the rest.

Thomas Merton's numerous and varied writings also leave the reader with the same initial challenge of where to begin. And with Merton's corpus, as with biblical literature, different readers will choose different touchstones.

I can see now that my choice of touchstone for Merton was affected by events of the fall of 2006—Pope Benedict's speech at Regensburg along with the violent reaction to that speech in the Islamic world, Iran's nuclear program, and the increased violence in the civil war in Iraq and also the war in Afghanistan.

In those difficult months, I felt drawn to one of the most oft-cited and important moments in Merton's journey, his epiphany on the corner of Fourth and Walnut Street in Louisville on March 18, 1958. His vision of the radical unity of the entire human race in God was just what I needed, a perfect contrast to my world as it was splintering apart and retreating further into camps.

> In Louisville, at the corner of Fourth and Walnut, in the center of the shopping district, I was suddenly overwhelmed with the realization that I loved all those people, that they were mine and I theirs, that we could not be alien to one another even though we were total strangers. It was like waking from a dream of separateness, of spurious self-isolation in a special world, the world of renunciation and supposed holiness. The whole illusion of a separate holy existence is a dream. Not that I question the reality of my vocation, or of my monastic life: but the conception of "separation from the world" that we have in the monastery too easily presents itself as a total illusion: the illusion that by making vows we become a separate species of being, pseudoangels, "spiritual men," men of interior life, what have you . . .
>
> I have the immense joy of being *man*, a member of a race in which God Himself became incarnate . . .

> Then it was as if I suddenly saw the secret beauty of their
> hearts, where neither sin nor desire nor self-knowledge can reach,
> the core of their reality, the person that each one is in God's eyes.[2]

How odd that a celibate Trappist monk should describe his moment of awakening in the language of love. And Thomas Merton clearly fell hard. The people on the streets of Louisville that day were no longer "alien" to him, but rather part of him as he was part of them. A brilliant sense of unity dawned as he plumbed the Incarnation, God entering humanity, in a more personal and radical way.

Before that epiphany, Merton had found Christ in the cloistered life of the monastery, in a life separate from the world. And before that day, his writings had extolled the cloistered life so brilliantly that scores of men had been drawn to Gethsemani.

In Louisville, on that fateful day, Merton saw Christ in the faces of everyone passing him on the street. Several years later, in *New Seeds of Contemplation* (1961), Merton would express this insight as seeing the mystical Christ in the people around him. "For in becoming man, God became not only Jesus Christ, but also potentially every man and woman that ever existed. In Christ, God became not only 'this' man, but also, in a broader and more mystical sense, yet no less truly, 'every man.'"[3]

It has been nearly sixty years since Merton's experience on the Louisville corner of Fourth and Walnut. The experience was a watershed moment in Merton's life, sometimes called his "second conversion." And in my returning to it, I found his epiphany to be a watershed moment in my own post-9/11 thinking. The more I have pondered Merton's experience, the more I am convinced that his experience in Louisville touches the wound where our healing must begin.

After his epiphany in Louisville, Merton remained in the monastery, but the horizon of his heart expanded dramatically. The new Merton took a "vow of conversation," as one of his subsequent books would be titled, a conversation with anyone seeking truth and reality whether that person was religious or not. His radical about-face might best be viewed as a new interpretation of the words carved over the monastic gate at Gethsemani: *"God Alone."* Merton's turning toward the world was, in essence, a deeper turning toward God, to the mystical Christ present within the human race.

Thomas Merton's Trappist training had prepared him for that moment. Trappists are technically the Order of Cistercians of the Strict Observance (of the Rule of St. Benedict). In that sixth-century rule, St. Benedict advises the monks to take special care in showing hospitality to guests: "Let all guests who arrive be received as Christ, because He will say: 'I was a stranger and you took me in'" (Matthew 25:35).[4]

The reference to Matthew 25 is significant. In that passage, Jesus demands a new way of treating not just one's neighbor, but also the stranger. The litmus test on the day of judgment will be this—how has one treated Christ as He is met in those who are hungry, thirsty, naked, sick, or imprisoned?

> Then the righteous will answer him, "Lord, when did we see you hungry and feed you, or thirsty and give you something to drink? When did we see you a stranger and invite you in, or needing clothes and clothe you? When did we see you sick or in prison and go to visit you?"
>
> The King will reply, "I tell you the truth, whatever you did for one of the least of these brothers and sisters of mine, you did for me." (Matthew 25:37–40)

With this text and the Rule of St. Benedict in mind, Merton's experience in Louisville seems to be a flowering of his Trappist training. But that maturing happened in such an unexpected setting and so deeply within him that he seemed, like St. Paul, to have been given new sight.

SEEING HUMANITY ANEW

Merton's initial reaction to this vision of the human race as the mystical Christ was one of relief, as if he were no longer required to hold up a wall. "This sense of liberation from an illusionary difference was such a relief and such a joy to me that I almost laughed out loud. And I suppose my happiness could have taken form in the words: 'Thank God, thank God that I *am* like other men, that I am only a man *among* others.'"[5] In a journal entry from March 19, 1958, the day after his Louisville epiphany, he wrote, "As if the sorrows of our condition could really matter, once we began to realize who and what we are— as if we could ever begin to realize it on earth."[6]

In the aura of his epiphany, Merton did not forget that the human race is prone to "absurdities" and "terrible mistakes." Yet more important is the truth that God in Christ has become a member not only of the church or her monastic communities, but of the entire human race. The Trappist monk who had left the world to be with Christ had found Christ where he least expected—in the world. "A member of the human race! To think that such a commonplace realization should suddenly seem like news that one holds the winning ticket in a cosmic sweepstakes."[7]

I reread Merton's Louisville epiphany in the month before I traveled to New Mexico to begin interviewing, and I realized that what Merton experienced in Louisville is the antidote to the tragic dualistic thinking—good versus evil, us versus them—that dominates the worldviews of both our adversaries and ourselves. We, too, have been holding up a wall, one we are trying to raise even higher in this time of heightened insecurity. Merton stumbled onto a very different view of humanity.

It is common for religions, especially Christianity, to focus on the *absence* of God at the center of every human. St. Augustine wrote the famous line in his *Confessions*, "We are restless until we find our rest in thee, O God." Merton, however, saw the *presence* of God in every human being. In our egotism and greed, we are unaware of our true nature—and that makes us extremely dangerous as well as lost—but Merton saw the "secret beauty of [others'] hearts, the depths of their hearts where neither sin nor desire nor self-knowledge can reach, the core of their reality, the person that each one is in God's eyes."[8]

For Merton, God's future can only begin when we see the human family in a new light. "It is like a pure diamond, blazing with the invisible light of heaven. *It is in everybody*, and if we could see it we would see these billions of points of light coming together in the face and blaze of a sun that would make all the darkness and cruelty of life vanish completely . . . I have no program for this seeing. It is only given. But the gate of heaven is everywhere."[9] And later he wrote, "If we believe in the Incarnation of the Son of God, there should be no one on earth in whom we are not prepared to see, in mystery, the presence of Christ."[10]

This was my touchstone in Merton's writings and in the project. His epiphany was like a flash of lightning, and I had heard the thunder of it nearly fifty years later. Nothing has moved me so much since 9/11, in this age of separation, disunity, and terror, as has this vision.

OUR WORLD AS HELL

Thomas Merton's epiphany is not an invitation to don rose-colored glasses. He was not trying to "teach the world to sing in perfect harmony," as the old Coca-Cola commercial went. Equally insulting to Merton's message and memory is the erroneous conclusion that he would advise us—or our adversaries—to no longer defend ourselves.

Merton's epiphany was a flash of light, and as such, that light exposed the shadow. If heaven was glimpsed in greater clarity by Merton, so was hell. Only four years after his epiphany in Louisville, Merton described his Cold War world as a mirror of hell.

Hell is where no one has anything in common with anybody else except the fact that they all hate one another and cannot get away from one another and from themselves.

They are all thrown together in their fire and each one tries to thrust the others away from him with a huge, impotent hate. And the reason why they want to be free of one another is not so much that they hate what they see in others, as that they know others hate what they see in them: and all recognize in one another what they detest in themselves, selfishness and impotence, agony, terror, and despair.

The tree is known by its fruit. If you want to understand the social and political history of modern man, study hell.[12]

Study hell. What an amazing bit of advice from someone who touched the edge of heaven in his epiphany. It is not a stretch to conclude that our age has become another reflection of hell. And we cannot exit this hell by pretending it is just the way the world works.

Yet Merton's description of hell on earth seems to describe perfectly the situation in which the West and radical Islam find themselves—each wants to get away from, even do away with, the other. But we cannot. We are stuck with one another and, as Merton suggested, with ourselves. This state of being is unbearable.

But if hell is unbearable, it is not inevitable. If we could read the Louisville newspaper from March 18, 1958, the day that Merton experienced his epiphany, I am sure that we would find a city plagued by racism, murder, rape, and other acts of inhumanity. Hell was in Louisville the very day that Merton experienced heaven.

In a passage that echoes St. Augustine's contrast of the city of God and the city of man, Merton argued that the human experience, whether in Louisville or Baghdad, Washington or Tehran, is not determined by the external circumstances (even a state of suffering and war), but how we choose to live within our time of crisis.

In the furnace of war and hatred, the City of those who love one another is drawn and fused together in the heroism of charity under suffering, while the city of those who hate everything is scattered and dispersed and its citizens are cast out in every direction, like sparks, smoke, and flame.[13]

At any given moment, Merton would counsel, the world is simultaneously flying apart in hatred and coming together in unity. All the world is Louisville. As Cardinal John Henry Newman wrote, heaven and hell may be the same place. For those who love only themselves, heaven (being in the presence of God and others) is hell. For those who love God in others, heaven is already known. We cannot choose the time in which we live, but we must choose between heaven and hell in this life.

THE TEMPTING ILLUSION OF HATE

If our world is hell, then that hell has arisen from certain recognizable human factors. Merton saw our world as a broken body, indeed, the broken body of Christ. The human race, however, is lost in a very different view of itself, living within an illusion of division, fear, and insecurity, of murder and war. And so we live as in "the unquiet city of those who live for themselves and are therefore divided against one another in a struggle that cannot end, for it will go on eternally in hell. It is the city of those who are fighting for possession of limited things and for the monopoly of goods and pleasures that cannot be shared by all."[14]

Is this not how our world lives, whether we are thinking of the Shia and Sunni in Baghdad, Israelis and Palestinians in Gaza and on the West Bank, or vigilantes and the streams of immigrants along the Rio Grande? Beneath our divisions, disunity, and greed lies fear—fear of others and fear of our own vulnerability. Yet, because we were created by God to want peace, we cannot accept as normal this life of fear and hatred. Despite our desire to carry on as before, we find this time of terror and uncertainty to have both physical and spiritual costs.

And here is where Merton's analysis of our human predicament is most startling and for that reason most noteworthy. Merton understood hatred not in the usual way as a sin, vice, or problem, but in a phenomenally different way, as a distorted human attempt to achieve *peace*!

"Hatred tries to cure disunion by annihilating those who are not united with us. It seeks peace by the elimination of everybody else but ourselves."[15] Fill in Darfur, Baghdad, Chechnya, or Kabul, and we see how clearly Merton knew our present world. Our dreams are filled with the hope that our adversaries will disappear or be made to disappear.

WAR: THE HELL IN OUR MIDST

From the first paragraph of *Seven Storey Mountain*, we see that Merton was always thinking of the human experience of war. But before his epiphany in 1958, war seemed part of the fallen world from which his vocation had separated him. His vision in Louisville brought him back into the world, and the pain of that world was now something he felt compelled to address.

"At the root of all war is fear: not so much the fear men have of one another as the fear they have of *everything*," Merton wrote. "It is not merely that they do not trust one another: they do not even trust themselves. If they are not sure when someone else may turn around and kill them, they are less sure when they may turn around and kill themselves. They cannot trust anything, because they have ceased to believe in God."[16]

In this appraisal of modern war, Merton noted how we all live under the threat of imminent attack. If that was true in the Cold War, it is perhaps even more the case in the age of terror. We seem to live between frightening news bulletins. Who can predict what tomorrow will bring?

Merton understood this fear to be rooted in our hatred, not of the enemy, but of ourselves. "There is in every weak, lost, and isolated member of the human race an agony of hatred born of his own helplessness, his own isolation. Hatred is the sign and the expression of loneliness, of unworthiness, of insufficiency. And in so far as each one of us is lonely, is unworthy, each one hates himself."[17]

But admitting such self-loathing is unbearable, and so our denied sense of insecurity sets in motion a chain of events all too common in our present age.

"We have to destroy something or someone. By that time we have created for ourselves a suitable enemy, a scapegoat in whom we have invested all the evil in the world. He is the cause of every wrong. He is the fomenter of all conflict. If he can only be destroyed, conflict will cease, evil will be done with, there will be no more war."[18] It is as if Merton had been listening to both al-Qaeda's diatribes against the West and American foreign policy statements.

Merton offered a second appraisal of war, one closely linked to his Louisville epiphany. The long and sorry parade of human history is nothing less than the endless dismemberment of Christ's body, he argued. "His physical Body was crucified by Pilate and the Pharisees; His mystical Body is drawn and quartered from age to age by the devils in the agony of that disunion which is bred and vegetates in our souls, prone to selfishness and sin."[19]

Pondering Merton's epiphany and its significance for our time has made matters clearer for me, but not easier. Through his "Louisville lens," we see not only what is happening to the human family, but also what is happening within the life of God. Homelessness, genocide, hunger, and war are all forms of deicide. "Christ is massacred in His members, torn limb from limb; God is murdered in men."[20] Is there a greater tragedy to war than the belief that peace and freedom lie on the other side of one limb trying to amputate another?

HEALING WILL BE EXCRUCIATING

Thomas Merton wrote that the refining love of God is the only remedy to our broken world. That may sound like standard Christian rhetoric, but Merton never treated such love as easy or abstract. On the contrary, he went to great lengths to explain the painful and difficult sacrifice this treatment would be.

If war is the tearing of Christ's mystical body limb from limb, then healing, Merton suggested, will be akin to "resetting a Body of broken bones" without anesthetic.[21] Worse yet, Merton understood that hatred's grip on us would not surrender easily. "Hatred recoils from the sacrifice and the sorrow that are the price of this resetting of bones. It refuses the pain of reunion."[22]

Merton's respect for the awesome power of hate is what separates his hope from that of humanism and reveals how deeply Christian is his hope for healing. When we pretend as humans that we are naturally kind and merciful and can freely choose to extend love to others, "our hatred is merely smoldering under the gray ashes of complacent optimism."[23]

For Merton, the hatred that undergirds this life of hell can be truly defeated only in the cross. Christ "suffered the pathological cruelty of His own creatures out of pity for them. In conquering death He opened their eyes to the reality of a love which asks no questions about worthiness, a love which overcomes hatred and destroyed death."[24] As the Nicene Creed affirms, for our sake and our salvation, Christ defeated hell by entering it fully.

Despite Merton's confidence in the power of the cross and resurrection, these acts of God do not change humanity in some automatic way. Rather, Christ's passion offers humanity a *chance* for healing, and that chance asks a great deal from us. The illusion of separateness, fear, and hatred that dominates and makes this world such a dangerous place remains a powerful temptation. "To serve the hate-gods, one has only to be blinded by collective passion. To serve the God of Love one must be free, one must face the terrible responsibility of the decision to love *in spite of all unworthiness* whether in oneself or in one's neighbor."[25]

And here Merton isolated the most difficult demand of the gospel. The healing of the world does not begin with our loving, but with believing that God loves us despite our unworthiness. Healing begins by accepting the paradox of knowing that no one is worthy of God's love, yet God has chosen to love the unworthy. This paradox changes everything, including our attitude toward our enemies. "And until this discovery is made, until this liberation has been brought about by the divine mercy, man is imprisoned in hate."[26]

So how in our age-of-terror world can the human family begin to heal? Merton suggested that the path to healing is well-known, summed up most succinctly in the golden rule (treat others as you would want them to treat you). But for Merton, this basic rule of life that seems so natural, obvious, and simple is utterly *unnatural* in our lost, broken state. God has given humanity the solution, but we have yet to *learn* how to practice that solution.

The fact that we do not feel such compassion toward others, especially our enemies, is no excuse. Merton takes a very radical stance on this point. "And if for some reason I do not spontaneously feel this kind of sympathy for others, then it is God's will that I do what I can to learn how. I must learn to share with others their joys, their sufferings, their ideas, their needs, their desires. I must learn to do this not only in the cases of those who are of the same class, the same profession, the same race, the same nation as myself, but when men who suffer belong to other groups, even to groups that are regarded as hostile. If I do this, I obey God. If I refuse to do it, I disobey Him."[27]

How easy it is to dismiss Merton's advice as "pie in the sky." Yet, consider the conclusion of Thomas Kean and Lee Hamilton, co-chairs of the 9/11 commission, in *Without Precedent: The Inside Story of the 9/11 Commission.* "In Indonesia, when the US military delivered aid and support for tsunami survivors, support for the US in the country skyrocketed—and support for Bin Ladin plummeted. That's a lot cheaper than war."[28]

Merton would have been the least surprised by this statement. As long as we are lost in the illusion of our separateness, insecurity, greed, and hatred will rule us, and military power will be necessary to defend ourselves from one another. But as the 9/11 commissioners have recognized, compassion, not military might, will end this war of terror.

ST. PAUL AND THOMAS MERTON: TWO LIVES CHANGED

The more I have reflected on Merton's epiphany in Louisville in light of 9/11, the more I am drawn to its similarities with St. Paul's epiphany on the road to Damascus.

> Saul was still breathing out murderous threats against the Lord's disciples. He went to the high priest and asked him for letters to the synagogues in Damascus, so that if he found any there who belonged to the Way, whether men or women, he might take them as prisoners to Jerusalem. As he neared Damascus on his journey, suddenly a light from heaven flashed around him. He fell to the ground and heard a voice say to him, "Saul, Saul, why do you persecute me?"
>
> "Who are you, Lord?" Saul asked.
>
> "I am Jesus, whom you are persecuting," he replied. "Now get up and go into the city, and you will be told what you must do."
>
> The men traveling with Saul stood there speechless; they heard

the sound but did not see anyone. Saul got up from the ground, but when he opened his eyes he could see nothing. So they led him by the hand into Damascus. For three days he was blind, and did not eat or drink anything. (Acts 9:1–9)

Merton's defining moment at the corner of Fourth and Walnut had several striking similarities to St. Paul's. Both Paul of Tarsus and Thomas Merton were about other business on the day that their lives were changed. Neither had any inkling that a life-changing experience was about to happen.

Both entered their experiences certain that God was to be found in the center of their own group. Paul had known God within Pharisaic Judaism, while Merton had found God at the center of his monastic vocation.

But the experiences of both men revealed that their understandings of God and the world were illusions. Paul met Christ as the living Lord of the very church that he had been persecuting. Merton had a similar awakening: the notion that being a monk cloistered from the world had drawn him closer to God was shattered.

And from their differing visions, both received new life missions. Paul's healing of blindness became a commission to bring spiritual sight to the entire world. Merton's epiphany in Louisville led him to take a new vow of conversation with the world.

There is, however, one startling difference between the two visions. The church did not treat the Damascus Road experience as a private mystical experience of St. Paul, but as a moment of transition for the entire church. The same has not happened with Merton's Louisville epiphany—at least not yet. Yes, Merton's turn toward Christ in the world did have an effect on Vatican II (1962–65). But for the most part, the church has treated Merton's vision as a private and mystical experience, not as a moment of transition for the church as a whole.

I believe this entire project could be summarized in this prayer:

that every person in the world would have Merton's Fourth-and-Walnut Street epiphany. What would happen in our world if, for just one human second, we would be given the grace to see our neighbors—the leaders of this world, the radio talk-show crazies, and our own enemies in that light of truth?

Merton himself expressed a similar wish. "And if only everybody could realize this! But it cannot be explained. There is no way of telling people that they are all walking around shining like the sun."[29]

BOUND FOR GETHSEMANI

As I packed my suitcases and equipment for my visit to Thomas Merton's own monastic home, the Abbey of Gethsemani in Kentucky, I wondered what would happen if the church *did* proclaim as a divine revelation what Merton had seen in his vision. What if we did view every person in this world as part of the mystical Christ? What would happen if we did see that every person in Darfur, New York City, Baghdad, as well as Louisville, is "walking around shining like the sun"?

At the Abbey of Gethsemani, I knew that I would be interviewing monks who had known Merton as their friend and, in many cases, their novice master. Were they living out Merton's epiphany? And if so, would these friends and students of Merton have a "word of life" for our broken world?

CHAPTER 7

Merton's Men

Abbey of Gethsemani
Trappist, Kentucky
January 24–26, 2007

In the photos of Gethsemani Abbey after World War II, the community is obviously bursting at the seams. The explosion of interest in monastic life by young men who had returned from the war meant that novices were sleeping in the dormitory's hallways.

A combination of factors lay behind this influx. First, many veterans returned from combat with burdens and a spiritual hunger that the mainstream culture of the late forties and early fifties could not satisfy. Second, America had helped win the war only to find itself caught in the new tension of the Cold War and the Nuclear Age.

Gethsemani Abbey experienced the natural upsurge of interest in monastic life that accompanies any age of uncertainty. But there was a special draw to Gethsemani for many of these men. At this Trappist monastery in rural Kentucky, these men were drawn by someone who had voiced their spiritual hunger—Thomas Merton, whose early autobiography, *The Seven Storey Mountain*, spoke powerfully and without cloying piety about the spiritual emptiness of the age.

In many ways, Thomas Merton was an enigma, even for a Trappist community such as Gethsemani Abbey. Here was a Catholic convert whose voice, as a Trappist monk, should have been silenced, his personal identity disappearing behind the limestone walls of Gethsemani. Yet, Merton, only thirty years old at the time, had been required by his abbot to write the story of his journey to Christian faith and then to monastic life. And from that isolated location, Merton wrote a series of books that made him one of the most widely read spiritual writers of the age.

Here was a young man who had spent his childhood and adolescence in Europe, in France and Britain in particular, and who came to the United States only during his graduate school days at Columbia. Merton did not become an American citizen until 1951. Yet his words resonate with particular insight with the American soul. Thousands of readers, including myself, sense that they *know* Merton and, more important, that Merton knows them.

And finally, here was a worldly young man, a poet and writer, who had never spent a day in military service. Yet his message hit home with those who had survived the worst war in human history.

A visit to Gethsemani today brings us to a far different community than the one that Merton knew. The schedule of prayer and work remains the same, but Gethsemani is no longer a secluded monastery. Women, who were once forbidden by the threat of excommunication from even visiting, can now come on retreat, stay in the guesthouse, and pray with the monks in the abbey church.

But perhaps the biggest difference between the Gethsemani of Merton's era and the present one is the size and average age of the community. Today, the monks who file into the choir stalls for the numerous services of the Daily Office are bald or gray-haired, stoop-shouldered, and even wheelchair-bound. Many of the choir stalls are empty. And most noticeably missing are the throngs of novices that characterized life at Gethsemani in decades past.

Many of these older monks were introduced to monastic life by Thomas Merton, who served as their novice master. When the idea first came to mind of traveling to monasteries around the country to interview monks and nuns about our current crisis, I realized that I must visit Gethsemani and interview "Merton's men." How had their years under Merton's instruction, as well as their subsequent decades at Gethsemani, prepared them to understand our age of terror?

This would not be my first visit to Gethsemani. I had come to the abbey on retreat at least a half dozen times before. But in those visits, I had entered into the silence of the place and rarely talked with the monks. Now, I would ask these monks to break that silence and share their "word of life" with an anxious world.

In this endeavor, I had the welcome assistance of Father Matthew Kelty. Father Matthew is a notable writer in his own right. He was also Merton's confessor at Gethsemani. Retreatants to Gethsemani have for years been drawn to the place, not just for its association with Merton and its opportunities to join in the prayer life of the monks, but also because of the chance to hear Father Matthew give a short talk following the service of compline. His wit, insight, poetic interpretations, and New England charm were ever present during these talks, another paradox of this Trappist house.

What was I hoping to hear? Obviously, I had hopes that these monks would still bear the influence of Merton on their spirituality and conscience. But I did not expect them to speak with one mind any more than had the monks from Christ in the Desert or St. Michael's Skete. Monastic discipline does not create clones, but rather individuated persons.

I was not disappointed in that expectation. The eight monks plus Abbot Damien whom I interviewed were greatly different from one another. Several of the monks, though hardly all, expressed their approval of Pope Benedict's Regensburg speech, when in an aside the pope chastised Islam for neglecting reason in thinking about God.

That view would be in sharp contrast with what I suspected would have been Merton's critique of the speech and in sharp contrast with the perspective of a noteworthy Catholic nun whom I would interview in the following weeks.

Several of the monks, including some who were military veterans, spoke from a stance of nonviolence similar to Merton's, while others did not. Some were fearful of what the near future might bring in terms of other tragedies, while several were what I could only call "obstinately hopeful."

I found all of the interviews at Gethsemani to be fascinating. Even though one monk explained why they did not engage in political debate in the community—they were certain that such a topic would lead to bitter arguments—the monks were both well informed about world events and candid.

Prior to my visit, Father Matthew had put up a description of my project and a sign-up sheet on the monks' bulletin board. While the older monks were willing to speak with me, their work and service schedules meant that the interviews were often conducted at a furious pace. At times, I felt as I were interviewing in a popcorn popper. My only hope was that my recording equipment would give me the chance later to reflect on what the monks had shared.

CROWDING AROUND THE TV

In some ways, the reactions to 9/11 at Gethsemani Abbey paralleled those of the majority in the country. The monks circled a TV set, much as did most Americans that day. A *New York Times* article reported the action of Father Matthew Kelty, who taped an American flag on his door in the aftermath of the tragedy.

In other ways, the monks of Gethsemani Abbey reacted quite differently than had our society as a whole. These distinct and divergent reactions reflect both the spiritual resources of the place and the highly personal political and spiritual perspectives of each monk.

I'll never forget the shock that they had of that other building when that plane banked. It banked and started toward that building. That made an everlasting impression on me . . . Within a couple of hours [of 9/11], we exposed the Blessed Sacrament and invited the retreatants to come down, even to the little area that we have if they wanted to sit there or to kneel . . . To me, by having the Blessed Sacrament exposed, it was the only way to accept or begin to understand something that was unacceptable or un-understandable. And this is the only place you can go when you have reached that point of surrender to "what in the world is going on?" And where can I go to find answers to this? And there wasn't any [answer] . . . When I said that there were no answers, I meant that the only place you could go was to God . . . It was a comfort to me. Of course, that is one of my strong devotions . . . It always has been.

—Brother Robert

Watching this, [I knew that] in a couple of hours . . . I would be leading back in the chapel in the monastery the Our Father. Can I stand before God and say, "forgive us our trespasses as we forgive those who trespass against us"? There was a lot to hang on that . . . I finally resolved it. I just said, "Lord, this is too much for me. I'm going to leave it in your hands—leave the judgment and all that can possibly be done to get beyond this and some way forgive those people" . . . That gave me great peace.

—Brother Raphael

In the tragedy of 9/11 and its aftermath, the majority of Americans focused on the horrendous loss of innocent life. Nothing of that scale had ever happened on our soil. The world suddenly seemed smaller, our adversaries nearer, our borders less secure. That view made it almost impossible for us to see what others in the world saw on 9/11, that "Goliath" had been dethroned. The size of the Twin Towers was matched by what some observers elsewhere saw as the hubris of their title—"World Trade Center" is eerily close to claiming to be the center of world. And what does the Pentagon signify if not the military heart of the world's last and greatest superpower?

Several of the monks at Gethsemani, however, had noted the terrifying irony of that day, when a nation without peer in so many ways—economically and militarily—found itself defenseless.

> I had very ambiguous feelings about the whole thing, because when the plane flew into the Pentagon . . . I had [been] more antimilitary for some time. The Pentagon certainly represented the military. The Twin Towers represented the capitalistic system. And by that time, I had a lot of negative feelings about it [capitalism]. I was sorry that three thousand people died, but I said to myself, "I wonder if those Muslims aren't onto something." In this world of ours, there is a tremendous amount of injustice, and the United States does in a way represent that. We have way more than our share of money, oil, everything and we're not sharing it equally or fairly with other countries.
>
> —Brother Frederic

> My first [reaction] was: "How could they do that? Who did it, and why? And then, what could we as a country have been doing or have done?" . . . I know something of what our country has done over the years to other countries . . . We're talking implementing democracy in Iraq; we torpedoed it fifty-three years ago in Iran . . . Time and time again, Guatemala, Chile, what we did to Allende, Bolivia, getting rid of Che Guevera, Castro . . .
>
> —Father Alan

The first thing that hit me was, "So there is the world's super-power on the ground—the world's superpower." And then the next thought that hit me, "I wonder when we're going to learn the lesson." That stuck with me for a long time . . . It [the United States] needs to learn that there is only one superpower, and that is above us. God is in control of the whole world, and He is the superpower.

—Brother Ambrose

PRAYER: THE INDISPENSIBLE WORK OF MONKS

A persistent stereotype of monks and nuns is that they are persons living in such isolation as to be out of touch with the realities of this world. Merton was himself frustrated with the pious image that many of his readers had of him. He resisted becoming a "plastic dashboard statue" that many wanted him to be.

In none of my visits did I find that stereotype existing. It is not monks who jump at every chance to be distracted by sports, the corner bar, and media intent on entertaining us incessantly. Monastic rules might be understood not as walls that keep the world out, but rather walls that keep the distractions away. Within those walls, the focus remains on the needs of our suffering world.

Merton sensed this on his first visit to Gethsemani Abbey. On the eve of Pearl Harbor and while the war was already raging in Europe, Merton credited the Trappist community's prayer life with holding the world together. Some of Merton's past students continue to feel the need to resist the trivializing stereotype.

It seems to me with a lot of people that that fear [of terrorism] has gone into the unconscious. This is a bad place for it to go, if you can't deal with it . . . Painting over rust is a thing that we tend to do. [The rust is] whatever it is that's bugging us. We're not really facing it. We're painting over it.

—Brother Raphael

Some people think, Oh, we're useless . . . No, [monastic life] is not like that. Prayer gives one the faith, the firmness, to stick it out or not be overwhelmed. See, that's the main thing [that] we're here for—prayer . . . We pray for everybody . . . We pray for those that suffered that day, we pray for those that are left behind; I add all those that are dying this moment, including what is going on in Iraq. I pray even for those guys that did [this] thing, that drove the planes. If we [as monks] don't do the right thing, if we don't live up to our vows, if we don't live up to what we're called to be here in this monastic setting, that's detrimental, in a sense, to the world.

—Brother X (name withheld)

There are people who come into their house at the end of work and [immediately] turn the TV on. With all due respect to the media, to the people in the media, what the media does to a great extent in this country is create this [artificial] world over here and then reports that world to you. So people get caught up in that.

—Brother Raphael

WHO FOR US AND OUR SALVATION . . . DESCENDED INTO HELL

One of Merton's most perceptive comments on modernity was that we, despite all the technological improvements, tend to make a hell of this life. The "things" cluttering our lives have proliferated, with our homes becoming as obese as our bodies. Meanwhile, we have stalled, if not regressed, in our capacity to live in peace with one another. As Brother Raphael sees it, the good that God is waiting to accomplish in our current crisis is restrained by our hell-bound insistence on being "left alone."

> There is a kind of wanting that goes with being God in His relationship with man. God wants this to happen, He wants to bring infinite good out of this . . . [God] puts Himself in that position [waiting on our free response], as He put Himself on a cross.
>
> My [take] on hell is that you're only there because you were selfish. You didn't care about your fellow man. "Get away from me." [You] build a wall around [yourself]. That's what you get—you float around for all eternity in an MRI.
>
> —Brother Raphael

ISOLATION: THE HELL WE LONG FOR

"Being left alone" seems the secret desire of most Americans in this age of terror. We would prefer not to know of Kandahar, Helmand Province, Basra, Somalia, Darfur, or Haiti. We wish history had never forced al-Qaeda and the Taliban upon us. We nostalgically recall a pre-9/11 world in which we were doing just fine without any of that. We were the last superpower, the master of all that we could survey, the nation above the fray. To cite Merton's terminology, we related to the world as if we were tourists visiting from a superior and distant civilization. Yes, the world was full of suffering, but we were somehow above that, looking down on the mess.

Merton's epiphany on the corner of Fourth and Walnut in Louisville exposes the idolatry of that dream and names as hell the very isolation we long for. That is why Merton's epiphany offers the most important message for our time, if we only had eyes and ears to perceive it. Merton was right in imagining how different the world would be if everyone could experience his own breakthrough, if everyone could see that those around us radiate sacred value. From the moment of his vision, Merton lived as one opened out to the entire human race. The world waits, God waits, for others to believe in the truth of his vision.

———————

I left Gethsemani and Merton's men with two powerful insights. First, hell is present in this world wherever and whenever human beings isolate themselves from others. That means that whenever nationalism, racism, religious tribalism, and classism fence off the Other, hell is here on earth. The second insight is the converse of the first. God is with us, lurking in the Other, our neighbors, the very ones that we wish to avoid. To recognize Christ in my neighbor is, as Brother René observed, to change everything. It is to escape hell.

> When I entered the monastery, the abbot told me, "There are only two people in the monastery—just you and God, nobody else." And I've never found anybody else. I mean if you give somebody a whack or a kick in the shins, Jesus is going to say, "You did it to Me." Actually, we live with Him alone [ending with laughter] . . . When God became man, it includes all men. If you're Protestant, Orthodox, Muslim . . . it includes everybody.
>
> —Brother René

Merton could hardly have said it better.

CHAPTER 8

The Other President
of the United States

Abbey of Gethsemani
Trappist, Kentucky
January 25, 2007

Abbey of Gethsemani
Jan. 18, 2007
Dear Dr Carlson

Recently, I read your letters to Fr Matthew and Abbot Damien. What follows is my recollection of my thoughts on "9/11":

That morning I was informed by one of our monks, who was using the Internet at the time, that a plane had flown into one of the "Twin Towers." Within an hour or so, he returned, and said (even more excitedly) that another plane had just crashed into the second Tower.

My very first thought was concerned about who could have been responsible for this . . . and more importantly, what could we (the United States) have done to provoke such violent acts?

A day or two later, my "insight" was confirmed when I learned that a wealthy Muslim (sheik?) had offered Mayor Juliani [sic] of New York a check for $10,000,000 to assist the survivors. He also said something like this: "Your Government should reevaluate the manner in which it treats third world countries." To my dismay, Mayor Juliani refused the $10,000,000!

Just thought I would share this with you.

I hope your visit to Gethsemani will prove worthwhile.

God Bless you and your Ministry!

Shalom,

Fr Alan Gilmore, OCSO

Thanks to Thomas Merton, the Abbey of Gethsemani is the best-known monastery in the United States. But the Abbey of Gethsemani had already been in existence ninety-three years when Merton came on retreat in 1940 on the eve of the US entry into World War II. His later reflection on that first visit still stirs me. "This church, the court of the Queen of Heaven, is the real capital of the country in which we are living. This is the center of all the vitality that is in America. This is the cause and reason why the nation is holding together. These men, hidden in the anonymity of their choir and their white cowls, are doing for their land what no army, no congress, no president could ever do as such: they are winning for it the grace and protection and the friendship of God."[1]

Merton's effusive words perfectly summed up my hope for this project, that I would find in monasteries what seemed so lacking in Washington: the spiritual sanity that could hold our world together.

The Abbey of Gethsemani lies south of Bardstown in the "knobs" region of north-central Kentucky. The "knobs," solitary and forested hills, rise stubbornly and form a perfect setting for Bourbon distilleries and isolated monasteries. Kentucky is Southern Baptist territory, that denomination's largest seminary being just thirty miles north in Louisville. But Gethsemani is hardly an anomaly, lying as it does in the heart of the Kentucky's "Catholic Holy Land." At the present time, the counties surrounding and including Gethsemani register a Catholic population of more than 50 percent.

The Abbey of Gethsemani is a Trappist house, meaning the monks are members of the Order of Cistercians of the Strict Observance of the Rule of St. Benedict. As that name suggests, the lifestyle at Gethsemani is strict even by monastic standards. The seven services of the "liturgy of the hours" take up nearly three hours a day. The sacred reading of *lectio divina*, physical work, meals without meat, and sleep from after compline (8:00 p.m.) to vigils (2:45 a.m.) round out the monk's day. Obedience to Christ through the abbot is demanded.

But for guests, Gethsemani offers few hardships. The rooms in the guesthouse rival a four-star hotel. While there is no TV, guests have access to the impressive library just down the hall, where books and magazines on spirituality, world religion, biblical studies, contemplation and mysticism, contemporary issues of the papacy, and, of course, Thomas Merton, can be found. The food at Gethsemani is both plentiful and tasty, with slices of the abbey's famous cheese offered at most meals. Comfortable lawn chairs line a veranda that looks out to the shady knobs and toward two statues on nearby hills. One is a bare cross, the other a statue of St. Joseph.

Unlike other monasteries, Gethsemani does not require its guests to share in the work of the community. Consequently, guests may use the time between services to read, pray, journal, stroll the grounds, or visit Merton's grave. While Trappists themselves have taken a vow of poverty, guests are welcome to visit Gethsemani's new and impressive visitors' center and gift shop. From some of the more caustic sections of Merton's writings, writings sold in this very bookshop, it seems likely that he would not have approved of the community's new enterprise.

THE STATE OF THE UNION, THE STATE OF THE WORLD

On my drive down to Gethsemani on January 23, 2007, I was reminded by radio newscasters that President Bush would deliver his State of the Union address that evening. For most of the twentieth century and now into the twenty-first, the State of the Union speech has also been a "State of the World" speech from an American perspective. With 9:00 p.m. being the time set for the speech, I knew that I, along with the monks, would miss it completely. Bedtime at Gethsemani is 8:00 p.m., immediately following the last service of compline.

Through official leaks, however, I already knew what the president would say. The year 2006 had been a difficult and watershed year for American foreign policy. More than one pundit had remarked on the precipitous erosion of American influence in the world. The war in Iraq was not going well. Afghanistan had been nearly forgotten. Osama bin Laden was thought to be hiding safely somewhere in Afghanistan or Pakistan.

History had clearly slapped the United States down in 2006, and the American people, as the midterm election had proven, were growing restless.

Being the first major speech of the post-Rumsfeld era, the 2007 State of the Union speech had the potential of signaling a major rethinking in Washington. But the leaks suggested that just the opposite would be true. The sobering analysis of the Iraq Study Group, recommending increased diplomacy with Syria and even Iran in dealing with the chaos of Iraq, would largely be shelved. Instead, a troop surge would be officially announced. Full speed ahead.

A MORE DISCORDANT UNITY

I had hardly settled into my room in the guesthouse before Father Matthew, my contact at Gethsemani, stopped by. He explained that I had been given the big room in the guesthouse because it would be convenient for the interviews. He also hinted that I would have a lot of business in the days ahead.

Two hours later, at compline, I scanned the community, wondering how many of the black-and-white-robed monks would stop by my room. I noticed something else during that service. The monks at Gethsemani stand in choir stalls lining both sides of the central aisle. Facing one another, the two groups chant the psalms antiphonally. That night, and in subsequent services, the monks on the right side were on tempo and in good voice. But the other side struggled a bit, with some monks noticeably dragging the beat.

That dichotomy, unity and muddle, symbolized my first day and a half at Gethsemani. On the first day, four monks stopped by for interviews—two in the morning session, two in the afternoon. All had had Merton as their novice master, and his influence on their perspectives was clear. While taking only slightly different perspectives on 9/11 and its aftermath, the four interviewees bolstered my impression that Gethsemani would offer a harmonious, Mertonesque voice.

The next morning, four more monks stopped by my room in the span of two hours, and it would be hard to imagine more discordant views.

To make matters worse, the first interview of the morning was with Brother Alan, the monk who had sent me the note about Mayor Giuliani. We talked longer than the thirty minutes allotted, which led to the other monks knocking and interrupting one another throughout the rest of the morning. Each monk had been permitted to break from work for his half-hour appointment with me, which left me barely enough time between interviews to reset my recording equipment.

By the time the last monk left my room in early afternoon, I felt frazzled. Any sense of unity from the night before, any sense that Gethsemani would form a tidy chapter in the book, had vanished. I felt the fatigue of a hunter who had tracked down four rabbits running in different directions. And more monks were expected.

Walking to the window, I gazed out toward the shadows forming on the knobs. I was overwhelmed and bone-tired. The divergent perspectives of the past thirty-six hours swirled in my head. My only hope was that some pattern would emerge later when I listened to the recorded interviews.

But I wondered how likely it was that that hope would be realized. One monk had questioned if Islam was even a valid religion. Another had questioned why 9/11 was any more noteworthy a tragedy than Darfur or abortion. Yet another told of an Irish mother by the name of Anne who claimed to be receiving messages from Christ.

Back in the 1940s, Merton had identified Gethsemani as the "cause and reason why the nation is holding together."[2] Now, sixty-six years later, I was struggling to understand what held Gethsemani together.

A loud knock on the door made me jump. Opening it, I expected to see one old monk who, that morning, had been lingering at the end of the hallway.

But it was Abbot Damien who stood in the hallway. I instinctively stepped back as he came into the room. Monastery guests have a natural curiosity about the abbot, wondering what type of person could lead a community of men of all backgrounds, ranging in age between twenty and one hundred. If Merton was right in calling Gethsemani the "real capital of the country," then this lanky man was the other president of our country.

I had not met Abbot Damien on my previous visits to Gethsemani, but I had observed him amid the other monks in choir. His stall is in the middle of the discordant side. His wooden staff of office is tall, as is the man himself. The previous abbot, Timothy, had been short and looked scholarly in his thick glasses. Abbot Damien is physically imposing. Though he is lanky, his shoulders suggest that he once hoisted heavy bags for a living. When Abbot Damien raps on the edge of his choir stall to announce the end of compline, the echo reverberates through the church up to the sleepiest guest in the balcony.

Now in civilian clothes, the abbot crossed my room and slumped into the chair. He ran his hand over his crew cut and confided with a yawn that he'd spent the entire day in Louisville on business.

"I wanted to stop by and see what all this is about," he said. His eyes locked on mine as I took the other chair.

Those eyes could be a problem, I thought, but I took a breath and asked permission to interview him for the project.

He shrugged in response. "Your sign-up sheet is full," but he added that he'd chat until the next monk came.

Somehow, no one knocked for the next ninety minutes, and somehow the busiest man at the monastery stayed to share his own State of the World.

"Let me tell you what happened on that day [9/11]," he began, "because I was the one who got the word, okay?" His comments would be peppered with "okays" and "you knows." Whatever educational level he had achieved, Abbot Damien wasn't embarrassed to let me know where he had started.

On the morning of 9/11, the abbot received a call from one of the neighbors, telling him that something big was happening. As the other monks had already told me in their interviews, Abbot Damien had let everyone watch the news on the monastery's sole TV in the infirmary.

"After lunch, we said, 'Let's go pray about this.'"

From my later reading of President Bush's 2007 State of the Union address, I discovered that he, too, had invoked the memory of 9/11: "Every success against the terrorists is a reminder of the shoreless ambition of this enemy. The evil that inspired and rejoiced in 9/11 is still at work in the world. And so long as that's the case, America is still a nation at war."

Abbot Damien's initial reflection on 9/11 was markedly different. He asked the big "why" question, "Why were we attacked?" I had already heard that question in New Mexico and was to hear it repeatedly throughout the project. Oddly, that question is one that I have rarely heard outside of monasteries. Perhaps it is a question that most Americans believe has been satisfactorily answered.

I draw from this contrast one of several possible conclusions. Either the monks and nuns whom I interviewed had not heard the administration's repeated explanation that our enemies hate us, hate our freedom, hate democracy, hate civilization, and are part of an axis of evil in the world, or they undoubtedly had heard that rationale and simply did not accept it.

"Why did they do this? Why do they hate us?" Abbot Damien posed. "If a person hates you, you know, what do you do? Do you just hate them back? How do you counter hatred?"

I sat quietly as Abbot Damien posed his own questions to answer. As was true of other Americans, the abbot was puzzled as to why a whole mass of people who we'd tried to help over the years had turned on us. But unlike many Americans who believe the record of American generosity should end further national introspection, the abbot pushed further. "[We] who have everything . . . of course, we're generous, but the world is still the same. The people are so poor, and they're starving."

The abbot's comment echoed a theme found in many theories as to the causes of terrorism. Violence flourishes in the soil of poverty, despair, and humiliation. To simply respond to the problem with superior military power will not end those conditions but only spread that dangerous mix.

Back in Washington, President Bush's State of the Union address had acknowledged the spread of violence but did not consider how our actions might have contributed to that increase. The president admitted that the five years since 9/11 had been sobering ones, and he conceded that the war in Iraq was going badly. He even admitted that our enemies had increased since 9/11, not decreased. But in the speech, there would be no questioning of our role in this. Instead, the president spurred the nation forward with the belief that "it is still within our power to shape the outcome of this battle."

Abbot Damien's assessment was significantly different. Speaking of Iraq, he asked, "How come it just seems to be lost? We dropped a bomb in the middle of this whole thing and wonder why they're all attacking one another now, and there's no way to walk away. We just lit a bomb."

NOT TOO LATE FOR REFLECTION

I brought up Nathan Dungan's observation, that 9/11 had offered the nation a chance for introspection but we had largely missed that opportunity. When 9/11 happened, we paused on the question of "why" for only a few days before embracing a dualistic good-versus-evil scenario. We named al-Qaeda as the enemy, invaded Afghanistan, hunted down suspected enemies, identified an axis of evil, and finally "lit the bomb" of Iraq. With nearly each step we had taken, the nightmare had only worsened.

Abbot Damien considered Dungan's comment for a moment before agreeing that 9/11 was an opportunity, a chance to "find [out] who we really are as human beings." As if he had listened to the State of the Union address, the abbot added, ". . . in order to heal this, it's not running after people. It's changing ourselves, our attitudes toward other people."

Abbot Damien explained what he meant. "There's something that transcends national boundaries . . . a common element that we have to recognize in ourselves. And we're going to have to have leaders who are like this, that are willing to dialogue."

Dialogue was not the theme of the State of the Union address. But list-making was. The address contained a list of our enemies: al-Qaeda, Sunni extremists, Shia extremists, Hezbollah, and Hamas, with Iran unnamed but lurking in the background. That growing list was the administration's rationale for placing our hope not in dialogue, but in our capacity to destroy enough enemies to demoralize the rest. "Take almost any principle of civilization," President Bush asserted, "and their goal is the opposite . . . They want to overthrow moderate governments and establish safe havens from which to plan and carry out new attacks on our country."

President Bush's language suggested an encroaching plague, a prospect meant to terrify. And it worked.

What seemed largely unnoticed about the speech was how similar such language is to al-Qaeda's rhetoric about us. Chalmers Johnson reports that one week after 9/11, Osama bin Laden offered the three reasons for the attack, none having to do with hating freedom and democracy: 9/11 occurred, according to bin Laden, because US forces were stationed in the sacred land of Saudi Arabia, because US support of Israel had brought intolerable misery to the Palestinian people, and because sanctions against Iraq after the first Gulf War had brought the deaths of half a million Iraqi children. But as the war on terror has progressed, al-Qaeda's leader increasingly portrayed the West as launching a crusade against Allah and Islamic civilization throughout the world.

In war, it seems that adversaries begin to mirror one another's rhetoric. Both the US government and al-Qaeda have divided the world into two camps: civilization against evil. Both see peace in the world coming through the annihilation of the other. But since this is impossible, both seem to be promising unending warfare.

Even in early 2007, Abbot Damien could detect how this prospect had affected us as a nation. "That's another thing that 9/11 did to us . . . Now, all of a sudden, now we got so isolated [that] we have to protect ourselves from everybody from outside . . . Don't let anyone in. Whoever heard of putting a wall up along a whole country?"

Yes, it was a confusing dance in which the United States was caught up. On the one hand, the United States had pulled back and was seeking to secure her borders. On the other hand, we have stationed troops all over the world and continue to look down on everyone from our satellites. We want the world to go away, yet we cannot leave the world alone.

But Abbot Damien retained hope that our country could still learn the lessons of 9/11, a moment in our history that "forces us into this corner of reexamining ourselves as human beings, and we have to come up with something else . . . We've got to have an alternative to killing."

And a leader with the courage to propose an alternative to unending war was who Abbot Damien was looking for. What the world needs, he suggested, is someone willing to walk over to the other side and say, "Hey, I might get killed [for this], but we got to talk." He paused for a moment before adding, "Somehow we have to know that we're *one*."

LOVE CUTS THROUGH

The abbot leaned toward me and in nearly a whisper said, "Let me tell you something. Let me tell you what this is all about."

And that was what he proceeded to do. First, I needed to dismiss the stereotype of the monastery as a secluded community cut off from the world. "Society is one," he said. "We have [just] one unit."

A monastery faces the same challenges as the world, he said. "We dialogue in here, because we find that there's something inside all of us . . . that must be tapped. We have to get to know each other on a deeper level than we ever have."

Second, Abbot Damien added, I would have to understand at this time of crisis the importance of the contemplative vocation, something difficult to recognize in a time when action and reaction dominate the news. The monk or nun as a contemplative is often dismissed as a navel-gazer or an evader of reality. Even religious folk wonder about the usefulness of contemplation in a world plagued with massive problems.

But contemplation, if properly understood, Abbot Damien insisted, is a path to a deepened humanity, a truer way of understanding ourselves and one another. This is the main work of a monastery, he explained, and that work, even if ignored by the majority in the world, affects the whole. "The person who can rise as a human being raises all society, and the whole role of the monastery is bringing civilization, the evolution [of it], closer to what it's supposed to be through our own integrity—through our own rising to our better instincts—by our own humanity."

Thomas Merton's great contribution to the world, Abbot Damien suggested, was that he had "tasted" this humanity yet to be, "and in tasting it, everyone else participates in the taste."

And that was the very reason, Abbot Damien confessed, that he had himself entered the monastery thirty years before. He was looking for a chance and a place to go "over the edge in terms of the spiritual life, of getting deeper into life . . . And in getting deeper into life, you bring all the people with you. You don't have to communicate this . . . just the fact that the two of us are one, you know? One humanity."

The abbot paused so long that I looked up from my furious note-taking to see that he was fighting back tears. He gained control, lost it, and then regained it as he told me of the letters of compassion that had poured into Gethsemani, after 9/11, from all over the world. Everyone in the world was suffering after that tragedy, he said, not just Americans.

His voice gained strength as he said, "The whole world was affected, but you have to know that the whole world is affected by good in the same way . . . You have to understand this, that if we have a house of good people, this does the same thing" in a good way that "a catastrophe does . . . in an evil way. That's what we're trying to do [here]."

I tried to square Abbot Damien's vision of the unity of Gethsemani with the widely divergent interviews that I had conducted during the past two days. I told of one monk who expressed doubts about Islam being a valid religion, of another who believed that Christ is speaking through an Irish woman.

The abbot nodded. Gethsemani is "a crosscut of the church," he suggested, housing liberals, conservatives, and those struggling with the church and her policies. But in his thirty years in the community, he had noted that the monks keep "moving forward, moving forward, moving forward" through dialogue, always measuring themselves against the ideal. "The men here aren't [perfect], but they're trying."

I understood why the monks of Gethsemani had, in 2000, chosen this man to be abbot. His strength of personality and character were obvious, even as was his gentleness, necessary traits for someone who has to sort through his men's hopes even as he bears their fears.

Abbot Damien paused, as if waiting for me, and I decided that I would share something—Thomas Merton's equating the entire human race with the mystical Christ—that had repeatedly come to my mind as I interviewed monks and nuns and wrote about terrorism.

In Merton's view, the Incarnation, the belief that God became human in Christ, was not an abstract theological doctrine, not simply a creedal statement, but an actual transformation of the entire human race. As a drop of holy water is said to have the power to sanctify an entire ocean, as a spore of leaven affects the entire loaf, God becoming human has changed us all. The decisive moment of human history had come in Christ, the God-man, and, for Merton, this was the answer to the Cold War of his own lifetime. I swallowed hard and told Abbot Damien that I had come to believe that Merton's insight was becoming for me an answer to 9/11.

I do not think it was simply my imagination that something in the room changed. We both knew that we were talking about something crucial. And because Abbot Damien knew Merton's writings far better than I did, I waited in anticipation for his reaction.

But part of me was also listening for any sound in the hallway. I knew exactly what this abbot would do if one of the monks knocked on the door. He would rise to leave, and I would be robbed of what I had come to Gethsemani to hear.

But no knock came.

Yes, Abbot Damien replied, Christ is in "every human being, every human being." In God becoming human, he explained, God had "changed our definition [of human beings]."

Yes, I could see that this insight of the abbot's was what Merton had meant, and it set my mind buzzing. Sin is the power that breaks everything apart; sin is the power that separates us from the truth about ourselves; sin is what blinds us to others. Losing all sense of human unity, we fear the Other, which causes us to act in ways that make us the feared Other for them.

I thought of our society built on competition, an economy fueled by insecurity. Win or be devoured. Do whatever is necessary to be the last survivor on the island. That same spirit, that same demon, has driven humanity into every conflict in our race's history. Think victory, not solution. Dismiss dialogue as weakness. But below the facade, our hearts remain filled with terror.

I thought of my own fears, the fear of public humiliation, the fear of being exposed for not being exceptional, the fear of not having the answer.

"I'm seventy-three, okay?" Abbot Damien said, breaking into my thoughts. Yet it was only recently, he admitted, that he realized that his life is wonderful. "The whole deal is because I'm finally getting out of that [fear]. I don't have to be afraid of these people . . . Love cuts through all of that."

During a time of fear, the word *love* has the same problem as *forgiveness* and *dialogue*. If we are to grasp what love means in monastic life, we will have to dismiss its meaning as a feeling, even a deep-seated and stirring feeling, within us.

The love that Abbot Damien was talking about is the action that Jesus demanded in Matthew 25 when He taught His followers that they love Him when they offer water to the thirsty, feed the hungry, clothe the naked, and visit the imprisoned. That very understanding of love is the basis of Benedictine hospitality, where the stranger knocking at the gate is treated as Christ.

I had run into three of these other "Christs in disguise" when I had checked into the guesthouse two nights before. A trio of downtrodden people, two toothless, all in ragged clothes, was sitting listlessly in the lounge. They were the type of humanity we step over on the streets of every major city in this country.

I learned later from Father Alan that the three knew that Gethsemani *could not* turn them away. I had seen three ragged failures. I might have even felt pity. The monks saw Christ.

What would be the result if we who call ourselves Christians in the United States lived by the Rule of St. Benedict and saw the stranger, even the enemy, as a "Christ in disguise"? How would our "immigration problem," our obsession with building a wall on our southern border, look through such eyes? What if we understood that the fence was walling out Christ?

The abbot was not finished with me yet. Now, years later, I am still stopped in my tracks when I remember what Abbot Damien next said. In becoming human, God had not only changed human nature, he said. "*He changed His own.*"

I had not seen that coming, nor could I have. From boyhood on, I had been taught that God "is the same, yesterday, today, and forever." God changes His own Self? To this very moment, I sense that I am touching the edge of something of huge significance, something that is pulling me past a boundary that has existed within me for my entire life.

I realize now that my entire interview with Abbot Damien was inviting me to abandon the numerous levels of duality that we so easily accept. First to go was the assumed duality of monastic life and the outside world. There is, the abbot agreed with Merton, only one humanity. A monk is simply a human being, sharing the same humanity as the layperson, as the atheist, as the Buddhist, as the Muslim, as all of us.

Second to go would have to be the false dualism of dividing the world into us and them, neighbor and enemy. All humanity is part of the mystical Christ, for in this Christ there is no distinction between slave or free, male or female, Jew or Gentile, Muslim or Christian, Islamist or secularist. Again, the abbot agreed with Merton. There is only one humanity, the humanity that Jesus assumed.

And finally, if I grasped what Abbot Damien was saying, the hard line dividing God and humanity had been forever bridged. In Christ, God had entered humanity, and, in Christ, humanity had forever entered God. God is not out there, over there, or up there. God has chosen to be with and in humanity—forever. There is, the abbot asserted, only one humanity—a God-permeated humanity.

And the one God is a humanity-permeated God.

Merton's vision of this truth allowed for no sentimentality. War is not downplayed but exposed for what it truly is, a continuous attack on the mystical Christ. War is the ongoing crucifixion of God, the crucifixion of ourselves. In war, we tear our own body limb from limb.

Viewing war in that way, Merton maintained that the eventual healing of our world will be terrifying, akin to bones being reset without anesthesia. And that healing, Abbot Damien added, was waiting for each of us to make a critical decision.

"I'm the one who has to be converted, you know," he said. "If I'm open to everyone who walks down the street . . . peace will be there." He offered the example of unity between religions. "It depends upon how much I can love the Muslim or love the Jew." If there's no wall between us, "then that's how I restore unity to the world, and . . . to myself. And then the unity in me is in Jesus, because Jesus is the heart of my soul. He's the one who is coming out of me . . . My response to everyone in the world has to be like that."

The abbot recommended that I consider the point made by the theologian Karl Rahner, who believed that the Christian of the next generation will have to be a mystic. "What the mystic is," Abbot Damien explained, "is the man at the core of civilization, at the core of what the human being is all about," someone who is "capable of relating to the universe . . . relating to all peoples."

THE JOURNEY BECOMES PERSONAL

As the abbot rose to prepare for the afternoon prayer service of None, I felt keenly the difference between us as human beings. Abbot Damien was deeply inside the truth that he was talking about. Perhaps, I thought, he is one of the mystics that Rahner wrote about. A problem-solving, straight-speaking, crew-cut man, but a mystic nonetheless.

I knew that I was not inside that truth yet, but outside it. But also, thanks to the unplanned time that Abbot Damien had spent with me, I felt near it.

As we stood together by the door, I asked him a question that had been on my mind since New Mexico. Should I remain detached and simply record the thoughts of monks and nuns in this book? Or should I accept that this was also my own journey to find some light, some hope?

He nodded. "Somehow in its heart, [the book] has to be about you more than these people, how [you] evolved in this whole thing. You have to get an answer out of all this."

It wasn't the advice of an editor or literary critic but that of an abbot, and though I wasn't one of his flock, I sensed that he had looked into my heart.

When Abbot Damien left the room, I started to pack away the recorders and found myself crying—finally. During my days, especially the afternoons, at Christ in the Desert and St. Michael's Skete in New Mexico, I had felt the tears rising within me. But I never understood that urge, and I am not the type to allow tears to flow without a known reason.

The tears that afternoon passed quickly, but after listening to Abbot Damien, I finally knew why they had been lying in wait for me from the beginning of the project. I had never doubted the importance of the interviews, from that third knock on the door in 2006. But from that very first moment, I had felt a fear of what could happen. I imagined some seasoned monk, nun—even better yet, an abbot—telling me to my face that I was not the one to handle the job. Now, with the tears, I realized that this scenario was only partially a fear. It was also a deep-seated wish.

Part of me wanted to be told to get lost, literally, to be told to return to my life as a college professor in a small Midwestern town. Part of me wanted to be a Jonah in reverse, to be told to drop my sense of mission and return to my far edge of the world. But from the start in New Mexico, monks and nuns had been telling me the opposite. "God be with you on this book." "People need to think about these things, even when they don't want to."

And now with Abbot Damien, I finally admitted that, yes, I had to get an answer out of all of this for myself.

WHERE THE FUTURE IS ALREADY PRESENT

I fell asleep early and heavily that night, but about one o'clock in the morning I awoke and lay in the perfect stillness of the monastery. There were no cars passing outside, no birds singing outside my window.

I waited for some thought or feeling to surface, something to account for my waking, but there was nothing. I turned on the light and opened my journal, but at first no words came. I picked up a book to read until I could again drop off to sleep.

A couple of paragraphs into a chapter, I put the book down, aware that the emptiness I was feeling was in truth a kind of *something*, a new something for me. Somehow, I had awakened to find myself *inside* what Abbot Damien had been talking about. As I lay alone in that room, in the quiet of a monastery asleep or perhaps monks praying in their cells, I felt connected with every other person in the world. Or maybe I was simply connected with these men who had that connection. I had no mystical feeling; in fact, it didn't seem a feeling at all. I just knew that the whole amazing world, from the pain of Baghdad, to Las Vegas, to Havana, to North Korea, and to my quiet room, was all one piece.

I picked up my journal again and found the words pouring out. "I am with men in whom the world has already been healed." I thought back to the gentle monks and nuns at Christ in the Desert, the sense of Eden rediscovered. I thought of Sister Julianne, spinning 360 degrees in her chair as if she were the entire world rotating on its axis. I thought of young Father John, who somehow knew that 9/11 was his sin, my sin, our sin.

"I'm with people and I'm in places where the future is already present," I wrote. It was just as Father Alan had said the day before: "The world is already one; it just doesn't know it." But these men and women do know that truth. And because they live in that reality,

that truth exists as leaven in a world of roadside bombs and Amish children being shot to death in a schoolroom.

As I lay in that monastery bed, I, too, tasted the world both in its brokenness and as it would be someday—healed. I felt nothing, heard nothing, saw nothing. But I was *in* something. I was where the world was heading.

I didn't pray, but just turned off the light and lay in the dark.

Only God knows how long it will take us to arrive at our divinely ordained destination. Only God can possibly bear what sorrow lies ahead of us because we keep choosing dead-end roads. But at Gethsemani, I tasted what the future will be.

POSTSCRIPT

Now, three years later, as I read over my reflections on the visit to Gethsemani, and especially my interview with Abbot Damien, I realize how much of what was discussed that afternoon in late January 2007 still stirs me. Yes, the occupant in the White House has changed. Some would say that President Bush's "surge" in Iraq has been a success. And now Osama bin Laden has been killed. But the war of terror and the war on terror continue. The Taliban in Afghanistan and Pakistan are now the main target of US military operations, and countries as difficult to locate on a map as Yemen and Dagestan now worry both us and our allies. The unrest on the streets of the Middle East and North Africa adds to our collective uncertainty.

Clearly, the dualities that Abbot Damien identified as dominating our thinking in 2007 have not abated in strength over the past three years. The world is still divided into us versus them, and that dichotomy has found a new and prominent place in the Tea Party movement, which opposes health-care reform, economic recovery strategies, and other aspects of the Obama agenda.

There is much in our country and in the world to cast a heavy cloak of anxiety over everyday life. If anything seems true, it is that the world is even more broken now than in 2007.

And yet . . . what stays with me and gives me hope is Abbot Damien's deep conviction that our world has already been healed in Christ—we just do not know it nor act in light of that truth. World events in the past three years, as well as crises in my personal life, have mocked that insight. And yet Abbot Damien's conviction—that in the Incarnation, humanity and divinity have been forever changed—remains for me *the* key insight, one that has the power to save the human race.

I left my 2007 visit to Gethsemani with the cornerstone of this new vision. Insights from earlier and later visits to other monasteries have certainly contributed to what has become a new personal vision of God, neighbor, and enemy. But the interviews at Gethsemani, and the related reflection on Thomas Merton's epiphany in nearby Louisville, are clearly the undergirding foundation for everything gained through this project.

As I wrote in my journal on the night following my conversation with Abbot Damien, *"At Gethsemani, I tasted what the future will be."*

That taste is still with me.

CHAPTER 9

Others Are Waiting
for Us at the Center

Our Lady of Grace Monastery
Beech Grove, Indiana
March 23, 2007

An ancient Jewish legend relates how weapons were introduced into this world by fallen angels. There is a kernel of truth in this story, for the legend suggests that warfare is not a natural part of the human experience, but part of what is wrong with our world. Unfortunately, human hands learned early in our evolution to make weapons. Lagging further behind is the true alchemy of taking in a breath and transforming that breath into words of peace.

Words themselves can easily be drafted into the service of wars, as has happened once again in the war on terror. Dialogue, however, is noticeably absent. It is not just Osama bin Laden who spoke from a cave. The White House, 49 Downing Street, and the presidential palace in Tehran are also caves.

THE APPEAL OF ACTION

In the West, and especially America, we prefer action films for our entertainment. Our archetypal action heroes (Bruce Willis, Vin Diesel, and Jason Statham) struggle with expressing themselves, and in that reticence we are oddly reassured.

The iconic action figure has also infiltrated our political life. We no longer honor the skilled negotiator, for compromise is suspect. Diplomacy is now either foreplay for war or a synonym for weakness.

And yet no culture has studied the effect of words, cadence, metamessages and tone as carefully as ours has. We have made a science of discovering the right phrases to sell cars, package a candidate, or leverage public opinion on hopeless wars. Marketers can find the words to sell lard on a cardiac unit, but that is mere conjuring. We have focus groups down pat, marketing to a science, but finding the words that will bring peace eludes us.

Gandhi consulted no focus group before proclaiming *satyagraha*, the truth-force that would move the mountain of colonialism out of India. Martin Luther King Jr. hired no marketing firm to craft the vision of the Beloved Community that continues to live on and will one day defeat racism.

At some moment in the future, perhaps when our broken world seems to be at a point beyond healing, we will begin a serious search for the words—the sacred words—that will end this war.

Some among us, persons largely unknown, have already begun that search.

TWO VETERANS OF PEACE

In her book *Islam Is: An Experience of Dialogue and Devotion*, Sister Mary Margaret Funk wrote, "We who call ourselves Christians are at a turning point in our relationship with Muslims in our shared world. The wars in Afghanistan and Iraq, and the effort of the international community to combat terrorism, all require us to look deeply into the heart of Islam and its faith, its plurality of cultures and civilizations. If we do not, we miss a jewel in our midst and risk generations upon generations of conflict because of ignorance."[1]

I first heard of Sister Mary Margaret Funk (Sister Meg) when her face appeared on the cover of *U.S. Catholic*. I turned to the article entitled "Stay the Course" to see her photo alongside that of Dr. Sayyid Syeed. Both stood looking squarely into the camera, slight smiles on their serious faces, as two corporate lawyers might look as they enter a courtroom.

With Pope Benedict's earthshaking address at the University of Regensburg only four months before, the implications of the article's title ("Stay the Course") seemed clear. Dr. Syeed and Sister Meg were introduced as credible respondents to the pope's address. Dr. Syeed is the former secretary general of the Islamic Society of North America and a member of the Midwest Region Dialogue of Catholics and Muslims. Sister Margaret Funk is a former executive director of the Monastic Interreligious Dialogue between Buddhist and Catholic monks and nuns. She has also been a participant in the Dialogue of Catholics and Muslims and, together with a Muslim friend, Shahid Athar, authored *Islam Is: An Experience of Dialogue and Devotion*.

It was not so much her credentials as it was Sister Meg's way of responding to the questions in that article that led me to request an interview. Here was someone who practiced something out of the normal experience of most Americans—dialogue with the Other. Here was someone who could speak to the power of dialogue as well as its limitations and frustrations. And I sensed from the article that she had problems with Pope Benedict's recent comments about Islam.

THE POPE SPEAKS OUT ON ISLAM

I have read the transcript of Pope Benedict's Regensburg address. Speaking to friends at his old, traditional Catholic post in Germany, the pope focused on this same issue of dialogue.

As nearly everyone knows, the Islamic reaction to the speech was negative, immediate, and in some cases, violent. A great deal of speculation has centered on the pope's awareness of this possible outcome. Daniel Madigan, of the Institute for the Study of Religions and Cultures at the Pontifical Gregorian University, believes that Pope Benedict, "the first really functioning Pope in the post-September 11 world," understands his role to include "laying down challenges to Islam."[2] The Regensburg speech was certainly crafted to be one of those challenges.

Within days of my interview with Sister Meg, the pope was back on the covers of major American magazines. With George W. Bush being a lame duck president, the West seemed to have anointed Pope Benedict as its chief polemicist. The *New Yorker* of April 2, 2007, explored the pope's relationship to Islam, while the April 8, 2007, issue of the *New York Times Magazine* focused on his stance as an anti-secularist. In different ways, both articles returned to the Regensburg speech and asked: Is the pope on the right track after all?

The speech, as various commentators have noted, was not aimed directly at Islam. The intended audience was secular Europe, Pope Benedict's post-9/11 mission field. Picking up the thread of articles and addresses from his earlier days as cardinal and Prefect for the Doctrine of the Faith, the pope warned that Europe's divorce of faith and reason weakened far more than European Catholicism. The growing secularity of Europe weakened the continent precisely at a time when Muslim immigrants continued to "move onto the block."

Pope Benedict has argued that Europe is, by definition, the fruit of the providential dialogue of faith and reason in Christianity. To sever that dialogue and seek to live off reason alone is to disconnect the train from its engine.

Pope Benedict is indeed a theologian of first order. He thinks about big things, which greatly appeals to me. "While Europe once was the Christian Continent, it was also the birthplace of that new scientific rationality which has given us both enormous possibilities and enormous menaces . . . In the wake of this form of rationality, Europe has developed a culture that, in a manner hitherto unknown to mankind, excludes God from public awareness . . . A culture has developed in Europe that is the most radical contradiction not only of Christianity but of all the religious and moral traditions of humanity."[3] And again, "Europe is infected by a strange lack of desire for the future."[4]

Most Westerners, including many Catholics, yawn at such warnings. Pope John Paul II harped on the same theme, and Europe and the West routinely ignored him. But Muslims get the point. Rising secularity is a danger felt by Muslims living in Europe and those in Islamic societies affected by Western culture.

But the Regensburg speech did not speak to this shared concern with Islam. Instead, to support his claim that the dialogue of faith and reason has been best achieved in Christianity, the pope referred to another dialogue, this one between the Byzantine emperor Manuel II Paleologus and a fourteenth-century Muslim. In the now oft-repeated quotation from the speech, Manuel II scathingly assessed Muhammad as having brought nothing new to the human experience except "things only evil and inhuman, such as his command to spread by the sword the faith he preached." In a nutshell, the twenty-first-century Pope Benedict, sounding like the academic he was, repeated a fourteenth-century Byzantine emperor's dismissal of Islam.

Christianity and Islam are both, along with Judaism, Abrahamic faiths. The three religious share common roots and intertwining histories. There is a wealth of scholars well qualified to speak on Islam and reason. But Pope Benedict chose to cite a fourteenth-century

Christian emperor and, moreover, to call Manuel II Paleologus "erudite."

Pope Benedict's decision to quote Manuel II has become a defining moment in Christian-Islamic dialogue. And, as such, it is hard to see his decision to do so as wise. At the very least, the citation seems uncharitable.

Many Muslims would agree that there is a frightening lack of rationality in statements from al-Qaeda and other extremist groups. Screams of "Allah Akbar" (God is great) followed by "Death to America," "Death to Britain," and, after Regensburg, "Death to the pope" suggest something is amiss. When zeal trumps reason, we have a right to worry.

But the pope's comment on Islam, even as an aside, was not directed against radical groups, but against the prophet Muhammad and thus the religion as a whole. The pope's words joined those of other Western religious leaders who have publicly offered disparaging remarks about Islam. And that is what made the pope's remarks not only uncharitable but also unreflective on the history behind the situation.

CHRISTIAN EXTREMISM

Christianity has had its own despicable periods of extremism. One can imagine sixteenth- to eighteenth-century indigenous leaders in Central America and among the Pueblo peoples of the American Southwest evaluating the Christianity of the Conquistadors and their missionaries in language much like Manuel II's as quoted by Pope Benedict in his Regensburg address: ". . . and there you will find things only evil and inhuman, such as [the] command to spread by the sword the faith he preached."

Perhaps even more ironically, Manuel II's words describe all too well the horrific Fifth Crusade, when Constantinople was sacked by Catholic forces and many of the city's Orthodox priests and monks were put to the sword. The memory of that tragedy was so great that in 1453, only sixty years after Manuel II's derogatory comment about Islam, the Orthodox residents of Constantinople preferred subjugation by the Islamic Ottoman Turks to submitting to Catholic domination.

Furthermore, in the Regensburg speech, the pope claimed that Christianity's dialogue of faith and reason began at the moment when the prologue of John's gospel was penned. There is some merit in that argument, but it would seem fairer to admit that it was not until the Enlightenment that Christianity treated reason as more than faith's obedient servant.

It was in the wake of the controversial speech at Regensburg and its unfortunate reaction that Sister Meg chose to speak out.

THE EMPTY LABYRINTH

The *U.S. Catholic* article "Staying the Course" is a carefully worded response to the Regensburg speech. It is also a public commitment from both Dr. Syeed and Sister Meg to do whatever they can to continue their version of Christian-Islamic dialogue.

The article is gentle on the pope, as would be expected, given that one of Benedict's first acts as pope had been to remove the editor of *U.S. Catholic*. There are numerous references to the gains achieved by interreligious dialogue since Vatican II, vociferous praise for Pope John Paul II, and near forgiveness of Pope Benedict's Regensburg address from Dr. Syeed.

Sister Meg, on the other hand, spoke bluntly in the article. She referred to the ecumenical dialogue (dialogue between Christian groups) that is preferred by this pope as a waste of precious time in comparison to the crucial dialogue between Christianity and other religions. Moreover, she hinted that the Regensburg speech was not the only damage that Pope Benedict has done to Christian-Muslim relations. I wanted to interview this nun.

I arrived a half hour early at Our Lady of Grace Monastery in Beech Grove, Indiana, for our prearranged interview. Some fifteen years before, I'd been at the monastery for a conference, and I was struck with how little the place had changed over the years.

I'm a poor estimator of age, but Sister Meg seemed in her fifties or early sixties, old enough to have held numerous leadership roles and still young enough to be considered for important tasks. This was confirmed at the end of the interview, when she relayed that the Vatican was transferring her to lead a Benedictine convent in Ireland.

Sister Meg is slight, but she walks and speaks with purpose. Everything about her suggests discipline. In our interview, she spoke in short sentences, straight to the point, occasionally adding a chuckle or a wisecrack. Later, in reading several of her books, I found her writing style much the same. More than once, Sister Meg gave me a sense of what the writer Flannery O'Connor would have been like had she been a nun.

After escorting me to the library where the interview was to take place, Sister Meg excused herself to finish a prior duty. As I waited for her to return, I gazed out the window toward a rain-drenched labyrinth. Labyrinths, sometimes confused with mazes, were originally alternatives for medieval Christians who couldn't afford to go on pilgrimages to sacred sites. The labyrinth at Our Lady of Grace is a large one, almost as big as a tennis court, its pathway weaving back and forth as it moves toward the center and then back out by the same path.

The purpose of a maze is to confuse, to challenge the walker, like a mouse, to find the one way out. In a labyrinth, by contrast, the pilgrim cannot get lost. But the pilgrim will be delayed, the path taking longer to traverse than first thought.

Tom, a friend whose graduate work was on labyrinths and their revival in contemporary Christianity, explains that the meandering path of the labyrinth is meant to promote contemplation and prayer. It accomplishes this in several ways: first, by slowing the pilgrim down both physically and mentally. From walking a labyrinth several times, I have been impressed with how calming the experience is and how little the presence of others disturbs that calm. Second, some of the sharp turns in a labyrinth lead the pilgrim closer to the center, representing intimate communion with God, before suddenly leading the walker away from that anticipated goal. As with life, the pilgrim receives a glimpse of the goal only to lose sight of it as her path takes an unexpected turn. And, as with life, other pilgrims are at different places on the same path. Some are returning from the center, offering hope to those working their way in.

No one was walking the labyrinth at Our Lady of Grace on the rainy March afternoon of my visit. Later, Sister Meg told me that she rarely sees the labyrinth unused: people from the neighborhood, the retreat center, or patients or staff from the hospital adjacent to the monastery walk it almost daily.

Our Lady of Grace Monastery sits snugly in a neighborhood of smaller, middle-class homes in this southern Indianapolis suburb. A busy four-lane street runs past one side, and the parking lot of the next-door Benedict Inn was nearly full, reflecting perhaps the extensive programming on Benedictine contemplative practice that the monastery offers.

But the library was quiet, giving a sense of the solitude still possible in a house of eighty nuns. I set up my recording equipment, sensing that my time with Sister Meg would be exactly as she had promised over the phone. Right on time, she came in and sat down. Almost immediately, we began the interview.

9/11 DIVIDES THE MONASTIC COMMUNITY

Sister Meg's memories of 9/11 were very precise. Along with another nun, she was at the dentist that morning. She remembered that the dentist started to physically shake as the news came over the TV.

Returning to Our Lady of Grace, Sister Meg found the community in shock, with many gathering in groups to pray or to watch the news. Looking back on it, Sister Meg said, "This house got [the seriousness of] it right away."

The community's somber response contrasted sharply with what Sister Meg experienced on September 20, 2001, when she gathered with others to plan an upcoming Buddhist-Christian conference.

"I tried to radicalize the board quickly around [what had happened], and David Stender-Rast was one of [my] soul mates insofar as we saw the significance of [9/11]," she said. But the board president, a monk who'd been in Japan on September 11 and had therefore missed both the attacks and the American reaction, was a different story.

"I couldn't communicate it to him. He just kind of laughed about it and said this happens all over the world. I remember getting kind of angry with him." Sister Meg shuddered as she added, "We had to go to Europe together in November, and I still remember being angry at him."

To make matters worse, another member of the board admitted on September 20 that he believed in war. "I sank because I assumed at this very high level of dialogue that at least we all believed in nonviolence, and that was not the case."

Despite the fact that many of the speakers at the upcoming conference canceled after 9/11, the Buddhist-Christian conference did occur. "But it was very sobering, and it was a commitment that dialogue—I mean, it was a little naive—that dialogue was the answer to violence."

NOT ALL DIALOGUE TAKES US TO THE CENTER

In the *U.S. Catholic* article, Sister Meg stated what seemed the opposite viewpoint, that "the alternative to military intervention is dialogue."[5] What would she say to those who view talk as useless, even dangerous, in our time of crisis?

As with nearly all my questions, Sister Meg responded quickly, though those responses never seemed haphazard or defensive. Her mind just seemed to work very quickly.

"All dialogue would help to know each other as persons, but the real dialogue that would matter enough is dialogue of experience, and the same experience of ultimate concerns—the Holy, the Significant, the God language, or the no-God, whatever it is. And it's that level of dialogue that we, as monastics, were at."

But all that has changed under Pope Benedict. "You see, the pope has shifted," she said. "He closed the Office of Dialogue . . . and put it with Culture, which virtually says, 'There is no dialogue of experience.' He snuffed that out."

To explain the differences between the two types of dialogue, Sister Meg asked if I had ever heard of the Belgian abbot Dom Armand Veilleux. When I admitted that I had not, Sister Meg promised to e-mail me an article by Veilleux on monastic interreligious dialogue with Islam.

As she had promised, I received the Veilleux article by e-mail on the following Monday.[6] And, as promised, Veilleux's article proved helpful, especially in clarifying the context of Pope Benedict's Regensburg address.

Veilleux's article opens with the historical background for interreligious monastic dialogue. The source of that openness could be traced to Vatican II and especially the important encyclical *Nostra Aetate*. But it wasn't until 1968 and then 1974 that the dialogue between Christianity and Buddhism moved from scholarly papers delivered at universities to what Thomas Merton had practiced before his death, that being the more important sharing of religious experience. Veilleux comments that "their conversations were not about institutions or philosophy and theology, but about religious experience. Dialogue at this level was not only possible; it was mutually enriching."

The encouraging outcome of these initial meetings led to the establishment of the Dialogue Interreligieux Monastique (DIM), its purpose being to help Christian monastic communities "become attentive to the religious experience of their brothers and sisters from the other great monastic traditions."

Other encounters followed, where monks and nuns met at each others' monasteries. Beginning with monastic communities of the Far East, the exchange gradually led to encounters with Muslims.

John Borelli, associate director for the Secretariat for Ecumenical and Interreligious Affairs at the US Conference of Catholic Bishops, has offered a quick description of the basic practice of this early Catholic-Muslim dialogue, a dialogue of experience, not theology.

"If there is no spiritual dimension to our meetings, they are not interreligious dialogues. Catholics attend Muslim prayers and Muslims attend usually a morning or evening prayer service specially prepared for the occasion. The Catholics also celebrate Eucharist each morning. Our dialogues do not dwell on the past, since to focus only on history, whether positive or negative, and on traditional teaching is to avoid contemporary issues."

As Sister Meg had stated, it was this dialogue of experience and prayer that has been scrapped by Pope Benedict. In February 2006, British archbishop Michael Fitzgerald was removed from the Pontifical Council for Interreligious Dialogue and reassigned to Cairo.[7] Soon after, the Council was itself absorbed by the Pontifical Council for Culture,[8] which represented a victory for the Congregation for the Evangelization of Peoples.[9] Put simply, dialoguing and praying with other religions seems less important if the church believes those other religions need to be evangelized.

I remembered a film that contained images of Thomas Merton's last day of life. Merton was in Bangkok, giving a talk to Christian monks and nuns on the importance of dialoguing with and learning from Buddhist monks and even Marxists. As the camera pans from Merton's face to the audience, the viewer is struck with the steely stares of the Christian monks and nuns. They who had spent their entire vocations seeking to convert Buddhists and Hindus are not buying a bit of this dialogue stuff.

But Merton's paradoxical message, that dialogue with other religions does not weaken one's commitment to and experience of Christian faith but strengthens that faith, became the basis of the interreligious monastic dialogue that soon developed. Now, with Pope Benedict's closing down that form of dialogue, at least officially, the voices for conversion have won out.

Veilleux's sad reflection on this state of affairs is that "those who consecrated their lives to [monastic interreligious dialogue] are regarded as wishful thinkers or naive romantics."

THE DIALOGUE OF EXPERIENCE AS A PATH TO PEACE

A person might argue that the focus of dialogue between Christians and Muslims hardly matters so long as it continues. Veilleux and Sister Meg disagree. Pope Benedict's decision to highlight culture rather than experience, Veilleux argues, is to emphasize the *differences* between the religions and their understandings of God.

"There is only one God, whatever the name or names we give to this reality," Veilleux wrote. "Whoever has had a real experience of the true God, an experience that goes beyond all ideologies, senses a profound communion with every other person who truly searches for God."[10]

In our interview, Sister Meg offered a similar conviction. "We've got to see that everyone has the truth. And that's not relativism. That is just fact." If, in her words, "everybody's truth matters," then the dialogue of experience rather than contrasting cultures becomes essential.

For Veilleux and Sister Meg, the Regensburg address offers a perfect example of how the dialogue of culture gets it wrong. "Those who engage in the dialogue of religious experience are not interested in whether or not Islam is 'reasonable,'" Veilleux argues. "Religious experience worthy of the name is neither rational nor irrational; it is *beyond* reason. God is greater and other than that which we can know, say, think, or 'feel' of God. Of that every contemplative, Muslim or Christian, is profoundly convinced."

For Sister Meg, the Regensburg address was an example of papal "misspeak" that exposed the assumption of Western superiority that so easily goes unchecked in the dialogue of culture. "It really was taken very badly by the Muslims as a bruising thing. And he repeated it, that text, the full text, he repeated it three times." (In checking the speech, I discovered Sister Meg is right. The quotation from Manual II is mentioned three times.)

"It was not a casual [remark], if you examine it," she pointed out. "He meant it. And then also closing the Office of Dialogue and merging it with Culture is saying that Islam is not a revealed religion," she said. "[Islam] is an interesting culture and we'll, okay, stay in touch, but it's not the level of truth. So they [Muslims] were putting that together too."

I was beginning to grasp the impotency of the dialogue of culture in our post-9/11 world. With 9/11, the world split in two, each side in those tragic moments becoming the Other. As Muslim and Western cultures drift farther apart, each side is tempted to wish that the Other would disappear.

The West dreams of a future where the Middle East is at peace, where Muslims hurry from their mosques in their BMWs to eat at Olive Garden before ending up at the mall. We imagine a day when Islamic religious practices and values will quietly fit, as ours do, into busy secular lives. Perhaps the other side fantasizes the Washington Capitol becoming a mosque, as happened to the Church of Hagia Sophia in Constantinople. Perhaps they dream of sharia, not the Bill of Rights, becoming the law of the land.

Both visions are based on the defeat of the Other and on the unexamined assumption that the rest of the world needs to become a copy of ourselves. And that is what seems to most alarm Sister Meg, Veilleux, and others committed to the dialogue of experience about the Vatican's recent change of direction. The dialogue of culture promotes a conversation that focuses on the differences that separate us and thus further emphasizes the otherness of each side. In contrast, the dialogue of experience *needs* the Other to be precisely other. In the dialogue of experience, the existence of the Other in this world is part of God's plan.

Here lies the superiority of the dialogue of experience in promoting peace. The differences between the various religions become not a problem but, as Veilleux wrote, "so many facets of the indescribable beauty of God who is absolutely transcendent and yet very close to us."[11]

But what good has the dialogue of experience brought to our troubled world? In the end, is this interaction and prayer together any more than just talk by a few powerless people? While Veilleux admits that such exchanges offer no short-term fix, they may be the only alternative to Huntington's scenario of a "clash of civilizations": "This experience of God, this taste for God shared by simple Christians and Muslims whose hearts are moved by the utterance of the Name of God, gives them a common desire for peace and fraternal community, *even when all around them Christians and Islamicists are killing one another in the name of opposing and fundamentally anti-religious ideologies.* Muslims and Christians who share an experience of God spontaneously come together to look for ways to comfort this wounded world with the balm of mercy and pardon," he wrote.[12]

THE LOSS OF THE HOLY IN THE WEST

While Sister Meg shares Vielleux's long-term hope, she added a concern about the West, a concern that changed the course of our conversation. "The bigger problem is that people don't have [this kind of] experience."

Then what is the hope, I asked, if the medicine offered by the dialogue of experience is unavailable to Westerners?

But it is very available, she countered, even as she admitted that people would need "spiritual direction and this whole realm of sensitivities toward the Holy in practice. And we'd have to reduce and remove the afflictions that are dominating consciousness."

As Sister Meg expressed it, "as long as you have food-consciousness or sex-consciousness or thing-consciousness, you're not thinking God-consciousness. And so you can't get there. So you have to go back to these old ascetical practices in some form to remove those . . . afflictions."

I tried to pull together the various strands of her argument. The dialogue of experience between those who have "God-consciousness" is perhaps our only hope for lasting peace, yet the West is blocked from entering this dialogue by its addictions to food, sex, and things.

What are the chances, I asked Sister Meg, that the West's secularized way of life, a life of little or no God-consciousness, will change? Can history's flow be reversed?

"You know, God's grace is very available, but these afflictions are just hiding everything. But the monastic archetype is in every soul."

At this point, she seemed worried that I might take her talk of "God-consciousness" and "afflictions of the mind and soul" to be spiritual abstractions. "But [this is] not poetic; it's not Greek mythology . . . It's an alternative culture."

A LABYRINTH OF THREE LEVELS

Even assuming that this alternative culture existed, I asked Sister Meg whether this God-consciousness would contribute to peace in the Middle East.

Believing that the dialogue of experience can indeed contribute to peace in the Middle East, Sister Meg cautioned that this dialogue requires patience as the participants work through three spiritual levels. "I think the first level really is just your own vibrations, your own meditation. And if you can get your heart still, then your mind at peace, you know you really do send out those levels of radiation."

Her answer disappointed me. This blunt, no-nonsense woman suddenly sounded like the advice printed on the inside flap of a Celestial Seasonings Tea box. But, as she was quick to explain, achieving a peaceful mind with its radiating energy is just the first, or surface, effect that one can have on our broken world.

The second level, she argued, brings us to the real battleground—the human emotions that lie at the root of all human misery. She illustrated the difficulty of this level by describing a recent personal experience. The week before our interview, on March 19, she had tried to organize a peace vigil at the monastery on the anniversary of the beginning of the Iraq war. But the monastery's schedule was already full, and assistance from other community members hadn't materialized. What surfaced and spilled over in Sister Meg was a rush of anger.

Our culture often views anger as a kind of strength. Anger is not just useful, but essential in our competitive society.

Sister Meg comes from a different orientation, a monastic one, though I sensed from her probing insights into anger in her recent book *Humility Matters for Practicing the Spiritual Life* that she is quite familiar with this affliction. In the book, she quotes both the fourth-century St. Basil and the current Dalai Lama on this "affliction of the mind." For St. Basil, "anger is the single biggest detriment to the spiritual life." For the Dalai Lama, anger is toxic and "makes us sick."[13]

In our interview, Sister Meg talked of anger as a cage which a person enters one thought at a time and then cannot get out of. "The [lesson] of it would be to back off, which I did, going up to my room and even [coming] to prayers here in this little oratory. [I had to] just back out my anger because that was ego."

Backing out of anger, as Sister Meg described it, reminded me of the labyrinth outside the window. The only way out of the labyrinth is to retrace the steps that took one in. This backing out of anger, Sister

Meg said, has nothing to do with suppression of anger, but dealing with it point by point as it surfaces. "I had to apologize and literally ask for forgiveness and back out thought, by thought, by thought [from] that anger. It was gone within a day, but nevertheless that's the second level."

What Sister Meg clearly wanted me to understand was that this wisdom is not restricted to monks and nuns. But it is this type of wisdom, she suggested, that must be known and practiced in true dialogue with persons of other religions.

That brought us to the third and final level of dialogue. That level is "to listen . . . to the impulse of the Holy Spirit. You know, there are billions of things you can do. [But] what is it that this [convent] can do? What can I do?"

To explain, she remarked that she was already ten years into the dialogue with Islam when the United States launched its strike against Iraq. She was angry, but what could she do? "I was ready to protest and go to Washington and get into nonviolence." But she heard distinctly, "That's just going to make everybody mad."

The inner voice reminded her that her training was in religion, and that she had been involved in dialogue with Muslims for a decade. What had that prepared her to do? "Then I heard from underneath, 'Teach about Islam.' So then I decided to put my anger aside and write a whole book about Islam."

As the interview ended, I confronted for the first time that same question. Was this book, though monastically based, also a book about Islam and for Muslims? I remained uncertain if I could fully embrace her image of all religions offering different paths to the same summit of knowing God. But I began to believe that there may be another summit, another common meeting point, for all people of faith. And there, I realized, Muslims, Buddhists, and many others would be waiting for me.

CHAPTER 10

Interlude: Sister Peggy (Cecily)

Sisters of Loretto
Nerinx, Kentucky
March 3, 2007

I came to the Sisters of Loretto Motherhouse, some twenty miles from Gethsemani, with the intention of interviewing nuns who had worked closely with Sister Mary Luke Tobin, a warrior for peace and a close friend of Thomas Merton. Before leaving, however, I heard that another nun, a poet who had written about 9/11, was willing to speak to me.

Sister Peggy, or Cecily, had in fact lived with Sister Mary Luke Tobin for thirty years. A small, soft-spoken woman perhaps in her eighties, Sister Peggy had recently retired to the Motherhouse after years living and working with Sister Mary Luke in Colorado. In Denver, the two nuns were involved in a wide range of justice issues at the time of 9/11, one commitment being part of the Colorado Campaign for Middle East Peace. Prior to 9/11, the group had opposed the sanctions against Iraq, holding vigils but also sending representatives with medicines to Iraq.

On the morning of September 11, 2001, Sister Peggy was in the kitchen, stumped by a recipe. Calling a friend for assistance, the friend blurted out, "Peggy, do you have on your TV? You ought to turn it on, because something terrible has happened."

Within a week after 9/11, when it was clear that the US government was going to attack Afghanistan, the Colorado Campaign for Middle East Peace held a strategy session. "It was decided that if the United States started bombing, we would all meet at the state capitol for a vigil."

Precisely at the same time, Sister Peggy was asked by the Motherhouse in Kentucky to write a poem honoring the upcoming twenty-fifth anniversary in October of the Cedars of Peace hermitages, retreat cabins on the grounds of the Sisters of Loretto motherhouse.

Although an accomplished poet, Sister Peggy found the task of writing an appropriate poem under those circumstances to be difficult. How was she to celebrate a retreat area dedicated to peace when the bombing of Afghanistan could begin at any moment? She resolved her dilemma by writing a poem that spoke to both realities, the imminent war on Afghanistan and the community's long-standing commitment to peace. Sister Peggy set the poem about Cedars of Peace at the time of compline, when it was the practice of retreatants to gather before bedtime to pray for the needs of the world.

Shyly, Sister Peggy handed me a single sheet of paper with the title "When That Day Comes" at the top. The poem began, she explained, with a memo from the peace group.

WHEN THAT DAY COMES
CEDARS OF PEACE, 1976–2001

"If the U.S. begins bombing, meet at 5:30 the same day on the West steps of the State Capitol, Colfax and Lincoln."
—Memo from Colorado Campaign for Middle East Peace

When that day comes
may our hearts meet here at Compline
where the pleading chant
layered through the years
will comfort us.

As we huddle in our towns to mourn
may our hearts meet here
in the silence of these woods
where hope will temper dread.

Seven thousand times or so before
you have gathered in the dusk to pray.
We shall scan a frightful sky
when that day comes
but may our hearts meet here.

When that day comes
the smothered moaning of the dove
and sudden scramble of two
acrobatic squirrels may be the loudest sounds
to counterpoint our prayer.

We must gather with our somber signs
and urgent chants when that day comes.
As our hearts meet here at Compline
we scavenge for a whispered peace
against the scream that vengeance shrieks.

Afghanistan, the atlas says, holds stands
of cypress, juniper, and pine.
Are they the cedars' kin
and will they offer peace, we ask,
when that day comes?

May our hearts meet here.

—Cecily Jones SL, October 6, 2001

Sister Peggy sat in silence as I read and then reread her poem. When I looked up to thank her, she explained that she finished the poem on the day before the bombing of Afghanistan began (October 7).

"I felt that our government was motivated by revenge immediately," she said, "without thinking about other ways to respond. It was just all vengeance."

We talked together about the mood in the country during those terrible twenty-five days after 9/11 and before the bombing began. We recalled the promise of our government to strike back and strike back hard. America vowed to make them sorry that they did this. But did we? Our response against the Taliban was to bomb a culture back to the Stone Age that had never left the Stone Age. And was not our response just as al-Qaeda expected and even hoped?

During our brief exchange of memories, Sister Peggy's poem was never far from my thoughts. Here was what all of us who hoped for peace had experienced in those days before our nation's massive response. Here was the knowledge that a further tearing apart of the human race was about to happen.

But Sister Peggy's poem was more than lament about impending war. Here was the truth about contemplation, that contemplation is a *protest*, a refusal to concede the victory to hatred, vengeance, materialism, tribalism, or individualism. Contemplation can be the collective experience of a minority (a "whispered peace"), but that minority insists that a depth of living exists, even within those who are ignorant of that depth, where healing, wholeness, and unity can never be destroyed. Contemplation is radical in that it anticipates not the destruction of our adversaries but our reconciliation with them. As Sister Peggy's poem concludes, "May our hearts meet here."

CHAPTER 11

You Just Keep Turning the Prayer Wheel

Saint John's Abbey
Collegeville, Minnesota
June 20–23, 2007

Remote settings, tall spires, quiet cloisters, the only sounds being the birds singing and bells calling monks to pray—that is the common image of a monastery. Philip Groning's highly acclaimed film *Into Great Silence* (*Die Grosse Stille*, 2005), chronicling daily life in the French Carthusian monastery of Le Grande Chartreuse, reflects that stereotype. Long silent minutes pass as we watched monks praying in their cells, the barest flickering of a candle the only clue that we are viewing a movie, not a still photograph.

Saint John's Abbey is, in fact, located in a peaceful rural setting in west-central Minnesota. Loons cry from the lakes on the abbey's sprawling twenty-five hundred acres, and bells do call the monks to pray. But there the comparison to Le Grande Chartreuse ends.

Saint John's is a beehive of activity, with fast-walking monks scurrying from services in the abbey church to their diverse duties. Trucks pass through the grounds, belching diesel fumes, and arriving guests circle the parking lots, trying to find an open space.

The unusual commotion of the place stems from Saint John's being not just a monastery, but also a four-year liberal arts university of nearly four thousand students. Many of the monks live out their monastic vocation of prayer and reflection over and above, or, perhaps *within*, duties on the adjacent campus. As the brochure in the guestrooms makes clear, the monks are involved in many ministries, from education to spiritual direction to publishing.

Saint John's was the only place that I visited during the project where I felt the rush of contemporary American life. I was reminded of a conversation that I had with a fellow guest in January when at the Monastery of Christ in the Desert in New Mexico. The young man confessed that, after spending several years at Saint John's as a monk, he had left in search of a place of greater solitude.

Yet the busyness of Saint John's Abbey is as monastically rooted as is the extreme solitude of Christ in the Desert. Saint John's version of monasticism recalls the medieval period, when monasteries were the centers of learning, the protectors of culture, and the repositories of that culture's treasures. Although public institutions, such as universities, museums, and libraries, have usurped this role of monasteries, Saint John's carries on this more traditional monastic function and does so impressively.

Saint John's has made a particular commitment to nurturing the arts over its 151-year history. Photographs from the mid-nineteenth century show choirs and orchestras flourishing on the campuses of Saint John's and nearby St. Benedict's. Here, on Saint John's campus, Minnesota Public Radio was founded in 1967, with a young Garrison Keillor hosting a classical music program. The award-winning writer J. F. Powers, whose father served on the faculty, was a writer-in-residence at Saint John's. More recently, Kathleen Norris, author of the widely acclaimed *A Cloister Walk* (1996), has twice been a resident scholar at the Ecumenical Institute on Saint John's campus. The alumnus and noted potter Richard Bresnahan is currently artist-in-residence, manning one of the largest kilns of its kind in the world. On the other edge of campus, the Hill Museum and Manuscript Library has sponsored the publication of the Saint John's Bible, the first illuminated Bible in five hundred years. And elsewhere on Saint John's grounds is found Liturgical Press, one of the leading publishers of progressive Catholic thought.

If monasteries have personalities, Saint John's is an extrovert. Drivers zipping by on nearby I-94 have no trouble spotting the community's bell tower, reminiscent of a torii gate at a Shinto shrine, rising confidently above the tree line. Directly behind the bell tower sits Marcel Breuer's equally stunning Bauhaus Abbey church, a concrete hangar of a building that serves as the meeting point between university and monastery. In contrast to so many monasteries that are off the beaten path and hard to find, Saint John's seems to shout out, "Hey, over here. Want to take a look?"

"OH, HE'S ON VACATION"

I arrived at Saint John's Abbey in late June 2007, happy to be interviewing again after a hiatus of several months. I had missed the give-and-take of the conversations, the way the thoughtful comments of monks and nuns would cut through the numbness I so easily feel in the face of contemporary events.

Much had happened in the world since my interview in March with Sister Margaret Funk and with Cecily. Gaza, more ruin than society, was again a battleground, only this time the fight was between the Fatah party supported by the United States and Israel and the more militant Hamas.

In Iraq, the United States was pushing ahead with the surge, with

US lawmakers freshly back from junkets to Baghdad giving widely contradictory reports of that strategy's chances of success.

In Afghanistan, suicide missions were becoming commonplace, and the return of the Taliban was beyond a rumor. A continent away, Ethiopian troops, again surrogates for the United States, had invaded Somalia to repulse the Islamic Courts and reinstate the old warlords.

Tony Blair's prime ministry was coming to an end, as was the presence of British troops in southern Iraq. Not that southern Iraq had been pacified. The area was surrendered, all but officially, to rival Iraqi Shia forces. Perhaps this was a preview of what it will look like when America leaves Iraq, if not also Afghanistan.

Several days before I arrived at Saint John's, the British had knighted Salman Rushdie, author of *The Satanic Verses*. Islamic governments expressed outrage at what they perceived as an insult to Islam. It was hard not to see the elevation of Sir Salman as a thumbing of the British nose as their troops left Iraq. Nothing seemed to illustrate as vividly as did this knighting the gap of understanding between the West and conservative Islam, between freedom of speech and respect for God.

In order to avoid the traffic of the Twin Cities, I drove the north route from my cabin in Wisconsin to Saint John's. The route took me through the small-town America of the upper Midwest, where magnetic ribbons attached to car trunks and bumpers prayed for God to bless our troops. The prayers of Saint John's would not, I knew, be so one-sided.

I drove into Saint John's lush grounds and found the newly completed guesthouse. Dropping my suitcase and computer in front of the welcome desk, I inquired if the monk checking me in were Brother Roger, the guestmaster. Oh, no, he replied with a laugh. Brother Roger was on vacation in Hawaii and wouldn't be back at the earliest until Saturday.

Vacation? Monks have vacations in Hawaii?

A tongue of panic danced in my head as I tried to recall my e-mail exchanges with Brother Roger. I remembered, with his invitation, that he had asked how the interviews had been arranged at other monastic houses. In writing back, I had offered the example of Gethsemani Abbey, where Father Matthew had pinned a sign-up sheet on the community board. That had seemed acceptable to Saint John's guestmaster.

After typing my name into the computer, the substitute monk read what appeared on the screen. "It looks like you're here to work on a book project."

Relieved, I explained that Brother Roger had agreed to arrange interviews for my work.

Looking puzzled, the monk called over his shoulder to another monk in a nearby office. "Did Brother Roger say anything about setting up some interviews before he left?"

A voice called back that he didn't know a thing about that.

My best bet, the monk advised as he handed me the key to my room, was to wait until Brother Roger returned on Saturday. But then again, he added with a shrug, Brother Roger might not return until Sunday.

And my reservation is only through Saturday, I thought.

At vespers in the great abbey church, I gazed across at the sea of monks on the other side of the altar. Even though I was at one of the largest monasteries in the United States, it seemed possible that I would not be interviewing even one of Saint John's 150 monks. Unkind thoughts invaded my prayers as I pictured the guestmaster strolling in shorts on a Hawaiian beach, mai tai in hand.

A PROVIDENTIAL ENCOUNTER WITH
A PEACE STUDIES PROFESSOR

But something of my prayers must have been heard, for as I returned to my room, I met Father René, who happened to be filling in at the guestmaster's desk. There are some men who look like monks. There are other men who look like something else, but also happen to be monks.

Father René, tall, dignified, well-spoken, looked like the professor that he is, a professor who also happened to be one of the senior monks.

As Father René introduced himself as a professor of philosophy and peace studies at the university, my heart skipped a beat. *Peace studies!* I quickly described my project and asked if he would be willing to be interviewed. In his kindly voice, Father René replied that he would be very willing. And why not now, he suggested, while he was manning the desk?

Over my three-day stay, Father René seemed an angel who had been sent to open key doors at Saint John's. Through his direct and indirect efforts, I conducted five unplanned interviews. Each was memorable. I am indebted to his generous assistance.

COMMON TRAGEDY; DIVERSE REACTIONS

Between the moment that the first plane hit Tower 1 and the second plane's fiery echo, our nation seemed to stop. We inhaled, and in many ways, we have not exhaled yet. Yet, while united in fear, Americans reacted to the shock of 9/11 in very diverse ways. That was also true for the monks of Saint John's.

THE NOVICE MASTER—FATHER COLUMBA

September 11 is a busy day every year for the novice master of Saint John's Abbey. That is the day when novices are received into the community, and Father Columba, a slight monk whose office was that of the overcommitted academic and who also happened to be the community's novice master in 2001, remembered exactly where he was when he first heard the news. "I was sitting with the novices who'd arrived the night before, and that day they were going to have their formal liturgical reception. [I was] starting the retreat they have as part of their first few days in the community when my sister phoned me." Taking the call, he heard his sister tell him simply to listen as she held a cell phone to her car radio.

THE WEBMASTER WITH THE GIFT OF TEARS—BROTHER RICHARD

On November 22, 1963, Brother Richard was a Christian Brothers novice living outside of Washington, DC. In that era, novices of his order were forbidden to watch TV or have any outside contact. Brother Richard remembered a simple sign being posted for the community: *"Kennedy assassinated. Rosary at 4 p.m."* "I am one of the few people in America," he said, "who . . . *doesn't* know where he was when Kennedy was assassinated."

In contrast, 9/11 was a live event all over the world, including Saint John's. Describing himself as "highly unsentimental" by nature, Brother Richard had earlier in his life prayed for the "gift of tears." Now, on 9/11, Brother Richard watched with others of the community as the planes hit the towers before, overwhelmed, he retreated to the privacy of his room.

But as the day progressed, Brother Richard was called away from his private grief. Joking that he had been webmaster at Saint John's Abbey since "Al Gore invented [the Internet]," Brother Richard spent the remainder of that horrible day huddled with Father Don Talafous, chaplain of Saint John's University. Out of that meeting came the community's first public response to the tragedy.

> Loving God, in this tragic time that affects us all, we come before you, our Rock and Refuge.
>
> We ask that everyone who is harmed in any way by the devastating events of Tuesday, September 11th, be held in your love.

We ask that peace enfold all who have been killed, that your strength and comfort be with all the injured and mourning.

We ask that compassion and love prevail over our anger and frustration.

We pray that the magnitude of this disaster will somehow bring victims, their families and friends new life.

We pray for children bereft of parents and care, for children whose innocence has been assaulted by these events.

We pray for those who committed these unspeakable acts. We ask that this horrendous event bring us all to more concern for injustice and hurt in our world.

We pray that this disaster impel human beings everywhere to work more ardently for peace and justice.

We ask that your Holy Spirit guide our nation and all of us in our reaction to this tragedy.

Be with us all, above all those mourning and suffering.

We ask this through the Savior, Jesus Christ, who blesses those who mourn and those who hunger and thirst for justice.

Amen

A WINDOW TO THE WORLD—BROTHER ALAN

Brother Alan was cutting hair in the monastery basement when he first heard the news. Rushing to one of the community TVs, he arrived in time to see the second plane circle and hit Tower 2.

He was staring at a scene that he knew well and loved, having spent a sabbatical in the 1980s in a Jesuit community in New York City that was also home to the Vietnam-era activist Daniel Berrigan. And Brother Alan had personal memories of the Twin Towers. Friends visiting during his sabbatical had been particularly fascinated by these massive buildings, structures so large that they had their own zip code and housed eateries capable of feeding fifty thousand people a day.

Recalling a brunch that he'd had in Windows on the World, a restaurant within the World Trade Center, Brother Alan said, "It was very weird . . . I was sitting next to the windows, looking down one hundred and four floors, and you'd see little planes flying below you." It was weeks after the interview before I realized that Brother Alan's vivid memory was also the last sight of many who died in the World Trade Center on 9/11.

9/11 AS TEACHING MOMENT—FATHER RENÉ

As was true of many college professors on 9/11, Father René elected to meet his classes. Educators know that all of life, even unspeakable tragedies, is a collection of "teaching moments" and needs to be addressed.

"I will never forget this statement that . . . a bright American student said. 'I can't understand why they hate us so.'" That was undoubtedly one of the most frequently expressed comments across the country that day. But in the same class, another bright student, a foreign-born Muslim, immediately replied, "'I can't believe that you can't understand why they hate you.'"

Today, a decade after 9/11, the gap of understanding between those two comments has only grown wider. The self-righteous belief that our enemies hate our democracy and freedom keeps us from grappling with the Muslim student's probing response.

Yet Father René also recalled another memory from teaching on 9/11, one that might be a hopeful sign. Freshman and sophomore students at Saint John's expressed the same desire for massive retaliation that swept the nation in those first days. To those students, Father Talafous and Brother Richard's prayer for patience and restraint undoubtedly seemed weak, if not cowardly.

Upperclassmen in the peace studies program, Father René was pleased to report, "were more reflective, and they also understood—a lot of them—the greater complexity of the situation and our support for Israel and how that played in." Good news for Saint John's, I thought, but how common was that across the country? With the help of my son Leif, I discovered that slightly over 250 colleges and universities in the United States offer peace programs or peace courses. In contrast, ROTC (Reserved Officers' Training Corps) is offered at more than a thousand institutions—including Saint John's.

"KEEP TURNING THE PRAYER WHEEL"—FATHER COLUMBA

In the immediate aftermath of the attacks in New York and Washington, DC, on September 11, Father Columba had returned to his duties with the novices. New life for the community had to be attended to, even on a day of death. In recalling that odd juxtaposition, Father Columba said, "We thought life as we know it was gone forever—and now we look back and say, 'Yes and no,' but that day it felt that way—and here we were, bringing these new members into the community. So that's a real monastic thing," he said. "The sun comes up, you go to church. The sun comes up, you go to church. You just keep turning the prayer wheel."

The prayer wheel has continued to turn at Saint John's through centuries of war and peace. During the first Gulf War, when Iraq launched missiles at Israel, the community opted for silent prayer instead of the traditional prayers of the Divine Office. "We just sat together," Father Columba remembered. "That was very powerful."

Ten years later, on the evening of 9/11, the community again broke with routine, this time electing to conduct a service normally reserved for August 5, the day when Saint John's annually commemorates the bombing of Hiroshima. "The psalms are chosen in reference to peace and conflict. Sometimes [the reading] will be from Martin Luther King; sometimes it will be from Gandhi," Father René noted. "And there is usually a Scripture reading as well [such as] 'My peace I give you.'"

If 9/11 was caught by Saint John's prayer wheel, the tragedy also pulled the community back to its main source of strength. "The psalms themselves give us such a deep historical, as well as religious, spiritual perspective," Father Columba explained. "All these things have happened before, and in the middle of it, the psalmist praises and thanks God. One minute you're lamenting, and the next minute you're wrapping it all up with a prayer of praise and thanksgiving." He paused for a moment before adding, "And so we do."

THE FRAGILE MIDDLE EAST

There is another link between Saint John's and the pain of the Middle East besides prayer. The manuscript preservation project, which Father Columba oversees, was at the time of the interview currently digitizing ancient manuscripts in Turkey, Syria, and Lebanon. Consequently, Father Columba has developed closer contacts with the beleaguered communities in the region than do many foreign correspondents.

I had always assumed manuscript preservation to be motivated by the deteriorating condition of old documents. Father Columba explained that Saint John's work in this area, however, had been motivated from its very beginning by trying to outrace war. War threatens not only people but also priceless historical records, and thus it can destroy a culture's past.

"Obviously, there is a concern about the long-term viability of particularly the Christian communities [in the Middle East] that have a lot of these manuscripts," Father Columba said. "And then the outbreak of the war between Israel and Lebanon last summer [2006], and the reappearance of instability in Lebanon has added a kind of poignancy and urgency to the work. It reminded us that that kind of instability or endangerment to manuscript and cultural heritage can happen anytime."

Manuscript preservation is not a new calling for Saint John's. The work began in the nineteenth century, when European monastic houses were closed by governments, their holdings dispersed, transferred to state collections, or lost. Photography became the preferred method of preservation in the 1960s when a nuclear confrontation in Europe, between East and West, seemed quite possible.

In contrast to the slower buildup of tension during the Cold War, present-day Lebanon illustrates how quickly the current style of war can endanger priceless historical records. "When we started the work in Lebanon in 2003, nobody saw [the present situation] coming," Father Columba observed. "The economic outlook was great. They were really proud of themselves for having put it all together after the civil war."

Matters changed rapidly after the summer 2006 war. While the Israeli assault did not dislodge Hezbollah, as had been the expectation, it did have a devastating effect on the Lebanese Christian community. On a subsequent visit to Lebanese Christian communities, Father Columba noticed that "people [had] lost their confidence in the future . . . I'm talking here about people with some education who may not have money, but they have means somehow."

To illustrate, Father Columba shared the story of the program's field director in Beirut, a young man with a master's degree in computer science and a father of three young children. "His two oldest children are very bright girls. And he looks around and says, 'What's the future for my bright daughters if it's a heavily Islamicized or conservative society?'"

Knowing Father Columba to be a sharp critic of the war in Iraq and US policy in the entire region, I asked what hope he held out for the Middle East.

"Do you want me to be honest?" he asked.

"Absolutely," I replied.

"I don't see a way out of this. It is so polarized right now, and the level of despair among people is so great," he said. "It's really tough to look into a crystal ball and see anything that looks like the hope we had, say, in 1993, the time of the Oslo Accords and the handshake [between Rabin and Arafat]." Father Columba paused for a moment. "That's a grim answer, and I'm not normally a grim person, but hey . . ."

9/11 AS A CALL TO UNDERSTAND

Sometimes it is only when you turn the pictures on the wall upside down that you see the truth. That saying of my wife's pertains to the common stereotype of monasteries, remote communities following arcane schedules of prayer and fasting.

Now turn that picture upside down. Beyond increased airport security and the anxiety experienced by families with members serving in Iraq and Afghanistan, day-to-day life in the United States carries on much as before for many of us. Most Americans, especially men, know far more about the standings of their sports teams than they do about events in the Middle East.

But at Saint John's, the tension and pain of our present world are inescapable. Saint John's, as other monasteries where I interviewed, carries on the practice of having one monk serve as lector, reading to the other monks, at one of the common meals. Father René told me that the community, while I was visiting, was hearing a history of US dealings in the Middle East.

Despite his background in peace studies, Father René had been surprised at what he was learning. The author had outlined a long and sorry history of superiority and entitlement that the United States had assumed in the region. From the United States' first dealings with Barbary Coast pirates in the early nineteenth century, "[we find] the same kinds of things [said] about infidels. They should all be wiped out, and they are terrorists," Father René said. "And what was really amazing was the way it took on a religious dimension, from our side, almost immediately . . . The do-gooders of the time said, 'We've got to go and convert them to Christianity, and then they won't do such awful things to us.' Then the others said . . . 'We've got to destroy every one of them.'"

The current xenophobia among some Americans is therefore not a post-9/11 phenomenon. With a wry smile, Father René recalled a visit to Saint John's in the 1980s from a Minnesota state representative who had come to the campus to convey President Reagan's warning of a possible invasion of the United States by Grenada. That tiny, Third World nation was, so the state representative told Saint John's community, in league with Cuba and Nicaragua. The three countries had formed a "triangle of power" which had already selected a site in Texas for its invasion.

Father René shook his head. "It was so absurd when you think about it, how people could buy that."

But fear can easily trump reason, as 9/11 makes clear. Referring to the current crisis, he said, "We use over and over again the rhetoric of security. Bush has used that phrase . . . 'We will make the world safe.' Not just safe for democracy, [but] so that [Americans] will not have to fear."

And that is a promise that can never be fulfilled, Father René noted. "I'm not encouraging fear, but we're just not secure."

9/11 AS A CALL TO LISTEN

For Father René, there are reasons that we as a nation have failed to grasp the hatred behind 9/11 and the widespread resistance to US efforts in the Middle East. Quoting a retired ambassador who'd recently visited Saint John's to receive an honorary degree, Father René remarked that "Americans are perceived as arrogant all across the world; they are perceived as refusing to listen, and they appear simplistic to everyone."

The chief flaw in our current national character is, for Father René, our failure to listen. Arrogance and simplistic thinking are the natural offspring of that underlying flaw. "Reflection even by the etymology of the word," he noted, "means we step a bit back and bend back. And I think we [as Americans] tend to bend forward as a people."

Taking a step back is the monastic way, and it may be part of the paradoxical wisdom that monasticism has to share with the country. "The way the [Benedictine] rule starts out [is] with the very first word 'listen.' 'Listen, my son, to the words of the master.'"

Perhaps monastic life is, at its core, a life devoted to listening—to God, to one's abbot, to one's fellow monks, to guests, to the stranger, and to one's own life. The numerous prayer services that define the monastic day, Father René observed, force the monk to listen. They service as deliberate "interruptions" to the chatter and activity of everyday life. And "that interruption constantly calls one back to say, 'Well, how would I see this [work] in the light of Christ?'"

But Father René's emphasis on the importance of listening is rooted in more than his monastic training. Listening was also a constant echo in the thought of Emmanuel Levinas, the noted Jewish philosopher who served as Father René's doctoral adviser at the University of Paris. What is especially critical for our modern world, Father René learned from Levinas, is learning to listen for the voice of God in the oft-forgotten voice of the poor and oppressed.

But there is more to true listening, he suggested, than even this rare openness to the whispers of those at the bottom. True listening means to weigh what one hears, one's sense of the world, and one's own life by some standard. For a Christian, Father René said, that standard is Jesus' command to "put away one's sword."

But are not we a nation in love with the sword? I asked. Has not one legacy of 9/11 been to ignore—to *not* listen—to anyone who appeals for peace and reconciliation?

I should remember, Father René countered, the perspective of Dorothy Day, the founder of the Catholic Worker Movement and one of his personal heroes. When asked one day if it bothered her that her speaking out against war since the 1930s hadn't made a difference,

Dorothy Day had responded ("and it's a response I love," Father René added), "'Oh, my worry is not about success. That's God's worry. All I have to do is what I ought to do.'"

After pausing a moment to let the story sink in, Father René recalled Father Alfred, a fellow monk at Saint John's, who is now deceased. "There was in [him] some sense of refusal to get perturbed by what was going on in the world. I mean, taking account of it, praying over it, but remaining a person that realizes that God [is] in charge, and you do what you can do, but then God worries about . . . the success."

Later, I heard Brother Richard offer a very similar perspective. Admitting as humans that "we're more at war than at peace," Brother Richard nevertheless found in monastic life an antidote to the despair that we so easily feel in the face of current events. "Real peace is a grace, a gift . . . [something] out of our hands," he said. "You have to think of it in that way as a grace that comes."

His hope for the Middle East is similar to what he saw happening in Northern Ireland. Peace will most likely come in small steps, not all at once or immediately. Thus, he added, the need for patience, a trait as central to monastic life as listening. "Monks realize . . . after thirty years that the progress one might have expected . . . is something you just have to realize [is] going to [come in] incremental change . . . even in yourself. And after a while, you take delight in very small victories."

For Father René, the peace studies professor, the wait might take *infinitely* longer. As he has confessed to students, Father René is not sure he could believe in God if there were no afterlife, a time when the suffering poor and innocent will finally receive justice. "It seems to me the vast majority of the human race has gotten the [short] end of the stick forever. And it's not that I want those who had the good end of the stick to be punished, but there has to be some justice, some reward."

This hope for justice too, he said, had also been a theme of his mentor, Emmanuel Levinas, who was convinced that the need for justice lies at the very heart of Scripture. "Charity is fine, but charity has to go only if there is justice already done," Father René said. "Charity is secondary to justice."

As he said those words—"charity is secondary to justice"—I had a strong sense of hearing an echo, of having been prepared to hear the importance of this point. During those same weeks of June, I had "met" the twentieth-century Chilean saint Alberto Hurtado, SJ, through a profile in *America*. I had saved the article with its arresting photo of the saint who had served the poor and homeless of his country. As Levinas had done, Hurtado also reversed the usual priority of love over justice. "It is easier to be benevolent than to be just," Hurtado wrote. Charity, he argued, "is a patch, an aspirin, whereas society requires an operation."

I left the interviews with Father René and Brother Richard convinced that they were right in hoping for a major cultural change, but I was also convicted of my own impatience and anger. These very traits had motivated our nation's response to 9/11 and the invasion in Iraq, and they were alive within me, even though my impatience and anger were directed at the Bush administration for those very acts. To discover a "word of life" through this project, I would have to *listen*, not for the message that the president needs to hear, not for something my country needs to reconsider, but what *I* need to hear. That was exactly what Abbot Damien had told me months before at Gethsemani.

But even admitting my anger and impatience, I felt I was missing something. Trusting in God to make matters right *someday* struck me as insufficient. There had to be something that God wants us, wants me, to *do*, now.

THE ONLY WAY OUT IS TO LOVE YOUR WAY OUT—BROTHER ALAN

With a mischievous smirk, Brother Alan leaned across the table in the monastic library to whisper, "I'm not one of the good monks here."

"What's a 'good monk'?" I asked.

"That's what I'm trying to figure out."

I met Brother Alan by accident, when I walked across campus to see the newest completed segment of the Saint John's Bible on display at the Hill Museum and Manuscript Library.

Two summers before, my wife, Kathy, and I had traveled to Minneapolis to view the traveling exhibit of the first completed portions of the Saint John's Bible, the first illuminated Bible in five hundred years. Saint John's had the vision, raised the nine million dollars necessary, and contracted Donald Jackson, the noted British calligrapher, to lead a team of artists and other calligraphers on the project. For those in the art and book world, the appearance of each successive portion of this amazing Bible has been as exciting as new Harry Potter installments for young readers.

As I walked through the exhibit of the new "Prophets" portion of the Bible in the Hill Museum, Brother Alan came from behind a desk and introduced himself. At the time, Brother Alan was curator of art and antiquities at the museum, but he had also been, for eight years, a member of the Committee of Illuminations and Text, the group from Saint John's that works most closely with calligrapher Donald Jackson.

The reason for my visit to Saint John's clearly interested Brother Alan, and I was gratified when he agreed to an interview later that afternoon. Due to the chanciness of our meeting, I had even less an idea than usual as to what to expect from this interview. I certainly had no clue that Brother Alan would begin to answer my nagging question of what 9/11 calls me to *do*.

As the interview progressed, Brother Alan shifted from personal memories of 9/11 and New York City to explain how his current work on the Saint John's Bible had helped him come to terms with that tragedy. He referred specifically to the passage in the gospel of Luke called "The Parables of the Lost and Forgiveness," a section that Donald Jackson had himself chosen to illuminate.

I knew the passage well, having taught the parables of the lost sheep, the lost coin, and the prodigal son frequently and never tiring of their power. Deceptively simple on the surface, Jesus' parables can still astound modern readers with their insights. In these particular parables, Jesus describes God as active, a shepherd searching eagerly for the lost, not a monarch or judge sitting passively atop some heavenly throne.

In his illumination for the page, Donald Jackson had chosen various symbols to reflect these stories of recovery and joy. "And in the middle of it are the Twin Towers," Brother Alan said.

Being an artist himself, Brother Alan was profoundly moved by juxtaposing that image with that particular text. "That image [in] those surrounding notions of forgiveness [was] really powerful for me," he said. "When he was talking about that page with us, [Donald Jackson] said, as far as he could tell, that these parables showed to him that the only way you can get out of something like this is to love your way out." In almost a whisper, Brother Alan added, "I think that [is] my favorite response [that] I've heard to that incident: 'The only way out is to love your way out.'"

Some messages we both grasp and, at the same time, do not fully grasp. That was true for me when I heard "love your way out." I had an instant sense, an inner acknowledgment, that this was divine wisdom, part of what I'd been searching for throughout the project.

At the same time, I realized that our nation had gone in the opposite direction from love after 9/11. Bowing to the legitimate concern for security, and with cultural patterns engrained over centuries, we had raced to avenge those deaths and reassert our dominant status in the world. Even some lifelong peace advocates had wondered aloud and publicly if 9/11 did not call for an exceptional response of strength. With few dissenting voices, we as a nation had chosen to "fight our way out." The horrendous attacks seemed to require that response. But in the process, it seems that we have only buried ourselves deeper in the rubble.

OUR MOST BASIC NEED IS MEANING

Security is a basic human need, but the need for meaning goes even deeper. We want our jobs to be meaningful, as we do our marriages, our friendships, our religious faith, and even our leisure time. We sell products on this same promise, that life behind a particular steering wheel or with whitened teeth and chiseled abs will be meaning-enriched. In every area of life, from the most important to the most trivial, our craving for meaning is insatiable.

And our tragedies? They, too, must yield meaning.

But meaning does not come cheaply. Meaning eludes us, and when we settle for false claims of it, we stumble, confused and blind. Meaning is that biblical pearl of great price. We remain restless until we find it, and once finding it, we would change anything, even our very way of life, to retain it.

Of course, there has been no shortage of religious interpretations to 9/11, all promising to reveal the meaning of our tragedy. Many conservative Christians have seen in 9/11 a frightening fulfillment of the book of Revelation and other apocalyptic texts. For them, 9/11 is a sign of the impending end of the world, a belief that invites only further disengagement with the world. I remember one fundamentalist who was elated when he heard the news of 9/11. The attacks proved that Jesus' return was imminent. For these religionists, the show is almost over. They are just waiting for the credits to roll up on the screen. Such a response to 9/11 demands no change, no reflection, no rethinking, and therefore remains meaningless.

The only way out is to love our way out. Donald Jackson has taken a more prophetic stance, challenging us to view 9/11 through the eyes of the Good Shepherd. With that unexpected and puzzling choice, Jackson has posed a question as much as an answer, and it is far from certain how readers will respond.

Brother Alan acknowledged that the Saint John's Bible does, in fact, give the reader a very active role in interpretation. "It used to be that the story would be told, and then they'd have a picture of the story for those who couldn't read well," he explained. "One of the things the committee said to [Donald Jackson] right away was 'We don't want a picture Bible, or a Bible storybook.'"

The committee's hope, Brother Alan explained, is that the image and text would create a conversation in which the reader could enter. "The image could lead you to new understandings of the text; the text could make you look at the image in a different way."

Through the parables, Jesus had invited listeners to think about God and neighbor in new and often uncomfortable ways. Much of the bite of the parables has been lost by reteaching them in Sunday schools as simple, rustic stories. Jackson, however, has recovered the parable's innate capacity to disturb by linking the images of the burning towers and the Good Shepherd. There is a paradox here, but also tremendous meaning.

The unexpected image of the burning towers in the Saint John's Bible will undoubtedly have a mixed fate. Some readers will simply miss the image completely. Others, seeing it, will draw back and turn the page as quickly as possible. But others will stop on the image and find it impossible to forget.

The only way out is to love our way out. Donald Jackson is right. The challenge of 9/11 is spiritual, not simply military or political. For Christians, this means that we must find Christ *within* the tragedy. Donald Jackson would point us in the direction of God the Good Shepherd, who searches for the lost. But who are the lost? Are they the victims buried in the debris? Are the hijackers also the lost for whom the Good Shepherd is searching? And do the lost include all of us Americans who are trying to find our way out?

What if the answer is all three? What if we all are those for whom God is searching—how would that change our perspective on one another?

The only way out is to love our way out. May God the Good Shepherd illumine our path.

CHAPTER 12

Feet of Clay

Richard Bresnahan's Pottery Studio
Collegeville, Minnesota
June 22, 2007

My wife, Kathy, became acquainted with the work of Richard Bresnahan through a summer art class in northern Wisconsin. At her suggestion, I had watched *Clay, Wood, Fire, and Spirit,* a DVD about this noted American potter who has been artist-in-residence at Saint John's University since 1979. I was impressed with what I saw. Upon graduating from Saint John's, Bresnahan was invited to train in Japan with the son of one of Japan's "living treasures." There, he was the first Westerner to earn the rank of master potter in that system. Returning to Saint John's after four years, Bresnahan proceeded to build the largest wood-fired kiln in North America. On its first firing in 1995, the "Johanna kiln" fired eight thousand pieces of pottery simultaneously over a period of nine days. It is no exaggeration to say that this man is a legend in pottery circles.

With my Friday afternoon at Saint John's free, I walked across the campus with the hope of finding Bresnahan's studio. My intention was simply to buy a sample of his work for my wife.

A monk who was also on a walk that afternoon pointed me in the right direction, and I found Bresnahan's studio with its doors open. Inside, the space was divided into several areas: a well-lit studio where a solitary man whom I recognized from the video worked silently at a potter's wheel, shelves of pots in front of which a young intern—I guessed a Saint John's student—was busy moving boxes, and a backroom in which hundreds of pieces of pottery were warehoused.

But where, I wondered, were the customers?

I stood in the studio/gallery for a few moments before Richard Bresnahan glanced up from his work, welcomed me, and returned to his wheel. He was physically both compact and strong, as if the years of working clay had also compressed him. I watched his hands effortlessly shape the clay for a few moments before I relayed my wife's keen interest in his work. He simply nodded at the acknowledgment. I was clearly telling him something that he had heard numerous times before.

In the brief exchange that followed, I managed to explain my main reason for visiting Saint John's. He looked up again from the wheel. "Ah, a writer," he said.

"More a professor," I clarified.

He expressed interest in the project, asking what other monasteries I had visited and what I was hoping to accomplish. As I answered his questions, he nodded or grunted in understanding and, at one point, added a sarcastic comment about the war in Iraq.

As we talked, I was struck again by the quiet of the room. The intern in the background worked efficiently and without needing direction. The whirl of the wheel was the only sound besides our voices.

Now, this, I thought, would be a perfect space to conduct an interview. But accompanying that thought was the reminder that Bresnahan was an artist, not a monk. Ah, I countered, but he is a potter who studied in Japan and is now living on the edge of one of America's largest monasteries. What would be his perspective on the rise of terrorism?

I have no doubt in retrospect that I would never have considered interviewing Bresnahan had my visit to Saint John's gone as I had planned. But Saint John's had been a crapshoot from the very beginning, with each unplanned interview seeming to arise out of nothing. Was Bresnahan another gift of the visit?

Bresnahan replied quickly to my request for an interview, saying that as long as he could keep working and did not have any other customers, he would be happy to oblige. But customers and visitors would undoubtedly drop by, he assured me. I raced back to my room for my recorders and notebook, convinced that the studio would be crowded upon my return, my chance at the interview lost.

But upon my return, the studio and gallery were as I had left them. I hurriedly set up the recorders, wondering again where the interview might fit—if it fit at all—into the project. I counseled myself to not make a problem out of this opportunity. The worst-case scenario was that I would at least have a good story to tell my wife. But I had a feeling that something unpredictable yet valuable lay ahead.

The interview began as had none other in the project. There was no warm-up, no small talk to establish an ease between interviewer and interviewee. When the recorders began rolling, a lid seemed to lift off one of Bresnahan's pots. Brimming inside was his hot anger.

Despite his earlier jab about Iraq, Bresnahan wanted to make it clear that he did not blame President Bush for the predicament. The origins of the current tension in the world, he argued, lay in a four hundred-year-old theology that viewed the earth as a "dead system," nature as a thing that we can use at will.

LOSS OF BALANCE AND DISORIENTATION

If we wanted to understand what had destroyed the human balance with nature, we should look back, Bresnahan argued, to the Industrial

Revolution and the migration of rural people into the cities. At first, Bresnahan's argument seemed a familiar one, the spiritual poverty of modern life linked to the loss of agrarian life. But with Bresnahan, I would hear an artist's perspective on what many—but, in the end, not he—considered irreversible.

First, he wanted to remind me of several fundamental truths. The role of the artist, Bresnahan asserted, has always been to "translate the culture" and consequently to provide "a stable structure" to society. During the period of urbanization, which most people at the time lauded as progress, artists throughout the world were in the minority in recognizing the threat to culture that accompanied the disbanding of rural communities. That was true, Bresnahan qualified, if the artists of the time were "moral."

That qualification—that the artist needs to be moral to fulfill his/her role—was not to be taken for granted. "When an artist doesn't react to his or her dreams, it's immoral," Bresnahan stated, his voice already strident. "That's the spirituality of the artist."

My first reaction to his comment was an instant realization that I was, for the first time, interviewing someone whose spirituality was not conventionally religious. That intrigued me. I wondered what contribution his artistic path could make to the "word of life" I was seeking. Yet even with that difference noted, I was also aware that his description of the artist was similar to a proper understanding of the biblical prophet—not as a foreteller of the future, as is so often misconstrued, but as one capable of seeing the underlying truth of the present moment. Later in the interview, Bresnahan would return to the unique relationship between the artist and the prophet.

And it was the artist who, at the beginning of the twentieth century, understood the connection between the mass migration to urban life and the rise of fascism. The loss of balance between human life and nature at the time—when "literally, whole systems collapsed; all human systems collapsed"—meant, he claimed, that someone had to be blamed. For the Nazis, it was the Jews. For the Italians, it was the Ethiopians, and for the Japanese, it was the Chinese.

THE FRATERNITY OF POTTERS

Bresnahan asserted that the only real resolution to the past century of scapegoating was in realizing once again the importance of art for preserving the last vestiges of true human life. While the world was splintering into two groups—the poor in the slums and the rich in their sterile, gated communities ("minimum security prisons with their cul-de-sacs," he offered)—it was the artist, and for Bresnahan, particularly the potter, who blessedly preserved a more ancient and healthy community. "Within the pottery family all over the planet earth, I can go anywhere. And if I'm a potter and I meet another potter and you [both] work with the earth, you are a family."

The potter is, of all the artists, he argued, the one most deeply rooted in the core of human experience. "[Pottery] is the oldest system for the healing of the human beings, for the storage of food . . . [and] seeds, the repository for those who have passed away. [Pottery] is the shell for the soul of the human being."

Unlike the ancient East, which was the first to see "the importance of the high-silicate world to human health," the West values pottery not for its perfect usefulness, but for its collectibility. And collecting art, rather than living with it, Bresnahan argued, kept art from fulfilling its healing role in culture.

He cited the example of schoolchildren visiting a museum where pottery was on display behind glass cases. Those same children would then go to a discount store to buy plastic bowls and pots, concluding that plastic and Styrofoam are all that are appropriate for normal life. The message, Bresnahan suggested, is clear—"Don't think that you can have any cultural quality in your life."

THE THIRTEEN-HUNDRED-YEAR-OLD CUP

We were no longer alone in the studio. Several customers and admirers had entered, followed soon after by others. By our agreement, the interview should have ended.

But these visitors, perhaps noting the recorders and my taking notes, hung back. Or perhaps they could feel the heat radiating from Bresnahan's staccato-like bursts. And Bresnahan, except for a brief nod to each who came through the door, kept his focus on the wheel. When he did look up and make eye contact, I felt his eyes burning into me.

As a contrast to the American "hands-off" experience with art isolated in museums, Bresnahan described a ceremony performed at the end of his apprenticeship in Japan. After sharing a cup of sake with Bresnahan, his teacher and mentor passed the cup back to his American pupil. The master explained that the cup that they had just used had been handed down from potter to potter for thirteen centuries. Whereupon, the master said to Bresnahan, "When it is your time, bring a young potter into your home and pass this on."

For Bresnahan, the value of the cup lay not in its age. The real importance of the cup was instead in its being tended so lovingly with *future* generations in mind. In that sense, the cup represented for Bresnahan how the entire natural world should be treated. "If you have a culture that looks at . . . transformation from one generation to the next, you're thinking seven generations ahead in your materiality—the way you build your environments, the way that you steward your soil . . . the way that you care for your neighbor—then what happens is that you cannot destroy your ecosystem. It's impossible." The cup's existence over the centuries, its promised future as much as its age, proved something immensely important to Bresnahan: humans are not destined to destroy the natural world. We "are [here] to balance out the ecosystem."

I have been one of those who enjoys viewing beautiful pottery, especially Southwest Pueblo pottery, on visits to museums. I even believe that I could distinguish a priceless pot by Maria Martinez of the Pueblo of San Ildefonso from lesser works from the same site. But Bresnahan was redirecting my attention from the pottery to the vocation of the potter, a calling both rare but also, in his opinion, potentially universal.

As he continued, I was struck by the similarity of his sense of vocation to vows taken by the Benedictine monks at Saint John's who live so close to this studio. Being a potter is not one aspect of Bresnahan's wider life, even as one could not be a part-time monk. One is either a monk or not. Similarly, Bresnahan's entire life—his view of the world, even his sense of home—is subsumed within his vows as a potter, vows that detach him from the American main-stream as much as do the vows of the nearby monks.

"You can't be a potter unless you dig and taste your own clay . . . You can't live in a home unless you have clay walls and [have] made your home yourself. It would almost be a sense of bipolar disorder to . . . buy a home in a suburb and then try and come here and make art," he noted. "[That] would be just an appalling way of having to get up and trying to look at yourself in the morning. Because you'd be living a lie."

"BEING TRUE TO YOURSELF" AND OTHER LIES WE TELL OURSELVES

"Living the lie" comes close to what Bresnahan considered the cur-rently pervasive American way of life. As evidence of our falsity, he cited the modern preoccupation of being "true to one's self," a goal far different from the traditional understanding of integrity.

"If you're going to be 'true to yourself,' that's that hollow voice yelling in a soundless cave. If you're going to be true to others, your self is understood." For Bresnahan, integrity is not being loyal to one's own narcissistic whims, but being loyal to that which brings balance to human community life. Those are the ethics of the Japanese community of potters with whom Bresnahan apprenticed.

He described a recent trip to China. In every city he visited, he witnessed alarmingly high levels of inhumanity, pollution, and industrial development "without any stepping back and saying, 'How did we get here?' and 'Where are we going?'" He described what he witnessed in China as the turning from the "propaganda of communism to the propaganda of absolute consumerism with not even skipping a beat."

While in China, Bresnahan heard that the authorities had sentenced to death the head of their environmental agency. "Not only [for] the pet food contamination, but [for] contaminated toothpaste that was putting thousands in the hospitals in China . . . [as well as] the contaminated medicines that had killed thousands." How and why had that happened? The answer, Bresnahan suggested, was the all-too-common motive of greed, the simple fact that the top ten administrators in charge of protecting the environment and the people had accepted huge payoffs to look the other way. What would have saved them, he added, would have been a desire to be "true to others," but instead they had settled for being "true to themselves."

ASSASSINATING HORSES; EXPECTING THE PROPHET

Bresnahan moved from his wheel to a shelf where he picked up an elongated piece of pottery. "The tube container [such as this one] was what all religions used to put their religious texts in and bury in the ground, whether it be Tibetan, Buddhistic [sic], Essene, everybody . . . . They [were] hiding the religion away to be rekindled."

He pointed to the rim of the pot and explained that he always incorporated the symbol of the horse in his contemporary expression of that particular container. "I chose the horse because in every culture, the horse is a prophetic messenger. Whether it be Hindu, Buddhist,

Islamic, early Christian, Jewish, any kind of multipantheon religion, the horse was the winged messenger."

He pointed to other symbols encircling the horse on the rim of the pot. "The horse is descending down out of clouds, and it has a half-drawn bull's-eye on its chest with three bullet holes that have hit the center of its chest. It's just been assassinated. Its neck is rearing up. Its mane is sticking straight out, and it's falling backwards."

More customers and admirers were now entering the studio, and some were listening in on our conversation. But no one would dare break into the bubble that Bresnahan had created around us.

"So why do we continually kill people who have answers for humanity, to carry humanity forward, to be the visionaries forward?" he asked rhetorically.

He picked up another pot and identified a variety of its symbols—a star, a tree, a cent sign, a Japanese yen, another tree, the sign of the lira, another of the British pound, another tree, and finishing with a downward arrow and a colon.

"If we always take the earth and exchange [it for] money . . . we will always have those who have and have not. We will have one religion at the throat of another religion because there's not enough water for that religion's goats to drink and there's not enough fuel for that religion's plants to be planted."

Pointing to a second row of symbols on the pot, he added, "So here in the next sentence structure is the baptismal water, the universe, and mountains—our universal symbols of why we're on this planet. And then out of the border relief is coming in a nuclear missile."

I was looking at an apocalyptic prophecy in clay. Did that mean that Bresnahan lived without hope for the future?

"We always solve our problems with holocaust weaponry, whether it was the bow and arrow, the chariot, the gun, the tank, the bomb, the airplane, the missile," he replied. "So [in] every firing [of the kiln], I have to draw [this] prophetic message to ground myself." The repeating pattern was his way, he added, of reminding himself that "when the prophetic walk through my door, I must care for them at all cost."

I thought of the nearby Benedictines, whose rule requires them to keep an eye out for Christ in the guise of every stranger. Similarly, Bresnahan is on the lookout for the prophet coming through his door. I asked him if his vigilance was a way of saving his soul.

The anger that had been stoked and restoked during our conversation seemed to dissipate. "I have no idea about that," he replied in a quieter voice. "But I know that what I am doing is important for my family—which I consider the human family on this planet. How my soul thing shakes out is not my decision."

Realizing that my overtly religious reference had caught Bresnahan off guard, I switched terminology and asked if he thought that his being a potter was saving his life. To that he readily agreed and added, "Having seen what others go through, I live in paradise right now. And as Zen monks whom I used to stay with say, 'If you live in paradise, take great pride in keeping it clean' so that every time you have a bowl of tea—and the path to tea is a path of clay—and, when you prepare the garden for a tea ceremony in the teahouse, you prepare it as if God were coming for tea. And in that simple bowl, you put pure water and green valleys that go into your soul."

WE ARE HERE TO HEAL THE WORLD

"I will tell you one final story," he said. In 1999, after a firing of the mammoth Johanna kiln, close friends of Bresnahan purchased a pair of cups for their adult son. When the son came home to Minnesota for Christmas, he walked into Bresnahan's studio and said, "My mom and dad sent me a pair of cups. I think they're the most beautiful things I've ever seen." Whereupon the young man asked Bresnahan to show him the kiln as well as explain the technical information behind the firing.

Bresnahan accommodated, taking the young man to see the very chamber in the kiln where his particular cups had been fired. When Bresnahan explained how water was poured into the kiln at high temperatures, the young man grew even more interested. He said, "I'd like to see your charts of the temperatures when you put water inside the kiln."

Once again, Bresnahan accommodated the strange request, explaining how the infusion of water had to come at a certain time of day to form hydrogen and oxygen clouds precisely when the sun was "coming on the other side of the planet and pushing [a] barometric pressure shift."

Back in the studio and sitting at the tea table, the young man said to Bresnahan, "You know, you're doing the same thing that I'm doing."

Bresnahan had been surprised. Was the young man also a potter? he had asked.

No, the young man explained. He was an astrophysicist whose doctoral focus was studying the Orion nebulae and star formation. "He said, 'What you're doing is the exact same thing I'm doing. Those flame clouds that are going through that clay are the same coloring clouds that give orange, blue, yellow, green [colors]—it's the same clouds that are fifteen hundred light-years of space, pull[ing] together hydrogen-oxygen clouds for new star formation.'"

"So when I look inside that kiln now, at 2,300 degrees," Bresnahan said, "I'm not looking at a pot. I'm looking at hydrogen-oxygen clouds, and I'm thinking about the universe." From an astrophysicist's perspective, Bresnahan was reliving the beginning of the universe with every firing.

Bresnahan described how he used the story with his students. He would alternate showing slides of the star nebulae with those strikingly similar slides of his pots in the kiln before asking his students, "Has anybody asked you lately why we're on the planet? What is our purpose for the universe?"

For the potter, he said, the answer to this persistent human question is clear: human beings are here to heal the world.

For the first time in history, Bresnahan argued, everything is in place for humanity to take care of all life on earth. The technological systems exist to provide what is needed for every human being on planet earth. But yet our thinking remains back "with Adam Smith," he said. The question that needs to be asked, he suggested, is, what can a person make that is not disposable or needs to be hidden behind museum glass, but can, he said, referring to the saké cup, still pour wine after thirteen hundred years?

RELIGION'S LAST CHANCE

To ask current Westerners to ponder such a question, to ask what can last a thousand years, is truly revolutionary, he suggested, because the question forces us to admit how little we know about something we're intrinsically connected with—nature. Bresnahan offered another example from his classroom, that being the husk of a wild rice seed. That husk is the perfect protection of the grain that is the basis of the Native American diet, a husk so well adapted to its purpose that it could lie dormant for seven seasons at the bottom of a lake bed if the water level is too high or too low for germination.

For Bresnahan, the wild rice husk represents the protective role of nature in our lives, a role that we have largely ignored in the modern experience. "We have a shell protecting us, and we have been oblivious to the shell for four hundred years. How do we change the theological [construct] to reinvigorate the understanding of that shell?"

I was struck by the fact that, after an hour-long interview, we were finally discussing the potential value of religion. I had assumed, without Bresnahan saying it in so many words, that pottery was his religion. Why, at the end of his argument, was theology important? I asked.

"Look at the options we got," he replied with exasperation. "We don't have a government that functions; we don't have a corporation with any ethics that functions; they're not listening to the artist. Who do we [have] in a modern society well placed enough to give guidance?" For Bresnahan the answer was obvious. Only religion could do this, if religion would "do its job."

But that task would be difficult, he predicted. Modernity bombards people with so much visual and verbal stimuli that it is hard to ferret out what is necessary for our human recovery and survival. And what was critical to that survival was the appearance of what he termed "the fifth-dimensional guide."

Bresnahan defined this fifth-dimensional guide as the type of person who would emerge from a dialogue between the theologians and the artists. No longer viable would be the isolated religious experience, an experience, once over, that allowed the person to flow effortlessly back into the shortsighted behaviors of contemporary culture.

Bresnahan concluded his thought by predicting that religions will have to work with artists to foster a new, whole way of life, one sensitive to the needs of the planet, or "religions are doomed. That's just the way it is."

HOPE BREAKS IN THROUGH A CHILD

I wondered if Bresnahan was commenting on the monks who lived so near to him. Were these monks, who had invited a potter to live in their midst and who work closely with international artists on the St. John's Bible, models of this "fifth-dimensional guide," or was Bresnahan expressing frustration at what had yet to be achieved?

I did not have a chance to ask that question. The interview ended abruptly and not as I had expected. The buzz of now nearly thirty visitors and shoppers, as they circulated through the studio and the back room of pots, plates, and cups, had risen to where it was becoming difficult for us to converse on top of that.

But it was not the crowds, and certainly not the prospect of sales, that ended our conversation. It was instead the appearance in the studio of an infant in the arms of her parents, a visitor who Bresnahan announced had "come all the way from the womb."

He moved to a long worktable where he placed a flat circle of fresh clay. After asking the parents to remove the baby's socks, he held the baby over the slab and slowly lowered the child until her feet pressed into the clay.

The room exploded into laughter and clapping. Smiling broadly, Bresnahan handed the baby back to the parents and explained when they could return to the studio to retrieve the fired plate. It was clear that I had just witnessed a tradition of the Bresnahan studio.

I had the odd feeling that I was observing an ancient ritual. I almost expected Bresnahan to announce to the crowded room that this child was now officially present in this world. The baby had been grounded, her tiny footprints preserved in the world's oldest artistic medium, the same material of the priceless saké cup, a material that, with care, could last thousands of years. The baby had been sealed with what Bresnahan accepted as ultimate reality—the earth.

Gone from the room were the dire warnings that Bresnahan had so recently expressed. It was as if the fire in a kiln had finally burnt itself out in the joy of the moment. A baby had been brought into this troubled and terror-filled world, christened by clay, with Bresnahan serving as the high priest. Perhaps, I thought, this artist lived with more hope for the future than he admitted to himself. For if this one child grew up *within* nature rather than separated from it, the child could help save the earth, even as nature, our fragile and mysterious husk around us, would save the child.

This was a hope that I could understand and could share to an extent, even if that extent was less than Bresnahan's. The interviews I had been conducting were pointing me more in the direction of how we view each other as human beings for a solution to our broken world than in our connection with the earth, even as I accept the interconnectedness of those two relationships.

Yet Richard Bresnahan had clearly left me with a challenge. Any proposed solution to the terrorism virus would not come from some minor tinkering with our present ways of being. That vessel will no longer hold water. We will need a complete shift of consciousness, and the message will have to be universal.

CHAPTER 13

The Scent of Holiness

Holy Transfiguration Skete (Society of St. John)
Eagle Harbor, Michigan
August 12–13, 2007

Driving to the Holy Transfiguration Skete means traveling through miles of desolate forest to reach an area in Michigan's Upper Peninsula known as the Keweenaw. The Keweenaw is itself a smaller peninsula in the shape of an arthritic finger that juts out into Lake Superior. Outside the remote village of Eagle Harbor and a few miles past an antiques shop named "The End of the World," summer residents and tourists round a bend on Route 26 and come upon the onion-domed church of Holy Transfiguration. Here, five men live out a demanding form of the monastic life under Ukrainian Catholic guidelines.

"FOLLOW ME"

In the Gospels, the first band of disciples seemed to form with a snap of Jesus' fingers. As easily as the world was created in Genesis 1 by a simple command from God, so Jesus in the gospel story had only to utter, "Follow Me" for the first four men to immediately leave lives by another lakeshore to become disciples.

As Jesus walked by the Sea of Galilee, he saw two brothers, Simon who is called Peter and Andrew his brother, casting a net into the sea; for they were fishermen. And he said to them, "Follow me, and I will make you fishers of men." Immediately they left their nets and followed him. And going on from there he saw Zebedee and John his brother, in the boat with Zebedee their father, mending their nets, and he called them. Immediately, they left the boat and their father, and followed him. (Matthew 4:8–22)

In our contemporary world, men and women are much less willing to answer the monastic call. Nearly every monastic house that I have visited is facing low numbers, has a clearly aging community, or both. When I left these houses and asked for their prayers for the project, they, in turn, routinely asked for my prayers—for more who will answer the call to monastic life.

Not surprisingly, I heard the same request when I left Holy Transfiguration Monastery. The daily work of running a monastery as well as a thriving roadside business (the Jampot) would be a challenge for twenty men to shoulder, much less five. I naturally assumed that their rigorous life of getting up as early as 2:00 a.m. to prepare the kitchen, followed by Divine Liturgy at 6:00 a.m. before a full day at the Jampot—baking, selling, and shipping—had scared off others looking for quiet cells, cloisters, and the life of prayer. Yet, the story of Holy Transfiguration has elements close to the instant "dropping of the nets" found in the gospel accounts.

THE PIONEERS: FATHER NICHOLAS AND FATHER BASIL

Father Nicholas and Father Basil began Holy Transfiguration monastery in August 1983 as a strict Benedictine Catholic order. Originally of Methodist background, Father Nicholas is the quiet and dignified spiritual head of the community, the one occupying the seat of authority both at the dinner table and in the morning Divine Liturgy.

Father Basil, as became clear in my first moments at Holy Transfiguration, is the designated spokesperson for the community, the one whose role in the community and at the Jampot it is to connect with the outside world.

That first year in 1983, the goal of the two men was simple—to survive the harsh winter. This they did by doing what so many of the locals have done for decades, picking berries and selling them to the numerous processors on the Keweenaw. Within three years, the pattern was reversed at Holy Transfiguration, when the two men began processing berries bought from other pickers. The impressive Jampot enterprise, offering pastries, jams, and jellies to passersby and through mail orders, was born.

With the jam and jelly business, the tiny community has successfully battled the economic challenge that plagues so many monasteries. But life on the spiritual front at Holy Transfiguration has not been as easy. In that first decade, when the relationship with the local and overseeing bishop of Marquette deteriorated markedly, the survival of the tiny community was in serious doubt.

Rescue came through an odd turn of events. In 1993, another bishop who had heard of the community's plight suggested a radical solution. The men should seek the protection of the Ukrainian Catholic Church, a tiny wing (only 2 percent) of the larger Catholic community. The Ukrainian Catholics, as part of the more monastically oriented Eastern Church, were eager to sponsor monasteries but also suffered the common monastic malady of few new recruits.

Holy Transfiguration's transfer to Eastern Catholic Christianity was consequently a boon for both parties, though the jurisdictional issues were a bit odd. Their overseeing bishop would not be in nearby Marquette or elsewhere in Michigan's Upper Peninsula, but hundreds of miles south in Chicago, the site of the nearest Ukrainian cathedral.

And Holy Transfiguration's motherhouse, her sponsoring monastery, was even farther away—in northern California. If Father Nicholas and Father Basil felt isolated before as monks on their remote piece of Lake Superior shoreline, the community's spiritual reorientation from Benedictine to Ukrainian Catholicism only intensified their isolation. Moreover, neither Father Nicholas nor Father Basil is Ukrainian (also true of the other three men who subsequently joined).

The two monks took the first step toward Ukrainian Catholic monasticism by traveling to Chicago to meet the bishop and discuss the possibility of Holy Transfiguration's adoption. The visit was also their first chance to observe Ukrainian Catholic worship. Finding much of the service foreign, they were not impressed. But they were undeterred. During the following Lent, the two men traveled to the monastery of Mount Tabor in northern California. Once again, they were struck by the foreignness of the Ukrainian service. Yet, at the conclusion of the service, when worshippers in the Eastern-rite service prostrated themselves in prayer, both men felt deeply moved. Yes, they concluded, this was a tradition they could embrace, one that would feed them spiritually as well as shelter them ecclesiastically.

The transition, formally made in 1993, has become yet one more issue to explain to puzzled customers of the Jampot. The monastic vocation is itself a stretch for many Americans to understand, and the jam and jelly shop has naturally led to the standard question, "What are you guys all about, anyway?"

But the additional step of becoming Eastern-rite Catholics confused customers and curious passersby all the more. The stunning onion-domed architecture of the new church, the Byzantine chant of the services, the icons adorning the walls of every room in the monastery, as well as the black caps and robes worn by the five men (even under their aprons in the Jampot) suggested, if anything, that the community was Orthodox.

That guess would not be far off. Except for prayers beseeching

God's blessing on the pope, the morning celebration of the Divine Liturgy of St. John Chrysostom at Holy Transfiguration is identical to Orthodox worship. Indeed, one of the goals of this small monastic community has been, since the transition, that it become a meeting place of the two branches of the church, Orthodox and Catholic, East and West.

This quest for ecumenical unity is given visual and dramatic expression in a side chapel of the monastery's church. Here stands a ten-foot silver cross, called the Holy Cross of Sorrow and Suffering. My first impression of the cross, with its two crowns of silver thorns at the beams' joining and at the cross's foot, was that it was a garish monstrosity, out of place in the traditional church.

But the story behind the cross won me over. In 1993, when the community moved from Benedictine to Ukrainian practice, the Byzantine chant taxed the men's voices. To increase their vocal strength, the men sought the help of a voice teacher in San Francisco, whom they consulted whenever they were visiting the monastery of Mount Tabor in northern California.

During these lessons, the voice teacher would frequently lament her financial situation. After all, she assured them, San Francisco is an expensive city in which to live. In response, the monks decided to help. Secretly, they began leaving whatever money they could spare on top of her piano.

In the late 1990s, the voice teacher wrote to Holy Transfiguration with a strange request. Would the monks send her their checking account number? The monks realized that disclosing such information was unwise. Nevertheless, they decided to trust her. On the next month's statement, Father Basil noted an extra $190,000 in the account. Through further research, he traced the increase to two deposits made by the music teacher.

Father Nicholas telephoned the unexpected donor to tell her that the community could not possibly accept such a large gift. "I did it, didn't I?" she replied. While clearly being generous, the woman also put certain stipulations on the gift. Part of the gift was to fund a fine arts program at the monastery that would benefit their rather isolated part of the Keweenaw Peninsula. The remainder of the gift was to fulfill a vision she claimed to have received from Christ. In the vision, she had been shown a large silver cross, with abstract shapes hammered into its surface. The crowns of thorns, also silver and encircling the cross at the intersection of the beams and at the base, was part of her vision as well. The cross was to comfort all visitors to Holy Transfiguration who were suffering, but particularly, she said, the cross was dedicated to the healing of the church's division, East and West.

Despite the plethora of artists on the Keweenaw, the monks had difficulty finding one able to fulfill the exacting requirements of the bequest. After the commissioning of one local artist fell through, the project stalled until the monks learned of another artist who had recently returned to the area. When they described the unique specifications of the project, especially the intricate silver work required, the artist was quiet for a moment before sharing that she had recently returned from Peru, where she had married a silver artisan. Could the two of them, she asked, work together on the project?

The married artists fulfilled the commission in 1999.

THE COMMUNITY GROWS

Throughout the project, my usual practice was to interview monks mature in age, such as Father Nicholas and Father Basil. Yet I was naturally curious to hear the perspectives of the younger monks, those at the beginning of the monastic journey. But only once, with Father John at St. Michael's Skete, did I have that chance.

Holy Transfiguration Skete did have three younger monks. I met them at dinner that first evening, but if they were curious about my visit, they hid it completely. From the group's spokesperson, Father Basil, however, I learned how each of the younger monks had come to Holy Transfiguration. Father Ambrose, slight of build and with close-cut hair and full black beard, was perhaps in his late twenties or early thirties. Having grown up in the area, he had initially been hired as a worker in the Jampot. From that experience, he stayed on as a monk and was ordained a deacon in 2007. As deacon, Father Ambrose is able to assist the priest in the Divine Liturgy by offering some of the petitions and wielding the censer.

Brother Ephraim is the newest and youngest member of the community, still a novice. Sporting a black eye from a fight when he first came to the Jampot with his grandmother, Ephraim is the son of two Methodist ministers. He returned to Holy Transfiguration on his own for a retreat and subsequently asked to stay. His introduction to Catholicism and monastic life came simultaneously. What had drawn him? I wondered.

On my second day at Holy Transfiguration, I sat on a stool in the kitchen of the Jampot and watched the three younger monks tackle their assignments. All were baking pastries that day, with jam and jellies being the next day's task. Brother Ephraim looked up from a tray full of cookies to ask why I was so interested in their views on 9/11.

As I had done at other monasteries, I explained the paradox that I'd found so intriguing in the project. Men and women who lived so close to one another in monastic life—eating, working, and worshipping together—nevertheless reflected not a shred of "group thinking" about 9/11 or the war on terror. In no interview did I hear those common echoes of politicians or the media: that "terrorists hate our freedom" or "Iraq is all about oil."

From another worktable, the last of the three young monks entered the conversation. Yes, he agreed with my point. Monastic life, contrary to what many assume, discourages all forms of rote thinking. The soft-spoken comment came from Father Sergius, who was delicately spooning jam onto long strips of dough. Fair-haired and studious-looking in his glasses, Father Sergius was very thin, his robes seeming too big for his slender frame. But with the entire community currently observing the fasting period preceding the Dormition of the Theotokos (the Assumption of Mary), none of the men looked particularly well fed. This was despite their being surrounded by pastries and sweets every day.

The story of Father Sergius's coming to Holy Transfiguration seems a page out of the gospel of Matthew. While flipping through TV channels one night toward the end of high school, Father Sergius caught a twelve-minute spot about Holy Transfiguration on Catholic TV. He immediately contacted the monastery for details and soon after announced his desire to join the monastery.

It shows the wisdom of both Father Nicholas and Father Basil that, despite the monastery's desperate need for vocations, they discouraged the young man from joining. Instead, they advised him to enroll in college. If at graduation he still felt called to their monastic life, he would be welcome to return.

Father Sergius did not wait that long, returning to Holy Transfiguration after only one year of college. He had heard the call to monastic life and had almost immediately heeded it. Together, the five men, two older, three younger, and none ethnically Ukrainian, practice the strenuous Eastern-rite form of monastic life on the northern shore of America.

WAITING FOR ME TO ASK ABOUT THE MIRACLE

My interview with the spokesperson, Father Basil, took place immediately after I arrived. Together we sat in what amounted to the monastery's living room, a couch and chairs balancing the dining room table at the other end of the room. I could not help but notice that one of those chairs was covered by an Islamic prayer rug. Except for the view of Lake Superior through the picture window, the room was one typical of any middle-class residence in the Midwest. As Father Basil told me later, the room had served as the community's sanctuary prior to the construction of the church. Consequently, we were sitting at the very site of a "miracle," in Father Basil's opinion, that had first occurred in their community three days after 9/11.

Later I realized how odd our interview must have seemed to Father Basil as he waited for me to ask *the* question that he assumed had brought me to Holy Transfiguration. But I had not heard the miracle story and would not have heard it had not Father Basil chosen to share it. My interest in Holy Transfiguration had originated in a comment made by my literary agent, whose son had visited the Jampot and Holy Transfiguration on several occasions and had been impressed by the special spirit of the community.

After contacting Holy Transfiguration, I also received a copy of their newsletter, *Magnificat*, which clearly revealed the experimental nature of the place. The community of five men seemed a perfect counterpoint to the larger and more historically rooted monastic houses of the Abbey of Gethsemani and Saint John's Abbey.

SCENE 1: 9/11

The "miracle" on September 14, 2001, came to Holy Transfiguration like the final scene of a play. The opening scene was one common to much of the world, that unforgettable moment when each of us first heard the news of the planes hitting the Twin Towers.

Holy Transfiguration heard the news from Father Nicholas's nephew, an artist who was to arrive that day for a visit. The call came at 10:00 a.m. local time, the nephew trying to explain that all flights had just been canceled.

"I was the one who took the call," Father Basil said. "He (the nephew) was hysterical . . . which was kind of surprising, because he never struck me [as someone] who would get flapped very easily. He was apparently watching it on the television, and he said, 'Oh my goodness, the tower is collapsing.'"

Father Basil immediately shared the tragic news with Father Nicholas, but, as it was a workday at Holy Transfiguration, life continued as usual. "We don't have a television hookup here. We don't watch television," Father Basil explained. "I guess I gleaned more information from customers as they came through."

SCENE 2: "I WANT MY COOKIES"

The 9/11 drama at Holy Transfiguration continued with an exchange with a neighbor, one that typified the initial reaction of the country to the tragedy.

Previous relations with these particular neighbors, described as "yuppies" by Father Basil, had been less than cordial. The couple was not religious, but over the years the wife had made a habit of coming into the Jampot for peanut-butter oatmeal cookies, her favorite treat. One summer afternoon prior to 9/11, this woman came into the shop only to find that her favorite cookies had already sold out.

The woman insistently asked, "Why don't you have these things? If you can't do them during your regular workday, you should work longer for your customers."

Father Basil reminded her that the community's primary responsibility was not baking but praying. The woman responded in exasperation, "I don't care about your prayers. I want my cookies!"

In those first days after 9/11, the woman was in a very different mood. "She came into the shop, much subdued, and came up to the counter," Father Basil recalled.

"'You've heard about the terrible thing that happened?' she asked.

"'Yes, yes, we've heard about it,'" Father Basil had replied, to which the woman responded, "'Oh, we all have to pray more.'"

Father Basil paused a moment in recounting the story. "I thought to myself, 'Oh, my goodness, maybe this woman's eyes had opened up.'" But sadly, within a short time the woman's focus returned to the cookies.

And that had been the pattern of the country, Father Basil suggested. The surge in church attendance after 9/11 hadn't lasted, but had simply been a "flash in the pan." As a country, we had returned very quickly to "demanding our cookies."

SCENE 3: THE SIGN OF ST. BENEDICT

What 9/11 had made the Holy Transfiguration community realize, Father Basil said, was that we could not simply count on the government to keep us safe. "This happened in this country with this almighty government. Well, not so almighty, after all."

Accepting this difficult truth might have been easier for monks, he felt, "because we don't set our hopes on this world at all anyway . . . Ultimately, it isn't in Washington's hands but God's hands." Continuing, he described 9/11 as just a "rather forceful reminder of that."

I moved to one of my standard questions. What texts or teachings had steadied or comforted the community or him in the wake of 9/11? Father Basil nodded, saying that he now understood where I was "guiding" the conversation. I must have come to Holy Transfiguration, he said, because I had heard of the miracle that had happened on September 14, 2001, the Feast of the Exaltation of the Cross.

"It was also the day that [President] Bush had declared a national day of prayer," Father Basil said. In a hushed tone, as if he were sharing a secret, he added, "But what happened here was most interesting. During the liturgy, and again it was in this room, this little space here," he noted, "Father Nicholas got an overwhelming sense of fragrance. He could smell something [but] it wasn't the incense he was using. It was something different.

"And after the liturgy, he really started sniffing around," Father Basil continued with a laugh. "You know, like, where is this scent coming from?" Once Father Nicholas mentioned the scent, Father Basil could detect it as well. "And [Father Nicholas] located it as coming from a relic. We had a relic of Saint Benedict, and it was on the altar. And from the little reliquary was coming this very powerful scent."

Father Basil had approached the relic to confirm that the scent was indeed coming from that source. "And we opened the reliquary, and . . . the scent just filled the whole room."

Father Nicholas brought the reliquary out of the sanctuary and called over the other monks of the community at the time, Father Ambrose and Father Sergius, to experience the miraculous scent.

"And [at the time] I thought about it," Father Basil said. "I said, 'You know, this is a consolation that was sent our way . . . because here it is, the Feast of the Exaltation of the Cross. It's a day of national prayer, and this relic of Saint Benedict, whom the Roman Church considers the patron saint of Western Civilization, is sending out this odor.'"

For Father Basil and the community, the message of the miraculous scent was clear. "No matter how dark things seem—and they seemed pretty bleak at that point—that this is not the end, that Western Civilization is going to survive and perhaps even prosper."

I wondered if Father Basil understood the irony of his story. The community of Holy Transfiguration had discerned a scent of holiness, a smell far different from that of cookies that, too soon after 9/11, once again controlled their neighbor's desires.

Father Basil added a postscript to the account of the miraculous scent. About a year ago, the community was invited to a little Orthodox church near Houghton, Michigan, to venerate a weeping icon of the Blessed Virgin that was touring America at the time.

"When we bent down to venerate the icon, there was the same fragrance, exactly the same as we'd smelled from the relic of Saint Benedict." The bishop present at the church in Houghton explained that "the fragrance of holiness is always there in the icon."

As I considered Father Basil's interpretation of the relic of St. Benedict, that the relic's miraculous fragrance promises the survival of Western Civilization, I was struck by how his view fit neatly with Samuel Huntington's theory of a "clash of civilizations." The future, Huntington had asserted in the 1990s, would be a series of conflicts between distinct civilizations, Islamic and American being two such cultures destined to clash. Was that how Father Basil understood 9/11? I asked.

In a certain sense, Father Basil said that he agreed with Huntington. The West placed their hopes in moderate, reasonable Muslims, with al-Qaeda and the Taliban being cast as perversions of the faith. But it seemed to Father Basil that the only moderate Muslims in the world were those who have been westernized. The traditional-ists seemed desperate to preserve Islam as they knew it. "I think maybe it [9/11] was an act of desperation. I don't think that it was a calcu-lated . . . step toward world domination. I think it was an attempt, for a certain element of that culture, to lash out and try to hang on to their own traditions that they felt were slipping from them."

And what did Father Basil believe was so threatening about the West? Was al-Qaeda attacking Western culture's Christian roots, glo-balization, or secularity?

"More secularity than anything else," Father Basil replied. "If they were attacking Christianity, per se, they would have gone for a Christian symbol. They would have tried to blow up St. Peter's."

The terrorists do not seem to be against practicing Christians, he noted, with al-Qaeda having chosen to attack symbols of secularity and globalization. They were "probably looking at the US government as the agent or the spearhead of this encroaching global, secular, irreligious society."

But is not monastic life in its own way, I asked, also a rejection of secularity?

"In a way, you could almost sympathize with their fears," Father Basil said. "Many of the things [that] you read that strong Muslims feel are wrong with the world, we feel are wrong with the world too. And I'm sure that the pope in Rome and the Ecumenical Patriarch would also agree that these things are wrong with the world."

But understanding the monastic alternative to secularity came into focus only when I visited the monk's seemingly mundane work at their roadside market, the Jampot.

EUCHARIST AND WORK

At several points in our interview, Father Basil referred to the key role that the Jampot played in the life of Holy Transfiguration. During the summer and at other busy times of the year, such as at Christmas, the monks become so busy with baking, selling, and shipping that the 6:00 a.m. Divine Liturgy is the only service of the day. Only at those times of the year, when the demands made by the Jampot are lighter, do the men also observe an additional service at noonday and the evening vesper service. Keeping such work in perspective is a great challenge. Father Basil told the story of a monk who had left a monastery to take an eight-to-five job. Why? So that he could have his evenings free for prayer and reading.

But as a visiting priest had advised the men at Holy Transfiguration, "There are special graces, very great graces that come with this work." The community should not be concerned, he suggested, that their life did not at the present time reflect the stereotype of monastic life. That life might happen at Holy Transfiguration only in the generations to come.

In my interview with Father Basil, I asked if their work in the Jampot could itself be considered a form of prayer. Father Basil thought for a moment before acknowledging that some duties in the shop had contemplative aspects. "Much of it is quiet work. Granted that the machines are going constantly, the mixers and things like that. But much of it, like making jam, goodness, you stand there, and you stir the pot. You pick out the bugs that float to the top, and you make sure that nothing burns, and when it's ready you put it in the jars."

But Father Basil clarified that his own duties in the Jampot, to stand at the counter and "interface with the world," were less contemplative. "There's no way [around] it. Shopkeeping is not a contemplative occupation, because you're constantly having to deal with these people."

I inquired if customers, seeing the men garbed monastically as they worked, ever asked religious or theological questions.

Yes, that could pose a bit of a difficulty in busy times, Father Basil admitted. But he had also been surprised by the thoughtfulness of some of the questions and comments, especially those comments from young people. He described the recent visit of a family with two teenage sons. One of the boys, perhaps only thirteen, had remarked that he had heard that monks were always happy because they did without so many things.

"And I said to him, 'Well, there's a certain truth to that.' The more simply you live, the less frustration you're going to encounter. However," Father Basil had told the boy, "I wouldn't say that our lives are always happy. We have our trials and tribulations too."

But the boy's observation held a lesson for the monks as well. Visitors felt comfortable in the store, perhaps more than in the church, to share their thoughts about faith, religion, and life.

THE JAMPOT—ONE OF THE GREAT SURPRISES

I never imagined that the Jampot would play such an important role in my reflections on the age of terror. At other stops on my travels, I had observed the diverse ways that monasteries sought to be self-sufficient. Back in January, when at Christ in the Desert in New Mexico, I had taken my turn working in the bookstore. At nearby St. Michael's Skete, I had observed Father John dipping candles. At Gethsemani Abbey in Kentucky, I had visited the new gift shop packed with tapes, books, CDs, DVDs, and religious jewelry. And at Saint John's Abbey, I had been impressed with their variety of projects, especially the calligraphic Saint John's Bible. A month after my visit to Holy Transfiguration, I would assist Brother Luke, prior of the monks of New Skete, as he cleaned the cages of the German shepherd puppies raised, trained, and sold by their community.

Of course, I understood that every monastery had bills to pay. And Holy Transfiguration had first come to my attention through my literary agent's description of the Jampot. But as the project unfolded, I naturally focused on the interviews. How these same monks and nuns "rendered to Caesar the things that are Caesar's" (Mark 12:17 KJV) seemed tangential to my interests.

At Holy Transfiguration, however, the business side of monastic life could not be so easily dismissed. Father Basil made that clear at a light breakfast after the 6:00 a.m. Divine Liturgy on my second day at the monastery. As he hurriedly cleaned up, Father Basil explained that the four monks (Father Nicholas would be away on business in town) would follow their usual Monday through Saturday pattern and spend the day baking and selling pastries and jams in the Jampot. There would be little time for us to talk further, given the usual stream of customers in late August, but he said that I would be welcome to observe their interaction with customers.

Yes, I wanted to see the operation, I said, trying to sound

convincing. Having passed so many other jam outlets further south toward Houghton, I imagined a long day with little to interest me. And what I did not share with Father Basil was my harbored suspicion that the Jampot compromised their monastic vocation. I could not imagine anyone attracted to monastic life being satisfied with stirring and packing jam jars for eight to fifteen hours a day. Were the five men really businessmen who happened to be monks on the side, or were they monks who ran a demanding business?

In the end, the Jampot was one of the great surprises of my visits. For most of the morning, I watched as Father Basil, sometimes with Father Sergius's assistance, served a steady stream of humanity who came into the shop. Sometimes the twelve-by-twenty-foot room was so crowded with an Elderhostel busload of vacationers trying to work their way to the shelves of jams and jellies that I had to step into the kitchen, where the three younger monks were busy baking.

By lunchtime, I was exhausted, and my only work had been to take pictures and jot down notes. I left the four monks with their customers and walked the hundred yards back along Route 26 to the guest cabin. Firing up my laptop, I sat in the quiet room to organize my impressions of the morning. The words did not come easily. Something I had not anticipated was happening in the Jampot, but where were the words to describe that specialness?

As I began tentatively to write my reflections on the morning's liturgy, my breakfast with Father Basil, and the hours at the Jampot, I felt none of the frustration that I expected. Instead, I was overcome with a deep and unexpected sense of peace and rightness. When this peace had entered the room, or why, I did not know, but I was struck by a clear sense of fittingness to everything in those moments—the singing of the birds, the warmth of the sun streaming through the trees and the windows, the occasional car going by on Route 26, the scurrying of the squirrels and chipmunks, the icons looking down on me from the walls of this tiny cabin, and the steady breathing sound of the waves of

Lake Superior. In the hush, I sat perfectly still, my fingers quiet on the computer keyboard. Later a friend and mentor, whom I have learned to count on for his uncommon wisdom, reminded me that the goal of life is to experience wholeness not perfection. Life was whole in those moments in the cabin.

Absent in those moments were the desire for more interviews, the desire for publication, and even the desire to find the right words to describe those moments. In an odd way, the project had brought me to these few peaceful moments as some sort of end, even though those moments were occurring in the middle of the project.

What was it that had triggered these unexpected moments of calm? The longer I sat in silence and pondered that question, the more I realized that the answer lay back in the busy and noisy Jampot. Something in the way the two distinct cultures, American consumer and monastic, intersected in that tiny space held the source of the peace I felt. I realized that I had no alternative but to return to the Jampot for the afternoon, my eyes and mind open wider.

That afternoon, the number of customers in the Jampot seemed to increase. I watched and listened to Father Basil more clearly, sensing that the source of the peace that I felt was in his treatment of those who come through the door. There were other places not many miles away where similar jams, jellies, and pastries could be purchased more cheaply. And there would be many other places where those same items could be purchased far more quickly. With Father Basil usually being the only monk checking customers out, and with his gregariousness, the wait could be considerable.

On shelves along one side of the room were, by my count, sixty different kinds of jams and jellies, all neatly stacked and labeled. (*Poorrock Abbey* is the community's trademark.) In one of the rare lulls in the day, I commented on the extensive choices offered by the community. Father Basil frowned and said my count of sixty varieties seemed a bit off. Usually they offered seventy choices!

In addition to the jams and jellies, the community offered at least eight kinds of muffins, brownies, or other baked goods, all neatly displayed on trays and cake stands on the counter. None of these had labels, requiring Father Basil to explain repeatedly, with considerable humor, that day's pastry choices.

"This one is poppy seed but with raisins, walnuts, and orange rind, so not the *usual* poppy seed," he explained over and over again throughout the day. And at one point, after Father Basil had similarly described all seven bakery items, a Southern woman from an Elderhostel bus said, "You're evil. Why, this is the biggest muffin I've ever seen." (She had a point. She had selected a muffin nearly the size of a baseball glove.) She exclaimed, "This is a family-size muffin!"

"Well," Father Basil replied with a smile, "I suppose that depends on the size of the family."

It did not take me long to realize that commerce in the Jampot often provided a pretext for conversation. Some customers were obvious repeats, back for their favorite jams and also for this casual bantering with a monk. They dawdled, asking questions or simply sharing with Father Basil their pleasure at the tantalizing smells wafting from the kitchen.

In the midst of this leisurely give-and-take, an SUV pulled up in a cloud of dust, disgorging a family with teenagers. By the time the family hit the door, the father was already urging his wife and kids to make their choices quickly. I wondered how this example of our fast-paced society would disturb the mood of the store.

The more the father hurried his family, the more the kids used their headsets and iPods to resist passively. Finally, the father was able to corral his tribe and line up their choices on the counter. As Father Basil handed the man his bagged goods, he expressed a wish that the family would enjoy both the bakery goods and the beautiful day. The man paused and, to my surprise, replied, "I'm glad you're here. You monks are a real asset to this area."

Later in the afternoon and still without taking a break, Father Basil fielded another customer's question. "Sir, what is a rose hip?" After hearing Father Basil's patient explanation of the rose plant and the hips of it, the woman replied, "Well, I've learned something new."

Without missing a beat, Father Basil added, "We just keep learning."

The topic shifted to fruitcake, one of the Jampot's higher-priced specialties, and how to keep that item fresh until Christmas. Ah, Father Basil replied, it was indeed possible. The secret was counterintuitive, not to freeze the fruitcake from August to December but only to refrigerate.

Father Basil's common and yet uncommon treatment of customers led to theological questions from some customers. Others asked if the church was open for tours. No, Father Basil replied. All the monks worked in the store, but visitors were welcome to walk through the monastery's gardens. To those who expressed an interest in the spirituality of Holy Transfiguration, Father Basil pointed to a clipboard where customers could sign up for the community's newsletter. No obligation, he assured the customers. Still others asked to take Father Basil's picture. Of course, he always said.

Toward the end of the long day, a neighbor from down the road entered the shop to ask to borrow a wrench. As if the request were as common as asking for a poppy seed muffin, Father Ambrose emerged from the kitchen holding a Vise-Grip.

It was no surprise, then, when Brother Ephraim told me that the Jampot is listed in *Biker* magazine as "biker friendly." The truth seems to be that the Jampot is friendly to everyone, from busloads of Elderhostel travelers to bikers to young backpackers.

Fifteen minutes after closing time, as the monks were cleaning up, a couple came through the door. The woman was talkative, so pleased to find the Jampot still open. Her husband remained mute as the woman scanned the shelves and read aloud the labels on the jams. I knew exactly what would be said to the woman in most stores and shops in America.

After a few more moments of such meandering and reading labels, the woman turned to face Father Basil. In a stage whisper, loud enough for all of us to hear, she shared with the monk that she and her husband had had a fight outside.

Father Basil waited patiently at the counter while the woman returned to her leisurely tour of the shelves. Ten minutes later, the woman brought her muffins and bread choices to the counter and asked if she and her husband could pay separately.

"No problem," Father Basil replied patiently.

"We'll get over our fight," the woman assured Father Basil and perhaps her husband, who in the end purchased nothing.

"I hope the muffins and bread will help," Father Basil answered with the same warmth.

After the couple left, the monks closed up the shop for the day. I waited to walk back to the monastery with them. The pace was slow, the day having obviously taken a toll on the four men. I knew that after a light supper, the men would retire to the dormitory long before dark, only to rise again the next morning for another equally long day of work. Sunday was their only day off.

Despite Father Basil's warm invitation for me to stay another night as a guest, I announced that I would soon be leaving. I was exhausted, too, and I had only been an observer to their long day. As we said our good-byes, I told the men that I sensed that something extraordinary was happening at the Jampot. I confessed that I was struggling to find the right words to describe what I had experienced. I knew that what they offered customers, the interplay as much as the merchandise, exceeded what they had to do to pay their bills. Several of the monks smiled, perhaps a bit embarrassed, before Father Basil expressed his appreciation that I had understood that the Jampot was a ministry.

As I drove south toward Wisconsin, I remembered what a colleague and psychologist had told me nearly thirty years before. Soon after our first child was born, the psychologist pulled me aside to counsel my wife and me never to fight or argue when we were eating together as a family. Even a baby would take in the words and the food together, she explained. "Always make the message at the table consistent." Real nurturing, she added, was not just about the nutritional value of the food but offering words of love along with the food.

I thought of the Divine Liturgy that had begun that busy day. The liturgy was filled with divine words of challenge, love, and forgiveness. Those words transformed the morsel of bread and the sip of wine into food for the heart.

At the end of the morning's Divine Liturgy, Father Basil had offered *antidoron*, blessed bread, to the only guest that morning—me. But after the hours in the Jampot, I realized that Father Basil was no less a priest in the tiny store as he offered loving words along with the jams, jellies, and pastries. His blessing for the harried father, that he would enjoy both the food and the beautiful day, and his wish for the feuding couple, "I hope the muffins and bread will help," seemed versions of the "Peace be with you" he had offered throughout that morning's Divine Liturgy.

Noted American Orthodox theologian Alexander Schmemann maintained that God desires that we approach all aspects of life sacramentally. That is, there is nothing that God has created that is inherently secular. The destiny of everything in this world is achieved when we recognize its capacity to connect us mystically with God.

Was this what drew people back to the Jampot and the monks of Holy Transfiguration? Yes, the jams, jellies, and bakery goods were certainly special, these goods having achieved an impressive reputation in the area. But people drove the miles to the Jampot for a taste of something else, something lost in globalization but missing also in the cutesy, touristy shops elsewhere on the Keweenaw. The monks engaged in no overt "witnessing" or evangelism in the Jampot. Yet, here was an older, Christian-oriented way of doing business, the exact opposite of McWorld and Walmart.

The violence of our world has caused many to doubt if this realm of forgiveness, peaceful community, and hospitality to the stranger—all characteristics of the kingdom of God—still exists. I felt the kingdom of God at Holy Transfiguration in the liturgy, but equally so in the Jampot. Here, all of life is sacred. Here, one catches the scent of holiness.

Perhaps, I thought, the monks' secret is that they understand their work in the Jampot as part of their vocation, their way of feeding the multitudes in Christ's name and in His stead. Or perhaps it is the other way around. The monks see Christ as He comes through the door, hidden in the lives of the bikers, the backpackers, the Elderhostel travelers, the vacationing families, the squabbling couple, and the woman wanting to borrow the wrench. I have no doubt that Muslims traveling Route 26 have been viewed in that same sacred way as customers of the Jampot.

In the end, I have come to believe that both are true at Holy Transfiguration. In the gentle attention and warmth the customers experience from the monks, the customers are in the presence of Christ. Equally so, the monks are in the presence of Christ as He comes to them in the lives of their customers.

"Do you love Me?" Jesus asked St. Peter. "Feed my sheep" (John 21:17). That's what the monks of Holy Transfiguration are doing, six days a week, to customers of every conceivable background. Would that the world were more like the Jampot.

PART THREE

Overcoming Hate

CHAPTER 14

Light and Darkness

New Skete
Cambridge, New York
September 19–22, 2007

By September 2007, I had journeyed spiritually more than I could have imagined when my travels started. At the start of the interviews, my thoughts were quite simple. Something major was missing in the way we had responded to the horrific tragedy of 9/11 and to the continuing age of terror. But what was missing? My answer at the time was vague, but in a word, and speaking as a Christian, I felt that Jesus was missing. Our response to the tragedy would have been the same if Jesus had never lived, and that posed a great problem for many people. If Christ is the way, the truth, and the life, He has to matter in some meaningful way in this war on terror.

Sadly, Jesus has been drafted into this war. But Jesus as the banner-carrier of Christendom or Christian culture has, from the beginning, been unacceptable to me. Also unacceptable is the belief that Jesus is on the side of the Coalition Forces and approves of all that we have done in this war. This image, to others as well as me, is that of a false Christ.

Yet I did not deny our nation's right to defend itself. What I did deny was that the horrendous nature of the attacks and the massive death toll justified American Christians censuring Jesus' radical call to love the Other, even the enemy. I resonated as a Christian with Nathan Dungan's observation that 9/11 was an opportunity for introspection that we missed. In a sense, I began the project by looking backward to what had been missed in September and October of 2001 in order to find the way forward.

As this project progressed, however, the focus shifted. The early interviews in New Mexico and at Gethsemani Abbey, as well as my rereading of Thomas Merton in light of 9/11 and the age of terror, challenged me to construct a new understanding of Christ's relationship to our world. The cornerstone of this new understanding would be a radical understanding of the mystical Christ as present within humanity. The Incarnation is much more radical an event than is reflected in our brief Christmas festivities. The Incarnation means that Jesus has entered this world and lurks, albeit often in a hidden way, within the entire human race. I began to realize that I did not need to bring Jesus to bear on our crisis. What I needed to do was find Jesus moving in the midst of it.

Merton's epiphany at Fourth and Walnut in Louisville was the lynchpin of my new perspective. After rereading his account of that experience, I asked, what if Merton's epiphany were taken as a truth for the entire church and the world? And what if we accepted Merton's view of conflict, from the personal to the international level, as ultimately civil war within the mystical body of Christ? What if we Christians understood that God in Christ suffers wherever humans suffer at the hands of one another? Even as sin in all its varieties has one common characteristic—it always separates us from God, each other, and also our true selves—love, which is sin's opposite, always unites. Christ entered humanity to bring us to unity in Himself and with one another. That is the instinct and power within all of us, if we would live in harmony with that instinct and power.

To understand sin in this way is to say that "war is hell" in a very literal sense. Hell is the lived experience of separateness—of us versus them—in this world. Hell is the desire to push others away from us, to want the suffering world to leave us alone. Hell is the preference of sin, of separateness, of ignoring Christ in the Other. Hell is the belief that we would be better off on our own. As Brother Raphael of Gethsemani had expressed it, hell is life in a self-made, claustrophobic MRI machine. In that sense, 9/11 and our response are both experiences of hell. 9/11 was a radical act of separation—al-Qaeda wants to destroy us—and our response was to mirror that separation—we want to destroy al-Qaeda and the Taliban.

After his epiphany in Louisville, Merton's way of relating to the world changed dramatically. Merton began to take very seriously that Christ is present among us. We need look no further than the neighbor. And Merton found Christ in the neighbor, in all whom he met and corresponded with: Jews, Buddhists, Muslims, and even atheists. If Merton's epiphany was not a private experience but a truth for the entire church and world, the question then became, could those of us who had not had this experience directly still live by faith in its light and truth?

Certainly, that was Sister Mary Margaret Funk's approach to Buddhists and Muslims. Opening herself to the sacred in her dialogue partners, she met God in the process. And clearly, that was what Brother André of Christ in the Desert was experiencing as he chanted the psalms from the perspective of the suffering Iraqi civilians. Christ is suffering in Iraq.

A TURNING POINT

By late September 2007, I felt close to the end of my search. I had found Christ in 9/11 and its aftermath. The "word of life" that I had been seeking as a Christian is this—Christ is present in the neighbor, yes, even in those we consider the enemy. What problem in the world would not be approached with greater humility, creativity, and energy if we saw in our neighbor the presence of God?

By that date, however, I was also becoming quite exhausted. The summer of 2007 had not been its usual time of renewal, but a time of visiting monasteries, transcribing interviews, and writing initial drafts of chapters. My duties at the college had also changed, and, even as I welcomed the new opportunities, I also felt torn between the project and these new duties. Spare time was a thing of the past. And below all of that, I was in the midst of a spiritual awakening. I knew that I was at a turning point.

Unfortunately, I ignored a lesson that I have given to countless students over the years. I would challenge students with the image of the Roman arch as a metaphor for the human drive for meaning. The arch, I would explain, could support an incredible amount of weight. Only two things could cause its collapse. One circumstance that would cause the arch to fall apart is not having enough weight on the arch. Metaphorically, our lives fall apart when we do not have enough meaning, or "weight," on the arch. The stones loosen, and collapse of the arch soon follows. The other circumstance is far rarer, when we ask an arch to support too much weight.

The arch of my life was experiencing the latter problem. The project was constantly on my mind. Meanwhile, my new duties at the college were challenging and personally satisfying. I had a surplus of meaning in my life, and so how could that be a problem?

I was living in denial about the toll that these challenges were taking on my life. Despite enjoying my visits to the monasteries and working on the project, I felt that I was racing to reach the end of the journey as quickly as possible. Why, I wondered? My wife remembers me as distracted and distant over that summer. Perhaps, at some level, I knew that I was wearing down. I wanted to complete the project before the batteries gave out. This rushing was also fueled by a nagging sense that there was yet something more for me to discover. There remained one column in the Rubik's Cube of this issue of faith and terror that still did not line up. It was in this revved-up state of mind that I boarded the plane to visit the monks and nuns of New Skete in late September 2007.

My visit to the monks and nuns of New Skete made it clear how wrong I had been in my estimation of the project. There was not one column left in the Rubik's Cube, but several. New Skete would indeed be an ending. New Skete would also be another painful beginning.

TOUCHING AN EDGE OF DARKNESS

If Christianity has a parallel to the Chinese philosophic principle of yin and yang, I experienced that at New Skete. Beyond what I could have ever hoped for, I exited the tunnel that the journey had been and stood at peace in the light. Truly, at New Skete, the "word of life" for which I had been searching came into sharp focus.

But that was not all that I experienced at New Skete. I also touched the edge of a darkness that I realized later had been waiting for me. In interviews with two members of New Skete, a monk and a nun, the issue of enduring periods of darkness and loss of God were unexpectedly raised. Certainly, I did not probe for this issue. At the time, I would have wished that this issue of the loss of God would have never been raised. It did not fit at all with the light that I also received at New Skete. But I was to learn again the wisdom of St. Cyril of Jerusalem, who had so wisely said in the fourth century, "The dragon sits by the side of the road, watching those who pass. Beware lest he devour you. We go to the Father of Souls, but it is necessary to pass by the dragon." Before I could live in the light of this "word of life," the dragon would thoroughly work me over.

New Skete has an ethereal unreality about it. In rural upstate New York, near Cambridge, New Skete was the most distinct monastery that I visited. Upon arriving at New Skete, I was greeted by the yipping of puppies. Between the monastery proper—church, refectory, and dormitory—and the gift shop and guesthouse, lay the graveyard and the kennels for the German shepherd puppies. As Gethsemani is noted for cheese and fruitcakes, so New Skete is renowned for dog training, an activity that has led the community to being featured on the cable network *Animal Planet*.

On my way back to the guesthouse after supper one evening, I heard Brother Luke cleaning out the puppy cages. By hearing, I mean that I heard him joking with the puppies. The puppies were full of joy to see him, and I have to admit that he treats them better than most people are treated in the world.

In an odd way, the raising and training of dogs have brought people to New Skete who might never have visited a monastery.

> I came attracted to the dogs. I leave with my heart refreshed by the prayers and hospitality of New Skete. Thank you God!
> —Entry in New Skete guest book, June 2002

But the dogs were only the beginning of New Skete's uniqueness. Across from the community graveyard sat a small Russian-style church, and behind that a pool, rock garden, and a larger church. The smaller church was also the older, stemming from the period when the community was a Byzantine Franciscan House (Catholic).

I was bowled over when I first entered the newer church. While all monasteries, with their silence and spiritual peace, give off a taste of what heaven might be like, I felt as if I had truly stepped into another realm when I entered this church. The temple, as the worship space in Orthodoxy is called, is extraordinary. The ancient Byzantine churches in Ravenna, Italy, have friezes of saints and martyrs lined up on their side walls. The same is true of the temple at New Skete, except that the frieze on the clerestory here is updated with modern saints of various traditions. Here, unlike anywhere else that I have ever seen, one finds the icon of Patriarch Athenagorus with the Anglican archbishop Michael Ramsey on one side and Pope Paul VI on the other. Athenagorus and Pope Paul VI were the leaders who, in 1964, removed the nearly millennium-old anathemas against each other's church.

On the other side of the clerestory are icons of Dorothy Day, the founder of the Catholic Worker movement, Mother Teresa, and Edith Stein (St. Teresa Benedicta). Here, in this peaceful space, East and West are one; here the wound of the schisms plaguing the church have already been healed. Here it is really true, "on earth as it is in heaven."

THE LIGHT BREAKS THROUGH—BROTHER STAVROS AND BROTHER CHRISTOPHER

Brother Stavros (called "Stash" in the community) volunteered to be my first interviewee at New Skete. Citing equipment issues as my excuse, I turned down his invitation to conduct the interview while hiking a trail up one of the nearby mountains. Brother Stavros, short of stature, wiry, and in his sixties, was obviously very fit. His mind also was active, jumping from topic to topic, covering local geography, the saints, Rome's ancient churches, as well as literature and film. The conversation over dinner both nights made it clear to me that "Stash" has seen more recent films than I have.

Brother Stavros spoke rapidly and to the point. His forty-five-minute interview was astonishing in its breadth and depth. Brother Stavros had also been to Ground Zero, and it was clear from the beginning of our interview that his reflections on our age of terror had been heavily influenced by his visit to that site.

In January 2002, Brothers Luke and Stavros had been summoned to New York City by church hierarchs. Some visitors to New Skete had complained about the ecumenical smorgasbord of icons in the monastery's church. Others had felt that the community's revising of ancient liturgies had gone too far. After a three-hour meeting, the two monks left feeling depressed and angry.

The next morning, to clear their minds and recover some perspective, the two monks took the subway down to Ground Zero. By January 2002, an observation deck had already been built at the site. What impressed Brother Stavros was "first of all, the enormity of the space. And there was still smoldering; they were still removing rubble at that point. So you could still see it and smell it . . . But still, just the enormity of the space."

Perhaps Ground Zero, like Dachau and Hiroshima, is too vast and evocative to ever be fathomed in its entirety. As others before and after him, Brother Stavros left the visit with a few striking images. He remembered seeing, on one of the buildings adjacent to Ground Zero, black nets draped over the building to keep further debris or glass from falling down on the workers. "And it looked like a widow in mourning," he said.

"And what got to me were all the writings on this [observation] deck. People had written all kinds of stuff . . . And seeing flags from odd places, like who would even [imagine] a little flag from Wales?"

Brother Stavros also remembered an arresting sight on a later visit to New York City, when he came across photos of the missing still posted in one of the subway stations. Were some still living in the hope that friends and relatives would emerge out of the rubble? Also vivid in Brother Stavros's memory was the small Catholic church that, due to its proximity to the Twin Towers, had been transformed into a command center. When the building was finally returned to its sacred function, the church had been rededicated to the emergency workers who had lost their lives on 9/11. It was for that church, he remarked, that Sister Cecelia, the prioress of the Nuns of New Skete, had been commissioned to "write" an icon (painting an icon in Orthodoxy is considered a theological act, and thus icons are written).

When our discussion moved to consider the lessons of 9/11, Brother Stavros related a strange conversation that had occurred shortly after the tragedy. He had traveled to the Albany airport to pick up a prospective new member of the community. NPR was on the radio, and the program stirred the passenger to ask a question. "He asked me if I didn't think that we were coming to, since 9/11, a huge conflict, a cultural conflict, which of course is the hallmark of fundamentalism, and the right wing, the neocons." The passenger asked Brother Stavros what he thought of the emerging conflict between good and evil, between violence and peace. "And he, of course, *he* characterized Islam as representing violence, and Christianity as peace," he added.

While Brother Stavros was familiar with this simplistic view, he was dumbfounded to encounter it in someone interested in monastic life at New Skete. He recalled that the visitor was well educated, having once been a professor in an evangelical institution. "Here he is, seriously asking this question about violence and peace, and I said, 'How can you characterize Islam as the same as violence?'" The visitor had replied that that was the conclusion he had drawn from 9/11 and subsequent conflicts in the world.

Brother Stavros explained that he had felt duty-bound to try to enlighten the man. He told his passenger of his visit to relatives near Toulouse, France. The area, he explained to me, as he had to this guest, had been one of the hotbeds of the Cathar heresy.

"They can show you the rocks where [the official Catholic Church] threw men, women, and children by the thousands, *by the thousands . . .* in the name of Christ." He suggested to the visitor that any reputable Islamic scholar could similarly protest that al-Qaeda represents only a fanatical interpretation of Islam. "We [Christians] can't throw the first stone. We've done the exact same thing. So why can't we ask the deeper question: 'Where does this violence come from?'"

Brother Stavros concluded the story by saying that he realized that he and the visitor were "speaking two different languages." But beyond that, what most frightened Brother Stavros was the man's "absolute certainty" of what God would do, a trait mirrored in Osama bin Laden and radical Islam. Fundamentalism, it seems, is fundamentalism, wherever it is found. "People get seduced by this absolutism, and absolutism then feeds on power, and then power, of course, leads to violence."

I asked Brother Stavros to return to his earlier question, where does violence come from?

"We have to confront the violence [and] the lust for power that are in our darker human nature, I guess what Jungians would call the 'shadow,' that [is] primordial, that came with us out of the cave . . . One of the first [human] tools is the club. It means [violence] has been with us for a long time."

But what makes us human, he continued, is our capacity to make life more than just a struggle for existence. That is the "thinking in the heart" that Brother Stavros believes can counter the aberrant belief that "there is a God there who is pleased by wiping out parts of the population because they don't conform to its wish or its will as mediated through its conviction."

For Brother Stavros, the antidote to the absolute certainty fostered by fundamentalism is contemplation. A monk for forty years, but still sensing that he is a learner, Brother Stavros explained that one of the main lessons that he had learned is to be wary of certainty. A respect for mystery, not absolute certainty, is the mark of the person who "thinks with the heart."

His juxtaposing fundamentalism and contemplation brought to mind al-Qaeda's fierce hatred of the mystical tradition of Sufism in Islam. Contemplation is a foreign and suspect spiritual activity in fundamentalist circles. And that means that contemplative Christianity, Judaism, and Islam and fundamentalist Christianity, Judaism, and Islam lead to two very different attitudes toward violence and vengeance.

Fundamentalism, in whatever religion, presumes to know the divine plan and can act with certainty upon it. Contemplation of whatever religion, in contrast, has lost all presumption and knows that we only ever experience the hem of the divine mantle.

For Brother Stavros, it is a relief to admit this. Contemplation never brings any sense of certainty, but rather feelings of humility and awe as one confronts the mystery of God and reality. "And that to me is comforting to realize you can't get your hands on all of this, you can't [completely] grasp it. And so real contemplation is the awareness of more and more places where that is true."

It was then that Brother Stavros raised, as others had in previous interviews, what I consider to be the key insight of the project. Surely, my heart picked up a beat when he described the Incarnation as the entire world being "polluted" with divinity. Through a professor in nearby Albany, Brother Stavros had come to believe that Christ has entered every strata of human experience, including our doubts and anger. "I don't know how anyone can get spiritual growth *without* facing that woundedness, if not in their own life—and I can't imagine anybody's life is really spared that on some level if they're honest—but when you see things like 9/11 or other huge cases of suffering, like the war now."

For Brother Stavros, Christ is found within the "woundedness" of our world. For him, Christ was consequently very present on 9/11, in those who died, in those who were left with doubt and anger at God, and even in those piloting those planes.

Brother Stavros further suggested that a more contemplative response would have brought a different response on our part to this tragedy. In those early days after 9/11, when the world seemed to be holding its breath waiting for the US reaction, Brother Stavros was convinced that the strongest response would have been "to do nothing." But, he admitted, "That would have to come out of real genuine strength—not naiveté, but strength. And I knew it was hopeless." What would have been better, he suggested, was "a special Peace Corps . . . You can only beat up on Afghanistan so long," he added. "And especially, I'm thinking, after what the Russians did [there], I mean, this is just an exercise in retaliation."

This was a new piece of the puzzle for me to consider, one that seemed obvious once Brother Stavros stated it. Foreign policy arises out of a state of mind, and religions are powerful states of mind. Our nation had responded with fundamentalist certainty to an attack by fundamentalists who acted with a similar level of certainty. Both presumed to know the mind of God. Had Christians in this country taken a more contemplative approach, had we understood that God is found within the "woundedness" of our world, we who call ourselves Christians would have pressed and prayed for a far different response. Yes, we as a nation had a right to defend ourselves. But demonizing Iraqis, Afghanis, members of the Taliban, and even al-Qaeda itself has made us so calloused that we neither know nor care how many we have killed. War has that habit of "insect-ivizing" the Other—where other human beings become no more than pests that we are glad to be rid of.

With Brother Stavros, I felt that I could see the light at the end of the tunnel of my journey. In my subsequent interview with Brother Christopher, I would walk out of that tunnel into the blinding intensity of that light.

> Every time I come I experience the vision of what could be. Thank you.
>
> —Entry in the New Skete guest book, 2003

> Solzhenitzen [sic] ends his short story describing Matryona as that old woman without whom the whole village could not endure, nor the country . . . So it is with all of you on this holy mountain.
>
> —Entry in the New Skete guest book, 2006

BROTHER CHRISTOPHER

On my first night at New Skete over supper, the guestmaster, Brother Ambrose, invited me to explain to the community the purpose of my visit. I left that evening sure of one thing: Brother Christopher did not want to be interviewed.

Brother Christopher is another one of those monks who would stump the age guesser at the county fair. Blond headed and looking to be in his mid- to late-thirties, Brother Christopher was actually fifty-three at the time of the interview. Along with Brother Stavros, Brother Christopher was very sophisticated in terms of art, literature, and film.

What Brother Christopher was *not* enthused about was my project. He openly expressed doubts that the monks of New Skete, or monks anywhere for that matter, had any noteworthy viewpoints or reactions to 9/11 and its aftermath. His skepticism remained steadfast, even after I shared that this had not been my experience at any monastic house that I had visited. Despite his doubts, I could not help but be drawn to this sarcastic monk, who had over dinner expressed in an unforgettable way his problem with denominational narrowness. "When I get to heaven," he said facetiously, "I'm going to ask where the Orthodox men's room is."

A look of shock must have crossed my face when, on the following afternoon, I saw Brother Christopher drive up and approach the guesthouse. He announced that he had a break in his schedule and was willing to be interviewed. I never did find out what had made him change his mind.

Very early in our conversation, I realized that we shared several similarities. We were both converts to Orthodoxy and shared the same gratefulness for finding, or being found, by this ancient tradition. But while we had found in Orthodoxy our spiritual home, we both were uncomfortable with those who insist on Orthodoxy or any denomination being the "one true church." "Part of my life is to witness to a broader, more wonderful, more mysterious reality that I think the church really is," Brother Christopher said. And when I shared that I first became interested in theology for the questions, not the answers, he replied with a laugh, "Right with you."

His skepticism of the night before and any wariness on my part seemed to dissolve in that moment. This interview, I thought, is going to be fun.

"The God that creates a club is not a God that I believe in," he explained. "The church is not a club. It's something far more wonderful, far more mysterious, and *far* more dynamic than, I believe, than we can even fathom." What is essential, but difficult to do, he suggested, is to leave it to God to let what he referred to as "the mystery of the church" play out.

Brother Christopher believed that we in the church need to remember that God is far more concerned with the destiny, the salvation, of every being who ever lived. "So, chill, chill," he advised. "Somehow, beyond all of the confusion, all of the doctrinal differences, beyond the seriousness of those differences—because there are serious differences—rests a God who is big enough, and loving enough, to deal with it all . . . and who risks creating because God trusted that love was big enough to work it all out."

I thought of the icons in the monastery church, how their ecumenical nature was mirrored in Brother Christopher's belief that God, as God, cannot be bound to any particular tribe or tradition.

That same respect for God's "boundarylessness" was evident in Brother Christopher's reaction to 9/11. He summed up his initial reaction as a "mixture of horror, sadness, solidarity—being aware that people were jumping, having to make that sort of decision—prayer . . . anger, rage, curiously, as a part of it, frustration, that so many of the choices we've made from the standpoint of foreign policy seem to have been inviting this sort of consequence."

And prayer was what he remembered the community doing initially. "We tried to be present to the experience as it was happening, to be present prayerfully, since there was nothing we could do other than to simply be a witness of it and handle it prayerfully."

I asked Brother Christopher what that prayer was like. What was its quality?

"It wasn't 'O Lord, save those people,'" he replied. "It wasn't telling God what to do. It was, rather, trusting that even in the midst of this horror and catastrophe, God is God, and that ultimately, ultimately, God can redeem even the most profound evil." We both paused, as ironically, military planes from a nearby air force base flew over the monastery.

Brother Christopher also recalled that the community had a special liturgy on the evening of 9/11 after vespers. Through a phone call that day, they had discovered that a friend of the monastery had been devastated by the news that his sister had been a stewardess and his brother-in-law one of the pilots on the plane that crashed into the Pentagon. "So there was a real personal . . . connection. These were real people," he said quietly. "You know that mentally, but then when you hear the crying on the phone from a friend . . . who has just learned that his sister was one of the victims . . . what kind of words of comfort can you say?"

Nevertheless, he had not lost hope or despaired. He did not expect God to "fix it," but to be present in the tragedy so that despair, hopelessness, hate, or violence would not be the last word. "Love is ultimately the last word." But being healed by love would not be easy, he said, echoing Merton's viewpoint. Every human being and our nation as a whole would have to take a journey that would "tap and touch every emotion . . . [We] will not be able to avoid any of it."

But were we as a nation on that journey? I asked. Instead, were we not stuck, pretending that we are unconquerable, asserting over and over again by our actions that we are still the great superpower? Why has it been so difficult for even Christians in this nation to ask, "Where is the redemptive action of God happening, and how can we be part of that?"

Brother Christopher responded by first commenting on the wrong path that some Christians have taken. "When our gospel is reduced to patriotism and political payback and we're the instruments of vengeance and retribution that God lights on the world, give me a break. That's the simplistic, easy way out, and I think that when we take that bait . . . we forfeit the power of the gospel, the radicalism of the gospel, and Jesus is very sorry, very sad."

But the path toward healing is always present, and that path demands that we "taste" the humanity of our enemies, Brother Christopher said. He referred to the recent film by Clint Eastwood, *Letters from Iwo Jima.* "This is not a pro-war movie. This is an anti-war movie . . . The viewer [can] touch the humanity of the enemy, and see the enemy, or feel the enemy's emotion, and know [those emotions] to be our own . . . I think that [such empathy] complicates things, and that's good."

The real key to understanding where God's redemptive action is at work is to look at Jesus on the cross, Brother Christopher said. "What is going on there? What is Jesus doing? What is Jesus doing?" he repeated. "Is He simply saving this one person who says 'I believe in You'? . . . The one who signs a little booklet? . . . Is that what that's about up there? And if it's not about that, if it's something much more universal, how does that get translated, how do we take the seriousness of that act and really allow it to speak with the radical power that I think that act [of crucifixion] intended?"

For a third time, someone I was interviewing raised the Amish schoolhouse tragedy and that community's response. Brother Christopher denied that the community's response had anything to do with a desire to feel better or "holier." He even denied that the community's response was one of conscious forgiveness. "No, it didn't have anything to do with that. It had to do with trusting in a love that we can't even begin to fathom, trusting that and believing in that."

And our failure to trust in this unfathomable love had been our lost chance after 9/11. "We had an opportunity to not only heal our-selves . . . to receive healing, but also to help the world," he said. "That didn't necessarily preclude trying to bring to justice the perpetrators of the act, but we, in my judgment, have squandered that. And that's almost as big a tragedy as the act of 9/11 itself." Brother Christopher's words were coming in short bursts now, striking me like bullets from across the coffee table between us. "It was a *kairos* moment [a time of great significance] . . . and is this an opportunity where God can be seen? And make no mistake about it; we're not looking for a *deus ex machina* swinging down. At least I'm not. I'm not expecting all of a sudden Jesus coming down or the Rapture taking place . . . No, rather, we become the means of grace. We become God's hands, God's feet. We become the instruments of the gospel. *Or not!*" he emphasized.

Those who claim the name of Christ had not become God's instruments after 9/11. In a terror-filled world, we had taken another path, one tinged with Christian language but far from Christ's exam-ple. "Sadly, a lot of what is going on in the Mideast today, [and] not just in the Mideast, seems to be going on under the banner of a trium-phalistic Christian response that, frankly, sickens me," he said.

I felt that Brother Christopher was approaching the center, the ground zero, of my journey for a "word of life." Few would argue that 9/11 had been a *kairos* moment in our nation's history, a moment of tre-mendous potential meaning. But we had failed to understand that 9/11 was a moment of choice between heaven and hell, God and vengeance.

No, we had not become instruments of grace. We had not responded to 9/11 as instruments of the gospel. In our triumphalism, we had denied the cross. How, I asked, can the cross still speak to this tragedy?

"One of the powerful aspects of the mystery of the cross is the fact that the cross is not simply the execution of one man," he replied. "When I [say] that . . . crucifixion is equally as horrifying as the events of 9/11, how can that be?" he posed. "Through the cross, Jesus becomes intimate with our deepest suffering . . . This is not a God who is unfeeling, a God who is omnipotent, who is untouchable, who can't understand the pain of human suffering in its broadest level. Rather, this is a God who can look me in the eye and say, [or] not even say anything, but to allow me to know absolutely [that] this God, this person, knows my deepest suffering and knows my pain. And that's the very significance of compassion, where God is able to be compassionate to all human suffering." In that way, the God who suffers with us, he added, heals the loneliness that often comes with suffering. "In Jesus, I see . . . the authenticity of God's embrace of human suffering," Brother Christopher added. "In that, healing takes place, transformation takes place, and, I believe, forgiveness can take place . . . [as well as] forgiveness that comes from a point of deep mystery that none of us can really fully fathom."

"I think to understand 9/11 in relationship to the mystery of the cross is potentially a very fruitful thing," he continued. "Because the cross is not the last word. The paschal mystery is the paschal mystery. It's death *and* resurrection, and that's not just to make us feel good. It's not just saying, 'There, there,' to our emotions, because looking at these empty caverns of meaninglessness and emptiness, we couldn't bear it. So as a result we simply explain it in a way to make ourselves feel good. No, the cross and resurrection, the paschal mystery is the paschal mystery," he repeated. "And so, as we apply it to 9/11, how do we understand 9/11 in relationship to the cross? Like I said, the cross is not the last word."

I will never forget that precise moment as we sat across from one another, when an insight that had been lurking in the wings of my consciousness finally became clear. That insight would have meant nothing without the interviews that had come before. But that insight, now dawning, seemed to complete my journey.

If the cross speaks to 9/11, and the cross is horrible like 9/11, I said to Brother Christopher, that would mean that God the Father could have chosen, at humanity crucifying His Son, to destroy us. God could have responded as we did to 9/11: with vengeance. But God had chosen another path. He had raised Jesus not for His own sake, but for ours.

"That's right," Brother Christopher agreed.

I took another tentative step. "God raised Jesus for the murderers' sake."

"Right, right," Brother Christopher replied.

The choices we had on 9/11, I saw for the first time, were the same as God's options at the crucifixion. They were the same options that the Amish had after the schoolhouse shooting. Vengeance on God's part, on the Amish's part, is one possible response to suffering, to crucifixion. But in seeking to punish our enemies, we leave Christ, we abandon Him, on the cross.

In contrast, the act of forgiveness, two thousand years ago on Golgotha, and just months before in the Amish community, brought and brings resurrection. That is what mercy and redemption mean, the passing from death to life.

But we made the other choice after 9/11. We did not act as God did at the crucifixion of His only Son. We did not respond as the Amish had done. We chose crucifixion. We chose to destroy.

But the path to reconciliation and new life for all of us is still open. "I think what [the aftermath to 9/11 of war and vengeance] may occasion, curiously, is a new sort of listening as a country . . . a listening that has learned from what we've done, what has happened, the opportunities that we've missed. And, God forbid, let me say it in capital letters, REPENTANCE. I mean, can a nation repent? Well, Jeremiah thought so. Amos thought so. Can a nation repent? Why not?" he posed. "Who is to say that the experiences that this country is going through might [not] be the very things that prime the country to hear that word [*repentance*] in a way that we weren't able to five years ago?"

The path toward peace begins with understanding, Brother Christopher added, "that the real power is in weakness . . . weakness that is strong and as tough as the hardest metal, weakness that is vulnerable, that acknowledges the fact that we have made serious mistakes. That is weakness that can be respected, that can give people hope and can recreate new relationships. That's the *serious* mistake, the tragedy of post-9/11. The opportunity that was missed is that there was the opportunity to create new relationships with different countries, with different peoples, to come to new understandings."

The suffering of 9/11 had not broken us open to human suffering elsewhere. As Sister Julianne of Our Lady of the Desert helped me understand, 9/11 could have been a "bridge" to the world. In our insecurity, we have instead sought revenge abroad and built a wall at home.

Here was the "word of life," fully clarified, that I had been seeking over the past year. In our response to the tragedy of 9/11, we had replaced the God of the paschal mystery with the God of vengeance. The God whom Jesus embodied had made a far different choice. God had chosen forgiveness. God did not condemn the world for crucifying His Son, but raised Jesus for the sake of the world—for the sake of us who continue to crucify Christ in our actions toward others.

"That's right," Brother Christopher said. "That's right."

I sat back and exhaled loudly. I confessed to Brother Christopher that I felt overwhelmed by what he had raised for me to consider. I began the project agreeing with Nathan Dungan, that we had missed something in 9/11. 'What have we missed?' had been the most critical question that I had asked everyone throughout the project. Brother Christopher had helped me finally answer that question for myself. We had failed to understand 9/11 in light of the death and resurrection of Christ. We had left Christ on the cross.

For Christians to view 9/11 and the world of terrorism through the paschal mystery of Christ's death and resurrection will be difficult and complex. Such a stance does not mean condoning or ignoring what al-Qaeda did on September 11, any more than God, in Christian belief, ignored or condoned the sinfulness of humanity in crucifying His Son. No, forgiveness must mean, as the South African activist Malusi Mpumlwana suggests, *helping our adversaries recover their humanity.*[1]

What God revealed in the resurrection of Jesus was His desire to *heal* rather than punish humanity for our sickness of fear and hatred. The crucifixion and resurrection of Jesus were not done for God's sake but ours. The paschal mystery takes what Christians understand as the most heinous act in human history—deicide—and transforms it through a quality of love beyond human comprehension into the healing of humanity, the perpetrators.

For Christians to view 9/11 and the world of terrorism through the paschal mystery means a shift of focus. Instead of asking how we can eradicate al-Qaeda and radical Islamism, we should ponder another question—what will it take to *heal* religious terrorism?

At the end of the interview, I shared with Brother Christopher that I felt that we were spiritual brothers. He agreed and acknowledged that he had not had a clue what would come out in the interview. In fact, what we had talked about had surprised him. With a smile, he reflected back on his reservation the night before, that monks and nuns had nothing unique to say about the world crisis.

Now, he said, he understood.

As he left to prepare to officiate at the next service, I felt bathed in an almost blinding light. The journey had led me to find Christ in the entire human race. At New Skete, I realized that in war and vengeance, Christ continues to be nailed to the cross, joined in suffering with all of us. But God waits, Christ is left on the cross, until we acknowledge the humanity of our enemies and to see that healing comes through offering grace and forgiveness. The resurrection of our Lord and the human race, His mystical body, waits to happen once again until we are willing to forgive.

There remains, then, an opportunity for new life after 9/11. But we cannot bomb our way into that new life. Resurrection and new life cannot occur if we respond to our experience of crucifixion on 9/11 with more crucifixion of the Other.

> I have found such peace here—wholeness that I've missed. Perhaps someday I will tell you my whole story.
>
> —Entry in the New Skete guest book, 2006

LIVING IN THE DARKNESS OF GOD'S ABSENCE— BROTHER AMBROSE AND SISTER CECELIA

From the yipping puppies to the ecumenical icons in the temple, my visit to New Skete was filled with surprises. Nothing, however, was more unexpected on my visit than the topic that surfaced in my two interviews on September 21, 2007, with Brother Ambrose, the guest-master of New Skete, and Sister Cecelia, prioress of the nearby Nuns of New Skete. The two could hardly be more different. Brother Ambrose is one of those naturally funny people, the kind who habitually tell their experiences in stories, all of which are laced with a good deal of humor.

Sister Cecelia is the opposite, being one of the most introverted and measured persons I interviewed in the entire project. Unlike the animated Brother Ambrose, Sister Cecelia sat quietly except for when the two German shepherds of the convent bounded into the room and interrupted us. Toward the end of each interview, however, these two very different people broached the same painful subject of losing the sense of God's presence while living the monastic life.

Was I surprised to find in a monastery this sense of losing God? The honest answer is yes, I was surprised, which only shows how little I had thought about the trials of monastic life. There is a chiseled slogan on the lintel to the monastic enclosure at Gethsemani Abbey: *"God Alone."* That is the monastic ideal, where life is pared down to its spiritual core. The vows that monks and nuns take demand that they willingly forfeit some of the most valued aspects of contemporary life—autonomy, sexual fulfillment, and affluence—and those "deprivations" are what outsiders such as myself imagine are the great trials of such a life. Monastic life strips one of everything but God, but I found it easy to assume that God would be the ever-abiding constant.

But what if a monk or nun loses the sense of God's presence? How shattering it must be to rouse oneself in the early hours of the morning to chant the first service of the day, to work, spend time in spiritual reading, and meditation, and to retire for the night by nine o'clock, to greet guests who gush about God being so palpably felt in your monastery when you have lost that one remaining reality.

By his own admission, the lanky Brother Ambrose is a leftover hippie. He was once, in fact, the head of a motorcycle gang that competed with the Hells Angels. He had also operated on the fringe of the Weatherman movement in his younger years. The guestmaster of any monastery has to be someone who can put visitors, with their widely divergent motives for coming on retreat, at ease and make them comfortable in the strange surroundings and pace of a monastic house. Brother Ambrose's personality and background seem to make him perfectly suited for that role. His preference for wisecracks matched my own, and there was a great deal of laughter as he described his meandering journey to coming to New Skete. As with most monks and nuns I interviewed during the project, Brother Ambrose looked twenty years younger than his true age. He seemed very much like someone who had settled deeply and happily into monastic life.

This funny monk consequently rocked me when the joking stopped and he admitted that he had been living for years without a sense of God's presence. This was in sharp contrast with his experience when he first arrived at New Skete, which he described as: "[God is] the constant in my life. I never have to worry about it. I just know this. I have such a relationship, and blah blah blah blah."

But soon after settling into life at New Skete, he was thrown into what spiritual masters refer to as "the cloud of unknowing." In his typically colorful way, Brother Ambrose described the experience as "walking through some sort of mental eraser. You walk through it and your mind is wiped out completely." God became a stranger to him, and his life at New Skete has, since that time, been a struggle.

He spoke of the odd comfort that Mother Teresa's own spiritual emptiness, now made public from her diaries, has been to him. "So when this stuff came out about Mother Teresa, I said, 'Hey, I understand how you feel.' It's not that you disbelieve. You just struggle all the time. I'm struggling all the time. I'm still in that cloud."

I tried to imagine this man's life, the hours spent in New Skete's beautiful temple, participating in the Divine Liturgy every day, and being surrounded by fellow monks, nuns, and retreatants who feel God's nearness in this place.

One guest in the spring of 2002 wrote in the guest book, *"God is here! I am glad."* Well, Brother Ambrose was certainly not glad.

What, I wondered, went through this monk's mind when he sat in the temple and looked up at the icons of St. Francis, St. Simeon the Theologian, the popes, archbishops, patriarchs, and martyrs? Do those figures oppress someone whose heart seems dead?

Brother Ambrose was candid in acknowledging the painfulness of God's absence when he first entered that "cloud of unknowing." But gradually, as the months and even years have gone by, he has come to believe that God is always there when he calls upon Him, even when he feels nothing. "But I still don't know God, and I don't have an image . . . and yet I still haven't lost the faith."

Brother Ambrose was describing something that I had no desire to think about at the time. How did this piece fit the larger puzzle? My visits to the monasteries, my times of joining in the prayers of these communities and especially my interviews with monks and nuns had all given me a deeper sense of God's nearness than I had ever known before. There were times in listening to a monk or nun when

I truly felt God's listening presence in the room. It was this sense of God's presence that made the work of the project so enjoyable.

I looked at Brother Ambrose and wondered how he managed to stay.

A second interview that same afternoon, this one with Sister Cecelia, helped me answer that question.

A self-admitted introvert, Sister Cecelia spoke of how her extroverted and agnostic brother had fallen into depression after 9/11. His considerably affluent financial portfolio had been devastated by that tragedy, but his depression "wasn't because of the money." Working in Connecticut, her brother would regularly go into New York City on business. He began to frequent a restaurant across from the Twin Towers and had watched the buildings being constructed. "And [it was depressing] for him to think about the fact, seeing [the buildings] go up and realizing the hatred that would cause them to go down."

Her brother does not share Sister Cecelia's commitment to Christian faith. In fact, he blames religion for 9/11 and many of the problems in the world. While respecting her brother and believing he is still a very "spiritual" person, Sister Cecelia sensed that he had fewer resources to draw upon in a crisis. "I absolutely believe these people who don't believe in an afterlife suffer much more."

Not that she has always found God any easier to believe in than her brother. "I have gone through darkness where I didn't really believe in God and I didn't believe in an afterlife." Later, she explained that on one occasion this sense of God's absence had lasted for a year and a half. She then admitted that there had been other periods of feeling God-forsaken.

Many of the same questions that I had when Brother Ambrose expressed his similar experience of "the cloud of unknowing" floated through my mind. How did this woman manage to keep up this exacting way of life? Did she feel like a fraud?

Sister Cecelia posed the same question to herself. What do you do if you are in a monastery at the time and you have others depending on you? "You carry on when you are in that state . . . Tomorrow, I might lose that [sense of God's nearness] and be in the darkness, and I'm still going to have to go on."

How? I asked.

"Well, I grit my teeth and just realize that for now I have to go on. [At first, I thought] maybe tomorrow I will leave here. But I stayed. And after about a year or a year and a half, somehow or another, because I kept making myself go to church with the other people and praying, I mean, singing songs I didn't believe in, I eventually did come to some belief that there was a God."

I was mystified as I listened. A year and a half of feeling cut off from God, and this woman still stayed? I would not have, I admitted to myself.

As had Brother Ambrose, Sister Cecelia also referred to Mother Teresa's posthumous diary, in which the world's most famous nun shared her own feeling of suffering the absence of Christ. Yes, Sister Cecelia said, it is always a comfort "to realize that other people have to keep struggling and going on."

Why, I thought to myself, was this theme emerging now, at this ending point of the project? I dismissed the notion that this sense of God's absence was restricted to New Skete. I had read too many accounts of the same experience throughout Christian history and within the lives of the saints. Merton himself had said that a monk would not know until the very end of his life if he has wasted it. And Merton's Gethsemani Abbey was not named by accident after the garden where Jesus Himself experienced the absence of God.

But the back-to-back nature of the interviews with the same topic surfacing made a vivid impression on me. Were these two stubborn Christians experiencing what the families of those who perished on 9/11 had also experienced?

I felt a longing to attend the next service in the temple. It would be vespers, the last service of the celebration of the Feast of the Holy

Cross. Perhaps, after hearing of Brother Ambrose's and Sister Cecelia's struggles, I wanted to feel once again God's presence in that holy space. Or perhaps the truth was that I wanted to watch these two, knowing now what they have contended with, as they joined the community in chants and prayers.

I stared at their backs as the service progressed. Why did it feel as if they had given me a warning?

I looked over to a man, also a retreatant, whom I had seen in several of the services over my stay at New Skete. He was obviously another layperson, though I knew that he was not staying in the guesthouse. The balding, middle-aged man stood and bowed his head with the community, but his mouth did not move. As I looked at him more carefully, I realized that he was crying, and crying freely.

Shedding tears in a monastery by those on retreat is not an unusual occurrence. Often, the cause of a visit is a difficult spiritual problem. I was not the only one who came to hear a "word of life."

My normal practice is to respect the privacy of people who display emotions so openly. I assume that they are burdened with something overwhelming, and the last thing they need is for a stranger to be nosy. But something drew me to this man. I wondered, was it somehow linked to the pain that Brother Ambrose and Sister Cecelia had shared with me earlier that afternoon?

On our way out of the service, my path crossed the man, whom I will call John. He was still wiping away tears with a handkerchief and obviously losing the battle. I asked him if there was anything I could do. He paused and tried to speak. In faltering phrases, John explained that he had come to New Skete because the week before, his son had been killed in a biking accident. His son had recently been married and was taking a bike ride with his wife. A car rounded the bend and lost control for a mere split second, just long enough for the car to drift off the highway and strike his son in front of his son's wife. John broke down again as he said that he had come to New Skete to grieve for his son, a young man who had not been very religious. He was hoping for God's mercy.

Standing there, I found myself weeping with him. We were two fathers with sons about the same age, and he was enduring every parent's nightmare. I felt the great unfairness of the world.

Supper with the monks was a few minutes away. I walked in silence toward the old, little-used church with the onion dome and golden cross. I opened the heavy wooden door and entered into the darkness. Slowly, as my eyes adjusted to the dim light, the figures in the icons seemed to emerge from the front of the chapel.

I tried to pray for John, for his son's soul, and for his son's grieving young wife. But I could not. Surging up from within me was anger, not at the driver but at God. I had an overwhelming sense of the uselessness of a God who could not prevent a car from losing control or, if it lost control, prevent anyone from getting hurt. I felt ashamed to admit it to myself on this Feast of the Holy Cross that all I could feel was the powerlessness of this God and our human need for a more powerful deity. John had come to New Skete to pray for God's mercy. I felt God owed him an apology.

The irony of this experience was not lost on me. Throughout the project, I had held at bay—as if I did not share the feeling—any anger at God, a feeling that all religious families affected by 9/11 were forced to deal with. Had they not asked over and over again, "Could not God have allowed at least one of the planes to experience mechanical trouble and be held back?" "Could not God have caused one of the hijackers to lose his courage and tell the authorities everything?" Why was it that from the attackers' point of view, everything had gone perfectly, like clockwork?

Those questions I had understood, but I thought that I knew how they should be answered. But somehow John's isolated tragedy had severed my trust in God, a trust that had withstood years of reading and studying the horror of 9/11.

And the light that I had received from my interviews with Brother Stavros and Brother Christopher—light that had seemed to be the culmination of my journey—what had happened to that? Perhaps the brightness of those insights made this new darkness even darker.

For the first time, I wondered if Jesus had not factored in our response to 9/11 because God had seemed so absent, so impotent in the attack.

New Skete was an ending to my search. It was also the beginning of a search.

The Light Shines in the Darkness

In late 2007, a few weeks after my visit to New Skete, I crashed emotionally and physically. My descent would continue months into the new year.

Sleep was elusive. I could neither work on the project nor feel at ease in the classroom. My anxiety deepened as depression set in. I experienced a darkness and waves of panic that I had never known before.

For a while, matters only became worse. I felt unable to work on anything. My doubts about finishing the project mounted day by day. I went on medical leave from the college and began to take medication. Unfortunately, the first medications only accelerated my descent. I felt helpless, open to a self-loathing that I had never known before.

God was gone, and He seemed to have taken all hope with Him.

Only those who have experienced this type of hell know how weak, useless, and damned a person caught in its grip can feel. All was a kind of darkness, of fears without relief.

It took months for me to come out on the other side. Of course, I asked myself over and over again the logical questions. Had my digging into the horror and evil of 9/11 contributed to the darkness descending around me? Was the collapse caused by some letdown as my monastery visits came to an end? Had the unexpected anger at God that I had experienced at New Skete brought on my sense of desolation? I will never know the answer to those questions.

What I held on to during those difficult months was the love of my family and friends. I knew that many people were praying for me, even as I could no longer pray. Bits of the interviews with Brother Ambrose and Sister Cecelia also returned to mind. I did not understand at the time how their spontaneously shared experiences of the "death of God" fit into the project. Now, the memory of their candid comments offered hope that I would survive this ordeal. But I also doubted that I had their strength to endure this God-forsakenness as long as they have.

In my recovery, I was blessed with both a gifted psychiatrist and psychologist who took the spiritual life seriously. To my surprise, neither considered the interview project to be a problem, something that I should abandon for the sake of my health. Rather, they viewed the project as something to which I should and would return, once recovered. I marveled at their confidence and also at their genuine interest in the project. That interest struck me as both odd and significant. The psychiatrist who treated me suggested something that I had never considered, that my anxiety and depression, while not caused by the interviews themselves, could have been partially brought on by too much "light." And the psychologist predicted that I would be "better than before" once I learned that I was not in control of life and did not need to be.

Giving up control was precisely the most difficult aspect of the ordeal. Would I recover, as they promised, or was this what they said to all their patients? Would I look back at the project as that which sank me like a stone, or something that I was able to return to and finish?

The one constant in my life was the love of my wife, my sons, my extended family, my priest, my friends at church, my friends and students at the college, and even my psychiatrist and psychologist. In my debilitating state of uncertainty, that was the one certainty—that I was loved by so many. In my personal experience of crucifixion, I was truly powerless to fix myself. Hope for the future, for the first time in my life, was not grounded in what I would and could do, but in those who loved me and were praying for my resurrection.

After a hiatus of nearly nine months, I very gingerly stepped back into the project. I began without knowing if the stress would return, necessitating my abandoning the project, or if I could handle the taxing work of listening again to the recorded interviews and writing chapter drafts.

What struck me immediately, as I heard the voices of the monks and nuns as they answered my questions, was that these men and women now seemed to be interviewing me. My earlier impatience was gone, and I began to hear clearly the "word of life" that I had been seeking. And that "word of life" was now not directed solely at our suffering world, but at my personal experience of darkness.

The "light" that the monks and nuns offered on the recordings began to seep back into my life. But now it was not a blinding light, as it had felt in the fall of 2007, but an illuminating and warming light, one that was a call to a new way of living.

If the project had previously contributed to wearing me down emotionally, the work now had the opposite effect. The project was a definite part of my recovery.

I returned to Thomas Merton's epiphany in Louisville and pondered how that truth could be put into practice in my own life. The process of doing this came naturally, and the results were quite immediate. When I found myself thinking about an adversarial relationship I had with someone—in higher education, one does meet opposition—when I felt inclined to judge those persons and in the process separate myself mentally from them, I returned to the most important truth that Merton had experienced in Louisville: Jesus had joined Himself with their humanity as much as mine. God in Christ had made peace with them, and they had sacred value, even if they might live in total ignorance or denial of those truths.

In the process of practicing that awareness, I felt the separation from those people being bridged. I physically felt something mending within me.

When I returned to my college duties in the fall of 2008, I also noticed a significant difference in attitude. For my nearly thirty years of teaching at the same institution, I had come to hate one aspect of my job more than anything else—faculty meetings. Picture a packed room where highly educated egos clash and defensive postures dominate. I had learned to achieve some distance from the ordeal by bringing a book to read or grading to do. I would simply tune out until someone said something that could not be ignored. In the tension filling the room, it seemed that everyone was making judgments about others. "Which side am I on?" "What are our best arguments?" "Why can't those others see what is obviously true?" Those were certainly thoughts going through my head. Peace in the Middle East seemed more likely than peace in faculty meetings.

Perhaps unwisely, most colleges and universities begin the new academic year with one of these faculty meetings. That was true of Franklin College in the fall of 2008. And this particular faculty meeting held something of extra import. Over the summer, the academic dean invited me to present the results of research that I and a few colleagues had conducted over the past few years. Welcome back.

Such a request in the past would have thrown me into a type of self-induced torture as I prepared to speak to a room divided between some who expected me to be stunning and others who hoped that I would fall flat on my face.

But as I stood before that packed room of highly educated colleagues on my first day back in the community, I realized, with a sense of relief, that I was not in control. I could not make the presentation go perfectly, and I could not anticipate every critique of our research. I was surprised that I did not feel panicky but rather, curious. What, I wondered, would happen in the next twenty minutes? The diverse perspectives in the room were no longer a threat but of interest to me.

Previously, I had approached such occasions as might a conductor before a huge orchestra. How could I have all these musicians play together? That had been my chief concern. Now I realized how absurd, and also deadening, was that expectation. Others were not in that room to play the tune that I dictated. Our diverse and conflicting viewpoints were all part of the process that would help us understand more clearly the challenges before us.

In the months that followed, I no longer tuned out of faculty meetings by retreating to class work. Merton's epiphany at the corner of Fourth and Walnut could apply to anyplace in this world, even in a college faculty meeting. Christ had made peace with all of us in that room.

THE SEEDS OF RESURRECTION

Merton's epiphany also began to color my response to the daily news. Even though I am a news junkie, I have to admit that the news is often a recital of how much hell exists in the world. From military reports from Afghanistan and Iraq, to updates on al-Qaeda and the Taliban, to Iran's nuclear aspirations and its crackdowns on dissidents, to the rise of the Mexican drug cartels and the Tea Party movement, to the suffering of Palestinians in Gaza, to BP oil, to bloody uprisings throughout the Middle East and North Africa, the nightly news had previously been bearable because I had learned to psychically separate myself from it. I judged each news story based on my politics much as I had judged my colleagues in faculty meetings based on my campus politics.

I began to watch the news now with a different point of reference.

Yes, there is certainly a great deal of evidence that our world experiences ongoing crucifixion. Christ continues to suffer with and within those suffering in this world. The border vigilante movement, the racial hate groups, the judgmental tone of "tribal religion"—religion that pits one group against another—and triumphalist nationalism all promote separation within the human family. For these groups to exist, they must demonize the Other.

But now, in the midst of the daily litany of bad news, I found it possible to center on the truth that Christ, by the mercy of God, had joined Himself to everyone in those situations. While the issues separating me from these persons and groups did not suddenly disappear, these differences did not constitute the most critical factor. The most important truth was that Christ has made peace with all of us. And that means that there is a power inside of all of us—that power being Christ Himself—that yearns for unity and reconciliation, for wholeness.

And I also realized that the news contains seeds of resurrection, new life. From Doctors Without Borders, South Africa's Truth and Reconciliation Commission, Habitat for Humanity, Food for the Poor, Oxfam, Prisoners of Conscience, and UNICEF, resurrection is bursting forth wherever compassion is offered.

TRIPPING OVER THE CROSS

Not that the memory of the darkness that I had first experienced at New Skete and then tumbled into headfirst in the months thereafter went magically away. But as the gospel writer expressed it, there is darkness in this world and in our lives, but the light, even when that light seems feeble, is not overcome by that darkness. Brother Christopher had emphasized that the paschal mystery is both crucifixion and resurrection. In sharing John's grief at New Skete, I had wanted a God who was powerful enough to overcome the darkness by taking control. Could not an almighty God have prevented the death of John's son? Could not God have stopped the planes from crashing into buildings? And in my anxiety and depression in the following months, I had wanted a God to swoop in and instantly heal me.

I had tripped over the cross, what Christianity has always known is its chief stumbling block. The cross is the evidence that God in Christ overcomes the darkness by emptying Himself, by sharing the cruelty that we wage against one another.

Hope has returned to my life as I sensed that in my recovery, the love of so many people had helped me move from crucifixion to resurrection. That hope increased the more that I committed myself to this practice of viewing life through Merton's epiphany. I remain a news junkie. I am still concerned about world events, but I also sense that there is a divine power at work with and within us.

In a broad sense, the end of the human story is known. Our destiny is not the fiery apocalypse that some believe, unless we make that our end. Some Christians have already given up on the world and believe that darkness will only grow until God intervenes to rescue His favorites.

I wholeheartedly believe that our destiny as the human race is to journey toward the light, to discover the road to peace. And that peace begins when we see, as Merton did in Louisville, the sacred value of one another.

Right this moment, the light is overcoming the darkness.

RETURNING TO THE ANCIENT QUESTION

As human beings, we are insecure by nature. That insecurity lies behind the incredible sums of money, energy, and innovation that we invest in defense. That insecurity also lies behind the universal human hope for peace.

Our insecurities lead us repeatedly back to the ancient question, "Who is my neighbor?" Buried within that most basic question is a hidden one, "Who is *not* my neighbor? Who does God not expect me to care about?" War is a formal declaration that the Other is not the neighbor. To designate someone or some group as "enemy" is to insist that we do not have to care about them. They are not our neighbor.

Even religion can be used to label the Other. *Barbarian, Gentile,* and *nonbeliever* are terms that designate those who are not like us, those who are not our neighbors. Those labels identify those who need to change, to be converted, if peace is ever to come to our world.

I am reminded of the comment of a past student and friend, Frank, who wisely noted that "foreign policy begins in Sunday school." The policy of separation so commonly practiced has its roots in narrowly defining who is "neighbor." The belief that peace will only come if and when the world achieves religious uniformity is also to limit who is "neighbor." But violence and coercion can never bring peace.

The only foreign policy that can promote peace is one based on compassion toward those in need, even toward those whom we consider our adversaries. To forgive our enemies, as Jesus commanded, is not to condone or ignore their behavior. Again, that would be irresponsible and obscene. Rather, to forgive our enemies in this time of terrorism is to realize that our adversaries need our help in recovering their humanity,[1] even as we need the help of others, their forgiveness, to recover our own.

For in forgiving and loving the neighbors who surround us in this world, we meet God.

THE COMING RAPPROCHEMENT OF CHRISTIANITY AND ISLAM

Flash forward a year and a half. The "word of life" that I gained through the project had only grown stronger as I neared the end of chapter revisions in May 2010. That was when Khadija Khaja, a Muslim-American feminist who has written about Muslim reactions to 9/11, asked about the book. As I described how the book had profoundly changed my theology, she paused for a moment and said, "Muslims need this book."

I tried to imagine what she meant. For a day or two, I kept bumping up against the same mental obstacle. My search had led me to *Christian* insights, insights that many Christians, not to mention Muslims, would have trouble accepting. And that made me think ahead with some concern to an upcoming peace conference when Khadija would interview me about the project. Would we have anything to talk about?

But then the rightness of Khadija's words struck me. While Samuel Huntington's "clash of civilizations" argument has drawn much criticism, it is at least historically accurate to admit that Christianity and Islam have frequently met one other in battle since Islam's beginnings. The two cultures have tried the path of dominating and even destroying one another, and that path has led to a dead end.

More recently, as the contact between religions has increased, Christians, Muslims, and Jews have taken the opposite approach, to focus on what we have in common—Abraham as forefather, ethical monotheism, a belief in divine providence over history. But that well-meaning approach has also failed, at least with many Christians and Muslims. Any thoughtful reader of the New Testament quickly notices that Christianity quite self-consciously views itself as the fulfillment of Judaism, even as Islam views itself as the "end" (final revelation) that completes and surpasses Judaism and Christianity.

Yet Muslims do need something from Christians at a time when so many Christians fear Muslims, if not actively demonize Islam. The monks and nuns I interviewed led me to embrace a *third* way. Muslims need Christians to come to a maturity within their own Christian faith. It will truly be a breakthrough when Muslims and all non-Christians are viewed by Christians as having sacred and inestimable value.

In Christianity, the sacred value of every human being is grounded in the Incarnation—the belief that Christ has entered our common humanity. The Incarnation means that Christ both abides and lurks in the stranger. The Incarnation means that these "Christic" strangers can be found everywhere, from the refugee camps in Uganda and Somalia and Haiti to the homeless shelters of our major cities. The Incarnation means that even those whom we call enemies, be they in Tehran, in the caves of Pakistan and Afghanistan, or in white supremacist groups in Idaho, have been united with Christ by His Incarnation. The Incarnation also means that the Incarnate Christ is being both crucified in every moment of human suffering and being resurrected whenever that suffering is met by selfless acts of love.

Muslims will never agree with those beliefs, nor do they need to do so. But Muslims and the world as a whole need nothing more right now than for Christians to live fully within Merton's transforming vision. Only then can Christianity contribute to humanity's destiny of living together in peace.

The same must certainly be also true for Islam, Buddhism, Judaism, Hinduism and all other religious paths to meaning. Would I, as a Christian, wish for everyone to encounter Christ as St. Paul, Merton, and even I had? Yes. But Christians do not need Muslims to become Christians for God's dream for humanity to be realized. The world needs Muslims to come to a vision of God's love for all human- ity, as is found in Rumi. How the world would be different if Islamist terrorists bowed to the wisdom of these words of the Sufi master:

> Not Christian or Jew or Muslim, not Hindu, Buddhist, sufi, or zen.
> Not any religion or cultural system. I am not from the East or the
> West, not out of the ocean or up from the ground, not natural or
> ethereal, not composed of elements at all. I do not exist, am not an
> entity in this world or the next, did not descend from Adam and

Eve or any origin story. My place is placeless, a trace of the traceless. Neither body or soul.

I belong to the beloved, have seen the two worlds as one and that one call to and know, first, last, outer, inner, only that breath breathing human being.[2]

Similarly, the world does not need Jews to accept Jesus as the Messiah, but instead to more deeply live within the divine vision apprehended by visionaries such as the Orthodox rabbi Abraham Isaac Kook (1865–1935), who wrote:

The higher holiness abounds with love, compassion and tolerance, as the mark of is most radiant perfection.

Hatred, sternness, and irritability result from forgetting God, and from the extinguishing of the light of holiness.

The more intense the quest for God is in a person's heart, the more the love for all people will grow in him. He will also love the wicked and the heretics and desire to correct them, as he indeed corrects them by his great faith.

However, a person is unable openly to show love except to someone in whom he finds a good element. He will thus be able to direct his love to the dimensions of the good. He will not be hurt by the evil side in those people to whom he will extend love in meeting his commitment to love people, which involves being good and extending good to the wicked as well as to the good.[3]

This sense of universal sacredness is not unique to Western religions. For the world to grow in compassion, Hindus need only embrace Gandhi's path of *satyagraha*.

But there I will stop. It is not for me to lecture other religions but to increasingly "become" a Christian, to live in the wisdom that monks and nuns have shared with me, in the wisdom that Mennonites and Quakers have generously given to me, and especially in the light of Thomas Merton's epiphany at Fourth and Walnut in Louisville.

The world is not destined to share a common theology. In that sense, I disagree with Gandhi and Sister Mary Margaret Funk, who are convinced that religions offer different paths up the same mountain of knowing God. But not all religions have the common goal of knowing God. Some religions seek harmony with nature or a cosmic law, while others seek enlightenment. Thanks be to God, the survival of the human race does not depend on our overcoming those differences about ultimate reality.

Rather, the survival of humanity depends on our turning our attention toward another mountain, one where the differing religions of the world do offer different paths to the summit. The true common goal of religions is realizing, through our different paths, that the neighbor and even the enemy have sacred value. On that summit, we come together to see what Merton apprehended at Fourth and Walnut in Louisville—the divine light that radiates from everyone.

As the project ended, the religious tension in our country was rising alarmingly over the issue of a mosque being built 250 yards from Ground Zero in Manhattan. On TV, supporters and protestors were seen screaming at one another behind police lines. Politicians were weighing in on the issue, some trying to calm the waters, others stirring them up. The virus of Islamophobia, with its propensity for violence, is clearly escalating.

And on August 1, 2010, the day I completed this manuscript, the *Chicago Tribune* featured a story about a Florida church planning to burn Qur'ans as a public condemnation of Islam on the anniversary of 9/11.

There are two paths that Christians and Muslims can travel in the next decade. We can continue on the path of *divergence*, of demonizing one another, or we can take the path of *convergence*. It is time for Christians to use their power to change the conversation, to ponder Jesus' command to treat the stranger as our neighbor and to treat our neighbor not only as ourselves, but as God in our midst.

The Death of Osama bin Laden and America's *Via Dolorosa*

When I heard of the death of Osama bin Laden early in the morning on May 2, 2011, I froze, not knowing how to grasp the news. Stunned, I walked to the college and to my office. I knew that this day would be no ordinary day of teaching. I felt an obligation to interrupt course content to let students talk about the news. In more than thirty years of teaching at Franklin College, I had only once before let world events trump my teaching plan. That had been on September 11, 2001.

In the quiet of my office, I tried to center myself, to sink below the thoughts and images streaming through my mind. What was the world's greatest need in those moments? What was my greatest need that day?

On 9/11, I wished I could talk with Thomas Merton. Now, I wanted to talk once again with the monks and nuns I had interviewed for this book. And I knew the question that I would ask these men and women: *Is this the day we have been waiting for?*

Later that afternoon, as I tuned into the news, reporters announced that May 1, 2011, was indeed the day that many Americans had been waiting for. Vengeance had been served. They showed images of people celebrating in the streets and jubilantly waving American flags. Their joy felt alien to me, but I was not sure why.

In the absolute silence of my office, I saw again the faces and heard the voices of those whom I had interviewed. No, the death of Osama bin Laden would not be what these monks and nuns had been waiting for. There would be no rejoicing over the death of this man in the monasteries, of that I was certain. I knew that they awaited something far grander. These men and women are praying and waiting for peace.

For people of faith, peace is not the *absence* of anyone or any-thing—not the absence of Osama bin Laden, not the absence of al-Qaeda and the Taliban, not the absence of all adversaries who come to mind. Peace is rather the *presence* of mercy and justice, of compassion for the neighbor equal to God's compassion with us.

I looked out my office window to the front of our campus. The statue of Benjamin Franklin that welcomes visitors to campus had been painted red, white, and blue sometime during the night after the news had been disseminated. Was the death of Osama bin Laden the day my students had been waiting for?

I put that question to my afternoon church history class. What surprised me most was the immediacy and soberness of their responses. One student in the front row explained that this was the day many Americans had been waiting for, but that was not true for her.

Another student added, "We want to see peace. We are so tired of war." My students reminded me that they were in fifth and sixth grade when 9/11 occurred, and fear and insecurity had always seemed to be a part of their world.

Another student a few rows back commented that the way Americans were reacting showed that we hadn't learned anything from 9/11. A student to the side chimed in that our rejoicing over Osama bin Laden's death was similar to what we had faulted al-Qaeda for doing on 9/11.

I knew that my students, religious studies majors and minors, did not represent the sentiments of most students at the college. To a person, my students found something shameful in celebrating the death of anyone.

As I look back on May 2, 2011, that day will remain in my memory as one of the most chaotic days I have ever known. But I also experienced some coherence as the day went on, as my students' comments were supported by those of colleagues who stopped by my office or friends who e-mailed me from around the country to talk about their own mixed feelings. All understood the sense of celebration that was sweeping the country, but they also felt something far more somber. Over and over I heard them describe the day as feeling hollow and sad, and I knew that their sadness had no connection with a lack of patriotism.

The candor of my students, friends, and colleagues helped me explore my own mixed feelings of the day. Along with many, including American Muslims, I felt the relief of knowing that Osama bin Laden's power to misrepresent Islam was over. But I also felt what I can only call sorrow.

Throughout this book project, I considered it a near certainty that Osama bin Laden would be found and would likely be killed rather than captured. But I was also aware that al-Qaeda is not a hierarchical organization but rather a very fragmented and decentralized movement. Osama bin Laden was never the type of leader who approved, vetoed, or even knew beforehand all the actions taken by those who identified with al-Qaeda. Al-Qaeda and religious extremism would not end with this man's death.

I had no doubt that Osama bin Laden's death was a milestone event, but his death was not the "word of life" that I had searched for and found through the interviews.

On 9/11, America and the world took the first steps on a new *via dolorosa*, the path of suffering. Our response in Afghanistan, Iraq, and elsewhere had been further stops, or "stations of the cross," on our road to the cross.

The death of Osama bin Laden will be remembered by many people of faith as yet another stop on our national *via dolorosa*. And so it makes sense that many people of faith felt an odd sense of grief on that day. Brought back to us was the grief we'd experienced on other "stations of the cross," on 9/11 and its aftermath. The newly reopened wounds had yet to be healed. We were once again face-to-face with the brokenness of the world and God's sorrow over that brokenness.

And so many people of faith continue to wait for resurrection. We do not know when that time of healing of the world will come, but we do know from Jesus' life, death, and resurrection that the healing of our broken world will not come until we commit to helping our adversaries recover their humanity. Forgiveness, not the death of anyone, is the only exit from our *via dolorosa,* the only path to resurrection joy.

Peace be with you. May peace come soon to our sorrowful world.

Notes

Prologue: In Search of a "Word of Life"

1. Mary Margaret Funk, *Islam Is: An Experience of Dialogue and Devotion* (Brooklyn, NY: Lantern Books, 2003), 99.
2. Robert S. Ellwood, *Introducing Religion: From Inside and Outside* (Englewood Cliffs, NJ: Prentice-Hall, 1993), 10–11.

Chapter 1: "Where Are the Prophets?"

1. Hilary Timmesh, *Saint John's at 15: A Portrait of This Place Called Collegeville* (Collegeville, MN: Liturgical Press, 2006), 26.
2. As cited in Mari Grana, *Brothers of the Desert: The Story of the Monastery of Christ in the Desert* (Santa Fe, NM: Sunstone Press, 2006), 16.
3. Thomas Merton, *The Seven Storey Mountain* (San Diego: Harcourt Brace Jovanovich, 1976), 325.
4. Madeleine L'Engle, *Walking on Water: Reflections on Faith and Art* (New York: Macmillan, 1995), 31.

Chapter 2: Caught Between Paradise and Wilderness

1. *The Rule of St. Benedict in English*, chap. 48 (Collegeville, MN: Liturgical Press, 1982), 69–70.

Chapter 3: 9/11 Should Have Been a Bridge to the World

1. Mari Grana, *Brothers of the Desert: The Story of the Monastery of Christ in the Desert* (Santa Fe, NM: Sunstone Press, 2006), 139.
2. Thomas P. McDonnell, ed., *A Thomas Merton Reader* (London: Lamp Press, 1989), 304–10.

Chapter 4: Here We Have No Lasting City

1. Kathleen Norris, *Acedia and Me: A Marriage, Monks, and a Writer's Life* (New York: Riverhead, 2008).
2. Martin Luther King Jr., "The Drum Major Instinct," sermon delivered to Ebenezer Baptist Church, Atlanta, GA, February 4, 1968.
3. Ibid.
4. Mari Grana, *Brothers of the Desert: The Story of the Monastery of Christ in the Desert* (Santa Fe, NM: Sunstone Press, 2006), 139.
5. Ibid., 60.
6. From www.thekingcenter.org.

Chapter 5: 9/11's Most Taboo Word—Forgiveness

1. Thomas Merton, *Contemplation in a World of Action* (New York: New Directions Publishing 2007; orig. pub. 1973).
2. Ibid., 123.

Chapter 6: Thomas Merton: The Man at the Intersection

1. Thomas Merton, *The Seven Storey Mountain* (San Diego: Harcourt Brace Jovanovich, 1976), 325.
2. Thomas Merton, *Conjectures of a Guilty Bystander* (Garden City, NY: Doubleday, 1968), 156–58.
3. Thomas Merton, *New Seeds of Contemplation* (New York: New Directions, 1961), 294–95.
4. *The Rule of St. Benedict*, chap. 53 (Collegeville, MN: Liturgical Press, 1982), 73.
5. Merton, *Conjectures*, 141.
6. Thomas Merton, *A Search for Solitude: Pursuing the Monk's True Life* (New York: Harper Collins, 1996), 182.
7. Merton, *Conjectures*, 141.
8. Ibid., 142.
9. Ibid., emphasis added.
10. Merton, *New Seeds of Contemplation*, 296.
11. Merton, *Conjectures*, 141.
12. Merton, *New Seeds of Contemplation*, 123.
13. Ibid., 123–24.
14. Ibid., 78.
15. Ibid., 75.
16. Ibid., 112; emphasis in original.
17. Ibid., 72–73.
18. Ibid., 114.
19. Ibid., 71.
20. Ibid.

21. Ibid., 72.
22. Ibid.
23. Ibid., 75.
24. Ibid., 73.
25. Ibid., 74; emphasis in original.
26. Ibid., 75.
27. Ibid., 76–77.
28. Thomas H. Kean and Lee H. Hamilton, *Without Precedent: The Inside Story of the 9/11 Commission* (New York: Vintage Books, 2007), 327.
29. Merton, *Conjectures*, 140–41.

Chapter 8: The Other President of the United States

1. Thomas Merton, *The Seven Storey Mountain* (San Diego: Harcourt Brace Jovanovich, 1976), 325.
2. Ibid.

Chapter 9: Others Are Waiting for Us at the Center

1. Sister Mary Margaret Funk, *Islam Is: An Experience of Dialogue and Devotion* (Brooklyn, NY: Lantern Books, 2003), 16.
2. Daniel Madigan, quoted in Jane Kramer, "The Pope and Islam: Is There Anything That Benedict XVI Would Like to Discuss?" *New Yorker*, April 2, 2007, 58.
3. Pope Benedict, quoted in Russell Shorto, "Keeping the Faith," *New York Times Magazine*, April 8, 2007, 43.
4. Ibid., 42.
5. Mary Margaret Funk, "Staying the Course," *U.S. Catholic*, February 16, 2007.
6. Dom Armand Veilleux, OCSO, "Beyond Reason: Monastic Interreligious Dialogue and Islam," Monastic Interreligious Dialogue, from Bulletin 78, January 2007. Available at http://monasticdialog.com/a.php?id=798.
7. Kramer, "The Pope and Islam," 64.
8. Ibid.
9. Veilleux, "Beyond Reason," 2.
10. Ibid.
11. Veilleux, "Beyond Reason," 3.
12. Ibid.
13. Mary Margaret Funk, *Humility Matters for Practicing the Spiritual Life* (New York: Continuum, 2005), 46, 48.

Chapter 14: Light and Darkness

1. As quoted by Desmond Tutu in *The Words and Inspiration of Mahatma Gandhi* (Boulder, Colorado: Blue Mountain Press, 2007), 5.

Epilogue

1. As quoted by Desmond Tutu in *The Words and Inspiration of Mahatma Gandhi* (Boulder, Colorado: Blue Mountain Press, 2007), 5.
2. Jelaluddin Rumi, Sufi mystic, 1207–1273.
3. Abraham Isaac Kook, *Abraham Isaac Kook: The Lights of Penitence, The Moral Principles, Lights of Holiness, Essays, Letters, and Poems* (New York: Paulist Press, 1978), 237–38.

About the Author

David Carlson, PhD, is a professor and the Charles B. and Kathleen O. Van Nuys Dean's Fellow in Religious Studies at Franklin College where he has served since 1978. He received his education at Wheaton College, American Baptist Seminary of the West, and University of Aberdeen, Scotland. His scholarly interests include monasticism, Orthodox-Catholic relations, and the faith development of college students and adults. He writes columns on religion, culture, and politics for multiple newspapers and journals. David is married to Kathleen and is the father of Leif and Marten Carlson. He resides in Franklin, IN, and can be contacted at dcarlson@franklincollege.edu.